THE SUPREME COURT'S ROLE IN MASS INCARCERATION

The Supreme Court's Role in Mass Incarceration illuminates the role of the United States Supreme Court's criminal procedure revolution as a contributing factor to the rise in U.S. incarceration rates. Noting that the increase in mass incarceration began climbing just after the Warren Court years and continued to climb for the next four decades—despite the substantial decline in the crime rate—the author posits that part of the explanation is the Court's failure to understand that a trial system with robust rights for defendants is not a strong trial system unless it is also reliable and efficient.

There have been many explanations offered for the sudden and steep escalation in the U.S. incarceration rate, such as "it was the war on drugs" to "it was our harsh sentencing statutes." Those explanations have been shown to be inadequate. This book contends that we have overlooked a more powerful force in the rise of our incarceration rate—the long line of Supreme Court decisions, starting in the Warren Court era, that made the criminal justice system so complicated and expensive that it no longer serves to protect defendants. For the vast majority of defendants, their constitutional rights are irrelevant, as they are forced to accept plea bargains or face the prospect of a comparatively harsh sentence, if convicted. The prospect of a trial, once an important restraint on prosecutors in charging, has disappeared and plea-bargaining rules.

This book is essential reading for both graduate and undergraduate students in corrections and criminal justice courses as well as judges, attorneys, and others working in the criminal justice system.

William T. Pizzi is Professor of Law Emeritus at the University of Colorado Law School. He is a graduate of Harvard Law School and he also holds an advanced degree in philosophy from the University of Massachusetts. Following law school, Professor Pizzi was a federal prosecutor in the District of New Jersey before joining the faculty at Colorado Law where he taught for thirty-five years. He is one of the foremost scholars in the United States on comparative criminal issues. He has lectured abroad for both the Ford Foundation and the United States Information Agency.

THE SUPREME COURT'S ROLE IN MASS INCARCERATION

William T. Pizzi

Routledge
Taylor & Francis Group

NEW YORK AND LONDON

First published 2021
by Routledge
52 Vanderbilt Avenue, New York, NY 10017

and by Routledge
2 Park Square, Milton Park, Abingdon, Oxon, OX14 4RN

Routledge is an imprint of the Taylor & Francis Group, an informa business

© 2021 Taylor & Francis

The right of William T. Pizzi to be identified as author of this work has been asserted by him in accordance with sections 77 and 78 of the Copyright, Designs and Patents Act 1988.

Library of Congress Cataloging-in-Publication Data
Names: Pizzi, William T., 1943- author.
Title: The Supreme Court's role in mass incarceration / William T. Pizzi.
Description: New York, NY ; Routledge, 2021. | Includes bibliographical references and index.
Identifiers: LCCN 2020016705 (print) | LCCN 2020016706 (ebook) | ISBN 9780367331597 (hardback) | ISBN 9780367331399 (paperback) | ISBN 9780429318207 (ebook)
Subjects: LCSH: Sentences (Criminal procedure)–United States. | Imprisonment–United States. | Plea bargaining–United States. | Criminal procedure–Social aspects–United States. | United States. Supreme Court–Influence.
Classification: LCC KF9685 .P59 2021 (print) | LCC KF9685 (ebook) | DDC 345.73/0773–dc23
LC record available at https://lccn.loc.gov/2020016705
LC ebook record available at https://lccn.loc.gov/2020016706

ISBN: 978-0-367-33159-7 (hbk)
ISBN: 978-0-367-33139-9 (pbk)
ISBN: 978-0-429-31820-7 (ebk)

Typeset in Bembo
by Wearset Ltd, Boldon, Tyne and Wear

"This book contains an unorthodox, unusually interesting and highly stimulating account of the Supreme Court's impact on the American criminal justice system. The author's suggestions about weakening the system's intense adversary character include valuable comparisons with other countries in the common law tradition."

Mirjan R. Damaška, *Sterling Professor Emeritus of Law, Yale Law School*

"William Pizzi, long one of the keenest observers of our criminal justice system, has written a book brimming with insights and surprising connections. Anyone wanting to understand the phenomenon of mass incarceration will find here persuasive explanations in corners where others would not have thought to look."

Richard D. Friedman, *Alene and Allan F. Smith Professor of Law, University of Michigan Law School*

"As William Pizzi shows in this masterful volume, the American system of criminal procedure is like no other. It has been shaped by grand pronouncements of the Supreme Court that appeared to advance the rights of the accused but that, in practice, have produced their antithesis. By rendering decisions without much regard for cost or practicality and without the ability to compromise or adjust to changing circumstances, the Court has made trials so adversarial and so unworkable that they have almost vanished. Harsh leverage now induces defendants to sacrifice their rights, and assembly-line plea bargaining has led to the imprisonment of Americans at a rate unmatched anywhere else in the world. Pizzi's extraordinary knowledge of the procedural systems of other Western democracies as well as our own and his insight and unfailing good sense have produced a powerful indictment of a criminal justice system off the tracks."

Albert Alschuler, *Julius Kreeger Professor Emeritus of Law and Criminology, University of Chicago Law School*

"In his new book, Professor William Pizzi presents a unique and insightful take on the underappreciated causes of a critical public policy issue—Why are so many Americans in prison? In *The Supreme Court's Role in Mass Incarceration*, Pizzi exposes how many Court decisions that gave the surface of appearance of improving our criminal justice system have, in fact, backfired. Anyone with any interest in understanding why we have one of the world's highest incarceration rates—and is willing to entertain ideas that depart from the conventional wisdom—will find much to learn from Pizzi's work."

Paul G. Cassell, *Ronald N. Boyce Presidential Professor of Criminal Law and University Distinguished Professor of Law, S.J. Quinney College of Law at the University of Utah*

"Based on expert analysis of both Supreme Court jurisprudence and the criminal justice systems of other nations, *The Supreme Court's Role in Mass Incarceration* offers intriguing and important insights into the causes of perhaps the most significant criminal justice issue of our time. The book's diagnosis and possible treatments will challenge and engage all readers, scholars, policymakers and members of the public alike, who want to bring more justice into the law."

Gabriel J. Chin, *Edward L. Barrett Jr. Chair and Martin Luther King Jr. Professor, University of California, Davis School of Law*

"In a lively, thoughtful, and thoroughly original treatment, Professor Pizzi identifies a new culprit responsible for high U.S. incarceration rates: the United States Supreme Court. Pizzi demonstrates that by constitutionalizing vast swathes of criminal procedure, the Court has fuel-injected the system of plea bargaining to the point that it is so 'efficient,' and the incentives of its participants so warped, that no one, including defendants, can any longer take the risks of trial. This Court-induced plea-bargaining-on-steroids is a big reason, maybe the biggest, why so many Americans are incarcerated. Perhaps more significantly, Pizzi shows that the Court's piecemeal forays into process have left state systems little room for the kinds of systemic experiments likely needed to lead us back to reasonable levels of incarceration. This book was a breath of fresh air to everyone who has waited to hear about the cost side of such revered cases as *Mapp*, *Miranda*, and even *Gideon*. How stunning to see in these pages that the costs of those historic constitutional decisions are being borne largely by the very people they were intended to protect."

The Honorable Morris B. Hoffman, *Denver District Court Judge*

Writing a book in retirement puts stresses on others, especially my wife of more than forty years, Leslie. But she has been understanding and encouraging throughout. Her love is a blessing for which I am so very grateful.

CONTENTS

ACKNOWLEDGMENTS

As a comparatist who has spent time in courthouses in many countries, it is impossible to thank all the many people who went out of their way over the years to show me around, take me to interesting trials, help me with interpretation, and introduce me to others who could explain things to me when they could not. To all of them—judges, lawyers, investigators, court personnel—I wish to say thank you.

This book often compares the United States with England and Canada because they share our common law tradition, yet they do many things very differently. I spent quite a bit of time in England at various points in my career. An English defense solicitor, James Morton, did a lot to help me get around the courts when I was beginning to learn about the English system. My days visiting the Crown Court and magistrates' courts were much more productive after he had opened doors for me.

In Canada, I had considerable help from the Canadian consul in Denver, who put me in touch with lawyers in Ottawa from whom I learned a great deal. I also received assistance while visiting courts in Toronto from Justices Heather McArthur and Grant Dow, who sit on the Superior Court of Justice in that city.

As a former federal prosecutor, I was generally familiar with the federal system, but was not as familiar with state systems. Whenever I had questions, John Stavely and Noel Blum—county court judges in Colorado—were ready to assist. It was fun to be with them and I could see why they were excellent judges.

Another Colorado judge I must thank is Morris Hoffman who sits on the Denver District Court bench. He is a terrific trial judge, an excellent scholar, and a close friend. He is not responsible for any of the positions I take in this book, but if I have defended them well, it is only because of many conversations with him on criminal justice issues over the years.

I am very grateful to two librarians from the University of Colorado Law Library, Jane Thompson and Matt Zafiratos. They often helped me find materials, especially from foreign or historical sources, that I could not easily have found on my own.

The Law School has been supportive in other ways. Dean James Anaya gave me support and encouragement on this project. And Chemaine Chandler, my faculty coordinator, helped me get the draft into publishable form and gave me editing suggestions that improved it significantly.

INTRODUCTION

It is the thesis of this book in a nutshell that the Supreme Court has contributed to the rise in our incarceration rate because the so-called "criminal procedure revolution" made trials increasingly unworkable and indirectly led to a system in which plea bargaining dominates. We used to say that roughly 80 percent of our convictions came from plea bargaining and the rest from trials, but today trials are rare and plea-bargaining rates are usually at 97 or 98 percent.

As trials have vanished, the system can process many more cases since the time devoted to each is so short.

This is obviously a controversial claim and also a painful one for many of us academics who were educated in the Warren Court years and thought that strengthening the rights of defendants would make for a fairer, more just system, especially for those who are poor and facing a legal system that is intimidating.

But the Court was taking risks in what it was doing and this book will explain those risks and how some of those risks did not pay off. Building a strong system of criminal procedure case by case, isolated issue by isolated issue, is always going to be a major challenge. In addition, the Court does not have nearly the range of options that a legislature would have for tackling the same issues.

The book begins in Chapter 1 with a review of the historical rise in our shocking incarceration rate and, building heavily on the work of other scholars, will show that the standard explanations offered for the rise in mass incarceration—such as the claim that it was the "war on drugs"—are either wrong or insufficient to explain why the United States has grown to be such an outlier among Western countries in the percentage of citizens in our prisons and jails.

Chapter 2 explains the risks the Court took by trying to use the protections in the Bill of Rights to establish rules that would then apply in nearly every phase of criminal cases from the investigatory stage, to the pre-trial phase, the trial, and even the appellate phase.

One of those risks involved trying to apply the same procedures applicable in federal courts to state systems. Chapter 3 explains the differences between the federal system and state systems in the volume of cases, the types of crimes, and the range of crimes.

Chapter 4 explains why the "vanishing trial," as the near extinction of trials is often referred to, has a tremendous impact on the way crimes can be prosecuted. Trials are important for keeping weak cases out of the system and forcing a criminal justice system to look for alternatives for some less serious anti-social behaviors. When the system avoids trials except for the rare case, the healthy tensions that should exist between prosecutors and investigators or prosecutors and judges disappear.

Chapter 5 is highly critical of the Court's commitment to jury trials for all felonies and misdemeanors.[1] This is shown to be in sharp contrast with other common law countries where only a tiny percentage of criminal cases are tried to a jury. Instead, those countries give incentives to defendants and prosecutors to use nonjury trials for almost all criminal cases.

The latter part of the book concentrates on sentencing, which is a major problem in the United States. Chapter 6 gives background to this discussion by explaining how shifts in sentencing goals and other factors ended up diminishing the traditional broad sentencing authority of judges. The chapter also discusses some of the factors that led to an increase in harsh sentencing statutes, including a backlash against some Supreme Court decisions as well as the emergence of a powerful victims' movement. The combination of these factors has led to greater control of sentencing by prosecutors.

Chapter 7 builds on the power prosecutors have today by showing how some extremely harsh statutes can be used to coerce defendants to admit guilt and waive trials. Probably all common law countries have a trial penalty of sorts that encourages defendants to avoid trial or to keep the trial simple. The trial penalties in the United States can be extreme, however, as two cases highlighted in this chapter show.

Chapter 8 uses another common law country, Canada, to explain the way in which a strong commitment to proportionality in sentencing permits the Canadian Supreme Court to use its prohibition of cruel and unusual punishments to fend off harsh mandatory sentences. The chapter explains our Supreme Court's struggles with proportionality as a limitation on incapacitation and deterrence.

Unfortunately, the Court is not in a strong position for controlling harsh deterrent punishments because it created one itself when it based its exclusionary rule on the theory of deterrence. The chapter explains the serious problems with a rule that insists that deterrence requires punishments out of proportion to Fourth Amendment violations.

Chapter 9 explains the serious problems with sentencing in the United States. Even the issue of who should sentence is not easily answered. For a long time, judges had almost complete discretion in sentencing within rather broad sentencing ranges. This led to serious disparities as different judges had different sentencing philosophies and different ideas of the punishment that was appropriate to a given crime. On top of that, appellate review of sentencing is not our tradition. The upshot was an attempt to bring some consistency to sentencing through sentencing guidelines systems in some states and in the federal system. This chapter ends by describing the Federal Sentencing Guidelines and explaining why they were detested by judges and lawyers alike.

Chapter 10 continues the discussion of guidelines systems in discussing the most important reform effort of the last four decades—the American Law Institute's attempt to provide a model for states to use in making all sentencing phases fairer and more just for defendants. This comprehensive model was based on the state guidelines model employed in Minnesota and Washington, which had proven successful in taming the disparity in sentences and at lowering sentences.

Unfortunately, the American Law Institute's attempt to achieve important reforms to probation, sentencing, and parole was undercut by the Supreme Court. This is a tragedy as this reform had tremendous promise to reform not just sentences but also a whole range of related issues, such as probation and the collateral consequences of convictions.

Finally, Chapter 11 returns to the issue of the vanishing trial phenomenon in the United States. It begins by focusing on the experience in federal courts in the wake of a 2005 decision that made the Federal Sentencing Guidelines advisory. This freed judges to sentence as they had been able to before the guidelines. The prediction was that there would be more trials as prosecutors no longer controlled sentences. But, instead, trials sharply declined. This has puzzled commentators.

Chapter 11 contends that what is being overlooked is the inconsistent style of advocacy at trials compared to that at sentencing. A very extreme style of advocacy for trial contrasts with the muted advocacy needed at sentencing. One cannot shift easily from one style at trial and then adopt a more muted style for sentencing. Defense lawyers are opting to use their talents in plea bargaining and sentencing rather than at trials.

Finally, Chapter 12 reviews some of the reform efforts that have taken place around the country at a time when many citizens have come to realize that many defendants are being punished too severely. But the effect of reform efforts thus far on our incarceration rate has been modest—some would even say minimal. And these reforms have been directed to the "low hanging fruit" of reform: minor, nonviolent crimes.

This chapter explains why significant reform—cutting our incarceration rate by one-third or by one-half—will not happen until we face up to what the Court has done. We could do many things to make our criminal justice system stronger but, first, we must face up to the fact that the Court, in trying to reform our system for the last five decades, isolated issue by isolated issue, has ended up as an obstacle to reform.

Note

1 "Misdemeanor" in this book refers to minor crimes punishable by sentences up to a year, with sentences typically served in local jails. Felonies are offenses punishable by more than a year in prison and typically those sentences are served in prisons.

1

MASS INCARCERATION AND ITS "CAUSES"

Readers of this book will be fully aware of the way incarceration rates have increased in the United States over the last several decades as it has been the subject not only of books and articles in academic journals, but also many dramatic articles in the popular press. The *New York Times*, for example, published a front-page article in 2008 on the topic complete with an interactive chart that allowed readers to click on different countries around the world and compare incarceration rates. When one did so, it was clear why the headline of the article intoned that "Inmate Count in U.S. Dwarfs Other Nations'."[1]

The article noted—what is clear from Figure 1.1—that from 1925 to 1970, the rate was stable at roughly 110 people in prison per 100,000 people. At that point, the incarceration rate began to shoot up dramatically.

Similarly, *The Economist* featured a cover story in 2010 on the extreme U.S. incarceration rate, featuring a dramatic cover illustration of Lady Liberty herself peering out balefully from behind the bars of a prison cell. The article stated that "[n]o other rich country is nearly as punitive as the Land of the Free" and, as proof of that fact, it noted that the United States incarceration rate was five times greater than Britain's, nine times greater than Germany's, and twelve times greater than Japan's.[2]

The chart in Figure 1.1 includes more recent years, showing our prison population numbers starting from 1925 and continuing until 2017. What is, of course, shocking is the steep incline in our prison population that begins in the mid-1970s and continues sharply upward for the next few decades until 2009 when the number steadied itself and there has been a slight decline over the last decade.

Figure 1.1 shows that at the last date in the chart—2017—there are 1,439,808 citizens in our prisons. But this chart understates our incarceration problem because we have many more citizens incarcerated. Figure 1.1 does not include those being held in jails in the United States. In 2019, there were an additional 612,000 citizens in our jails. Adding together those in prison and those in our jails, the total is more than two million citizens incarcerated.

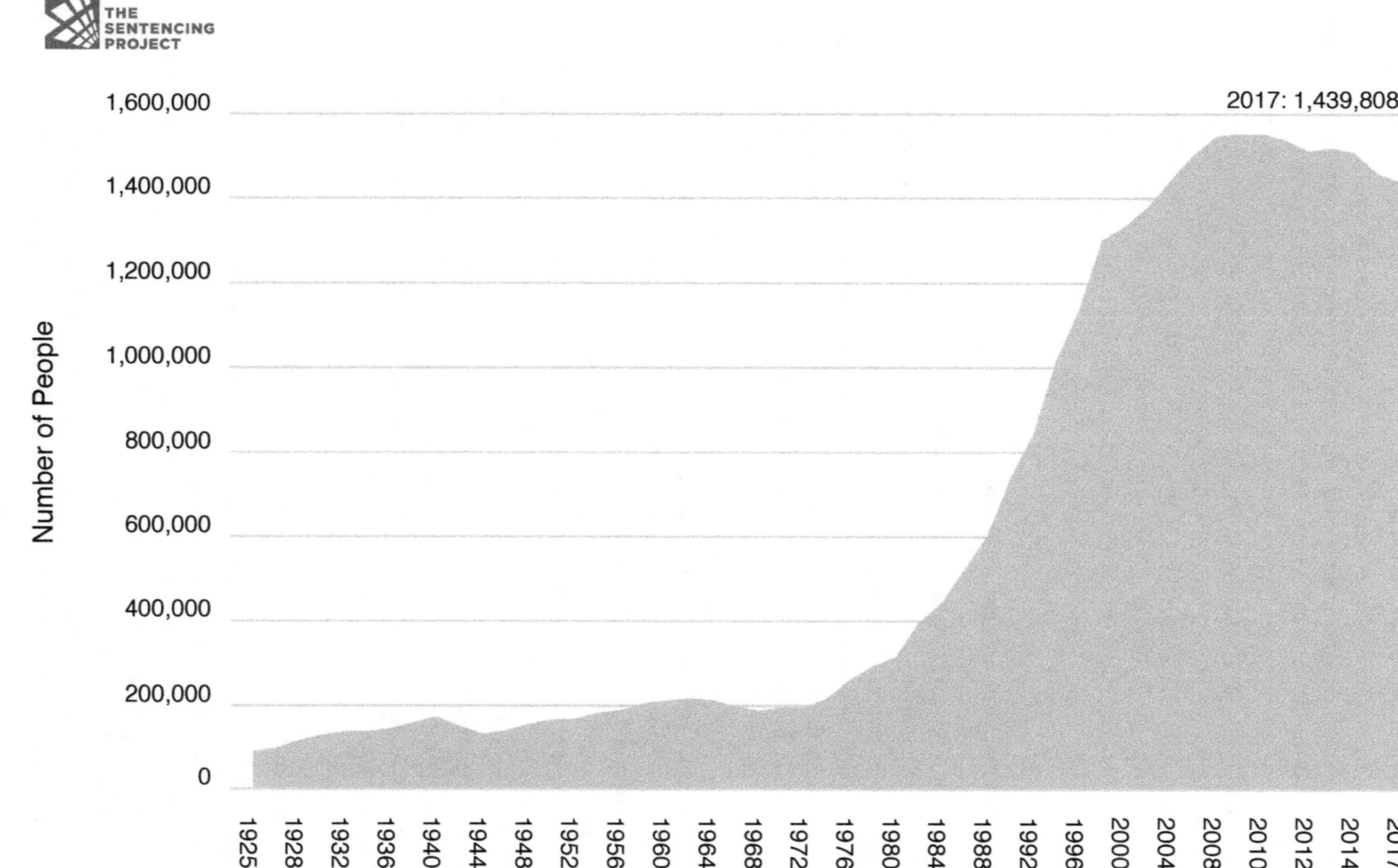

FIGURE 1.1   U.S. State and Federal Prison Population, 1925–2017.

Source: The Sentencing Project, www.sentencingproject.org/criminal-justice-facts/.

The above chart of prisoners is not completely bleak. Our incarceration rate has stabilized and even declined by several percentages since the high of 2009. But we cannot take too much solace in the decline, as it is slow. The Sentencing Project, an advocacy group which tracks incarceration rates (and constructed the above chart) reports that at the rate of decline achieved over the last decade, it would take seventy-two years to cut our prison population even by 50 percent.[3]

Another cautionary note on the decline is that a major part of the decline was due to a court order in California to address prison overcrowding. Michael O'Hear argues in an excellent book, *The Failed Promise of Sentencing Reform*, that if you take California's compelled reduction in its prison population out of the picture, even with drug sentencing reform in high population states like New York and New Jersey, we are closer to treading water on our incarceration rate rather than reducing it.[4]

Comparative Country Incarceration Rates

It would be easier to understand the sharp and sustained rise in our incarceration rate over the last forty years if it were a common phenomenon among other Western countries. But other Western countries have incarceration rates that have held relatively steady over the period when our rate rose sharply. As the *New York Times* and *The Economist* articles demonstrate, this comparison of our incarceration rate with other countries has been given quite a lot of attention in the press.

A more recent comparison of our incarceration rate with other countries—in this case, other Western countries—confirms that our incarceration rate is still extreme (see Figure 1.2).

In addition to the sheer number of citizens we incarcerate, the composition of that group of citizens is troubling as well. While black Americans make up only 13 percent of our resident population, they represent 40 percent of our prison population.[5] Black men are six times more likely to be incarcerated than non-Hispanic white men.[6]

Much has been written about the disproportionate effect of our incarceration boom on racial minorities. In 2015, one in ten black men in their twenties or thirties was incarcerated on any given day.[7] This takes a tremendous toll not just on those men who will have difficulties going through life marked with a criminal conviction, but on their families as well.

It has been estimated that of black males born in 2001, one in three will be incarcerated at some point in their lives compared to one in seventeen for non-Hispanic white men.[8]

These numbers make it imperative that we face up to our incarceration rate and try to determine what has gone wrong with our criminal justice system.

What Went Wrong?

The comparison with other countries is shocking and painful. Admittedly, we have more guns and more violent crime than most other Western countries, but hasn't that always been the case? Why would our prison population and our incarceration rate suddenly rise starting in the mid-1970s? Many countries have higher rates of property crimes including burglaries, car thefts, and the like than we do—why have they not seen the same dramatic climb in their incarceration rates?

Sometimes U.S. lawyers are resistant to conversations comparing the United States with European countries and prefer to end any comparisons with the refrain that European countries "have a

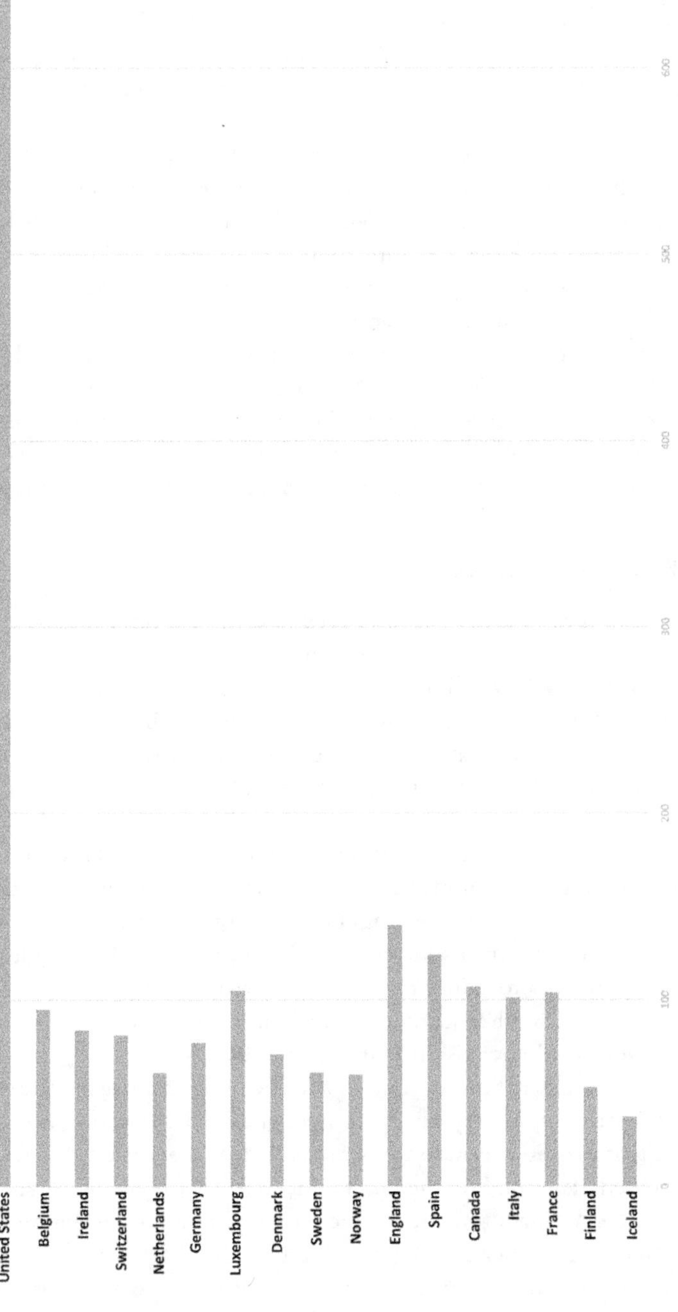

FIGURE 1.2   Comparative Incarceration Rates Among Western Countries.

Source: Author.

different legal system from ours." This is somewhat true—trial systems are quite different in many European countries, where judges play a more important role at trials and juries—as we know them—are rarely used.

But we cannot say that sentencing is a "different system" that would explain incarceration rates at one-third, one-fourth, or even one-eighth of our rate. There is no difference in sentencing procedures to suggest that sentences in the United States must be multiples of those dispensed for the same crime in Europe. Sentencing asks the same question in every country: having determined that the defendant committed the crime, what is the appropriate punishment for this offender for this crime?

More to the point, one does not have to look to continental countries to suggest that there is something wrong with what is happening in the United States. Comparisons of incarceration rates between the United States and the rates in England[9] and Canada are equally shocking. Those countries, like the United States, use juries for important criminal cases and their trials proceed roughly as do ours with a prosecutor bringing out the evidence against the defendant first and then the defense putting forward its defense to the charge.

While there are differences in their criminal justice systems from ours, some of which will be brought out in this book, their criminal justice systems share our common law tradition. Yet, the incarceration rates in the two comparison countries are much lower than our rate. The rate for England is 140 per 100,000 and that of Canada is only 107 per 100,000. The U.S. incarceration rate of 655 citizens incarcerated per 100,000 is thus four times that in England and six times the rate in Canada.

The Timing of the Rise in the United States

What is surprising about mass incarceration in the United States is the timing of the rise as well as how quickly it rose. In the period from 1920 through the 1960s, the U.S. incarceration rate was steady and moderate, maybe even lenient, with the rate holding fairly steady at roughly 110 citizens incarcerated per 100,000. But in the late 1970s, when it appeared things were getting better for most of our citizens, the incarceration rate began shooting up to a high of 755 citizens in our prisons and jails in 2009, declining slightly to the present rates of 698 citizens in our prisons and jails per 100,000.

The obvious question is why did our incarceration rate rise so sharply? This book will suggest that the criminal procedure revolution played a role in the rise in our incarceration rate. In a nutshell: as our system of trial and pre-trial hearings became more expensive, we moved almost exclusively to plea bargaining, which permits many more defendants to flow through the system and into prisons. Also, the criminal procedure revolution sparked concern and a backlash from citizens and this led to pressure for harsher sentences, which, in turn, made plea bargaining more necessary for defendants as they could not risk trial in many cases.

This thesis is not one of the standard "causes" put forward by others for mass incarceration. The standard accounts of mass incarceration vary, but three frequently put forward, almost reflexively, by lawyers and judges are that mass incarceration was caused by: (a) the war on drugs; (b) the rise of violent crime in the United States; and (c) the enactment of harsh sentencing laws.

These explanations have been shown to be incomplete to explain an incarceration rate shooting up from 110 citizens incarcerated per 100,000 to a level six times greater in four decades. In this chapter, I will consider each of these "causes" for mass incarceration. My goal is not to claim that they are not factors in the rise of our incarceration rate, but rather that these explanations are limited in explaining what has happened and that we need to consider another factor in the rise in our incarceration rate: the Supreme Court's criminal procedure revolution.

Mass Incarceration and the "War on Drugs"

When talking with lawyers and judges and the topic of mass incarceration comes up, it is very common to hear them assert reflexively that mass incarceration is caused by "war on drugs." We made war on drugs—so the explanation goes—and in turning our attention to drugs, we began to lock up more and more of our citizens, primarily black citizens, in a futile effort to curb our nation's drug habit. In the end, we have filled our prisons with nonviolent drug offenders who do not deserve their fate.

That many Americans would share this same explanation for our prison population is not surprising as this "war on drugs" explanation is repeatedly put forward on the national stage. None other than President Barack Obama himself put forward this thesis about our prison population in 2015:

> But here is the thing: over the last few decades we've locked up more and more nonviolent drug offenders than ever before, for longer than ever before. And that is the reason our prison population is so high.[10]

Statements like President Obama's are unfortunate, first, because they are inaccurate in describing our prison population, but, second, because they imply an easy solution: end the war by cutting drug penalties severely or even decriminalizing most drugs and we can then can get back closer to our historical incarceration rates.

This claim that we are locking up vast numbers of our citizens for nonviolent drug crimes repeats itself over and over. In 2012, Michelle Alexander, a columnist for the *New York Times*, wrote a whole book on the topic, *The New Jim Crow: Mass Incarceration in the Age of Colorblindness*. In it, she states, "The impact of the war on drugs has been astounding. In less than 30 years, the U.S. penal population exploded around 300,000 to more than two million, with drug convictions accounting for the majority of the increase."[11]

At the present time, every democratic presidential candidate vows to fix "our broken criminal justice system." But when pushed for solutions, their positions meld into the claim that "too many people are serving too-lengthy sentences for nonviolent crimes, including those related to drugs."

When you understand why offenders are in prison, you can see why those who have studied the prison statistics, such as the Prison Policy Initiative—a think-tank on prison policies—term it a "myth" that releasing nonviolent drug offenders will end mass incarceration. In an article in the *Prison Policy Initiative* in March 2019, the authors had this to say about the connection between our drug laws and mass incarceration:

> It's true that police, prosecutors, and judges continue to punish people harshly for nothing more than drug possession. Drug offenses still count for the incarceration of almost a half a million people…. Drug arrests continue to give residents of over-policed neighborhoods criminal records, hurting their employment chances and increasing the likelihood of longer sentences for any future crimes.

But at the state and local levels, far more people are locked up for violent and property offenses than for drug offenses alone. To end mass incarceration, reforms will have to go much further than the "low hanging fruit."[12]

Of course, there is a link between drugs and other crimes. Many violent offenses may have been triggered by disputes over drugs, by the craving for drugs, or by the effects of the drugs themselves. And, of course, offenders may commit property crimes in order to get sufficient resources to buy drugs. Unfortunately, we cannot put exact numbers on how many violent or property crimes are linked to drugs.

John Pfaff, a criminologist at Fordham Law School, who has probably done more with crime statistics and prison statistics than any other scholar in the field, has examined prison populations from 1980 until 2013 from many different angles. In his book, *Locked In: The True Causes of Mass Incarceration and How to Achieve Real Reform*, he shows that no matter how you define the war on drugs—whether you just use drug convictions or you broaden it to include anyone who would not be in prison if the United States had not prohibited certain drugs or enforced their prohibition, the impact of drugs appears to be important, but is secondary to other factors. He concludes that:

> as long as reformers argue that prohibition itself is a major causal factor of mass incarceration, they will likely be disappointed in the extent to which decriminalization, or even legalization, reduces crime, and thus the extent to which either reduces prison populations.[13]

Consider Pfaff's analysis of the composition of state inmates by conviction offense in the period from 1980–1990 and then in the period from 1990–2009 (state prisons hold 87 percent of those incarcerated in prisons in the United States). In the years 1980–1990, drug offenders made up 33 percent of those incarcerated. This was a period of high crime rates in the United States and also includes the period when the crack epidemic exploded on the scene, starting in 1985. But in the years 1990–2009, drug offenders made up only 14 percent of those incarcerated. By 2013, Pfaff reports that six out of seven inmates were in prison for nondrug related crimes.[14]

In other words, the number of drug offenders in our prisons has declined considerably and it has continued to decline since 2009. Yet, we still have an incarceration rate very near its historic high.

The bottom line then on the war on drugs as it affects our incarceration rate is that the picture often put forward of prisons full of nonviolent drug offenders, many of whom have no previous record, is not accurate.

There are still very good reasons for reforming our drug laws. One obvious reason: there is a built-in bias in the way that drug laws are enforced. When police are pressured or incentivized to go after drugs aggressively, they are likely to concentrate their efforts in poorer inner-city neighborhoods where drugs are sold on the streets rather than try to ferret out drug deals that occur in private homes, business offices, and other places more shielded from the police. This leads to more arrests and minor convictions for the residents of those neighborhoods.

And, of course, reducing drug penalties will affect our incarceration rate. Even if only 15 or 16 percent of those in prison are incarcerated for drug crimes, reforming those laws will lower our prison population and our incarceration rate. But it will not get us anywhere close to our historic incarceration rate or even get us halfway to that rate.

Mass Incarceration and Rising Crime Rates

One relationship that one would think should hold fast to explain mass incarceration would be the link between crime rates and incarceration rates. Is it not self-evident that as crimes rates go up, the incarceration rate should go up? Put simply, if there are more robberies, there will be more arrests of robbers, more convictions of robbers, and more robbers going to prison. This would seem to explain the rise in our incarceration rate from 1975 until roughly 1990, when our crime rate and our incarceration rate rose in tandem (this period of rising crime included the period when the crack epidemic gripped urban areas).

But this explanation has problem. First of all, crime rates were rising in all Western countries during that period, yet their incarceration rates did not explode the way ours did. A good example is Canada, whose crime rates track the rise and fall of the crime rate in the United States. Yet, Canada's incarceration remained steady in the years when crime rates in both countries were rising.

However, the real problem with seeing our incarceration rate as linked to a rising crime rate was what occurred in the United States in the years from 1993 to the present time when crimes rates were falling dramatically. The Pew Research Center reports that the FBI annual statistics on violent crime show a decrease of 51 percent between 1993 and 2018, while the Bureau of Justice Statistics shows a decline of 71 percent in that same period.[15] What happened to our incarceration rate during that period? It did not decline at all.

This seems strange. People who commit violent crimes often end up in prison. Should we not expect at least a 10 or 15 percent decline on our rate of incarceration if violent crime falls by 50 percent or more? Yet, our prisons stayed full.

The same paradox applies to property crimes in that period. The Pew Research Center reports that the FBI data puts the decline between 1993 and 2018 at 54 percent, while the Bureau of Justice Statistics puts the decline at 69 percent.

Figure 1.3 shows the combined crime rate for violent crime and property crime from 1960 to 2018. What is startling is that our crime rate has dropped below the rate in 1970, just before our incarceration rate started its precipitous climb to historic heights.

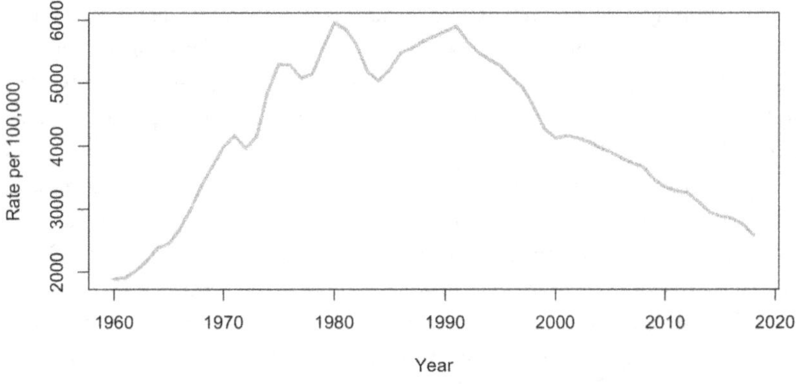

FIGURE 1.3 The Rise and Fall of U.S. Crime Rates, 1960–2018.

Source: Author.

This presents a conundrum: how can an incarceration rate be so impervious to a long-term decline in the rates of violent and property crimes? This book will suggest that part of the explanation lies in the fact that we are prosecuting far too many cases simply because we can.

Mass Incarceration and Harsh Sentencing Statutes

Another explanation frequently offered for the increase in our incarceration rate is "harsher sentencing laws."

There have been, of course, many harsh sentencing statutes enacted over the last four decades. For example, there were the infamous "650-Lifer Law" enacted in Michigan that threatened a life sentence to anyone in possession of 650 grams of cocaine or heroin and the so-called Rockefeller Drug Laws in New York which mandated a fifteen-year sentence to anyone caught with four ounces or more of cocaine or heroin (both now thankfully have been substantially softened). These laws threatened very long sentences to offenders, even if it was a first conviction.

Readers will likely also be familiar with Congressional legislation in 1986 at the height of the crack epidemic that created a sentencing disparity of 100:1 for trafficking in crack as compared to the same amount of powder cocaine. This had a sharp disparate racial impact since crack users and crack dealers were overwhelmingly black (Congress eventually passed the Fair Sentencing Act in 2010, which reduced the discrepancy between crack and powder cocaine to 18:1).

In addition to harsh drug laws, California and many other states passed very tough "three-strikes" laws, which punished offenders with long sentences, often life imprisonment, when a defendant is convicted of a third felony. The kinds of prior felonies that qualify for this enhanced punishment vary as does the exact punishment.

Harsh statutes no doubt have an impact on our incarceration rate and one hears news reports of prisoners receiving extremely long sentences that are disproportionate to the crime. In an article in the *Wall Street Journal*, a Colorado judge described giving a young person, who had robbed patrons in a restaurant a sentence of 146 years, which was just lightly over the mandatory minimum. He will be eligible for parole in 2065 when he will be almost ninety. It was a terrible crime, but no one was injured except the robber, who was shot by a patron who was armed.[16]

The connection of harsh sentences to our incarceration rate is complicated. The assumption would seem to be that we are putting more and more citizens into our prisons for longer and longer periods of time. To make it simple, if in year one we put away 100,000 prisoners for twenty years and continue to do that year after year, after a decade, we would end up with a prison population of a million prisoners.

But there is not the direct link one would expect between statutes with harsh sentences and incarceration. One major reason why there is not a link is that legislatures often pass harsh laws knowing that prosecutors will be highly selective in visiting these sanctions on offenders. Harsh sentencing laws—like so-called three-strikes laws—are used as a threat to coerce plea bargains, a subject to be discussed in Chapter 7, and this impacts our incarceration rate. But prisoners do not spend as much time in prisons as one might expect. We do read news accounts of very harsh sentences like the one just mentioned above in which the defendant in a robbery case received 146 years. Similarly, there are news accounts of persons sentenced to prison for long terms or even life for a singular drug offense, however, these make the news because they are exceptional.

Again, turning to John Pfaff's work, he reports that in many states half of all inmates are released in one to two years, and three-fourths are released within about three years. This holds true over a wide range of crimes. And Pfaff suggests these numbers may have even declined since 2000.[17] While there are many offenders serving sentences so long that the term of years is practically meaningless, the amount of time served in prisons has not changed noticeably over the decades. Median sentence lengths are often in the range of two to four years with 75 percent of inmates being released after six to eight years. Even sentences for violent crimes are not brutally long on average—the average length being 4.7 years.

What these numbers reveal is that we have enormous numbers of citizens being convicted of crimes and receiving relatively short sentences and these sentences pull down the average length of sentences when averaged with the sentences of prisoners serving extremely long sentences. In effect, what is occurring is a tremendous churn as large numbers of citizens pass through our prisons pulling down the average length of sentences. The Prison Policy Initiative report explains that each year many citizens are released from prison, but each year 600,000 citizens enter prisons. The jail churn is even greater with 10.6 million citizens passing through jails.[18]

In short, the picture of our prison and jail population at any given moment as including somewhat more than two million citizens does not come close to revealing the enormous numbers of citizens being impacted by a failing criminal justice system every year. Mass incarceration is more closely linked to the vast number of citizens *admitted* to prison and jails than to the length of sentences.

Again, this is not to downplay the injustices caused by harsh sentences or to deny that there are many serving sentences disproportionate to anyone's sense of proportion for their crime. But if we are aiming to cut our incarceration rate, we need to do something about the vast churn of inmates in and out of our prisons and jails each year.

Mass Incarceration and the Criminal Procedure Revolution

The timing of the steep rise in our incarceration rate is puzzling. One would think that our incarceration rate would have been much higher in the 1950s or 1960s when segregation was still state policy in many of our states and when the poverty rate was high. Yet, the rate began to increase sharply only in the period after the late 1970s—after civil rights for blacks had improved and after the federal government had passed War on Poverty legislation.

In addition, a set of powerful constitutional rights aiming to protect defendants—rich or poor—from the power of the state had been firmly put in place by the Supreme Court, beginning in the Warren Court years. The sweep of these rights is breathtaking. A right to a jury trial in a misdemeanor case, like a simple theft or shoplifting? A right of an arrestee after a crime to prevent any questioning by the police? The right of a defendant to have reliable evidence suppressed even where an officer acted in good faith and the crime is serious? All powerful stuff.

But something went wrong. The world became worse for defendants and we began putting away more and more of our citizens until our incarceration rate became something of a national embarrassment.

We can, and should, put some of the blame for our incarceration rate on legislators, on elected judges, on aggressive prosecutors, and, even, on the public that reacts emotionally to terrible crimes.

But we have to put a share of the blame on the Supreme Court as well. This book is intended to explain the risks in what the Court was doing and some of the mistakes the Court made in the criminal procedure revolution.

Chapter 2 will explain the risks the Court was taking in trying to make rules of criminal procedure by constitutional fiat.

Notes

1 Adam Liptak, Inmate Count in U.S. Dwarfs Other Nations', *New York Times*, April 23, 2008, available at: www.nytimes.com/2008/04/23/us/23prison.html.

2 Rough Justice, *The Economist*, July 22, 2010, available at: www.nytimes.com/2008/04/23/us/23prison.html.

3 Nazgol Ghandnoosh, U.S. Prison Population Trends: Massive Buildup and Modest Decline, *The Sentencing Project*, September 17, 2019, available at: www.sentencingproject.org/publications/u-s-prison-population-trends-massive-buildup-and-modest-decline/.

4 Michael O'Hear, *The Failed Promise of Sentencing Reform* (Santa Barbara, CA: Praeger 2017), xv.

5 Wendy Sawyer and Peter Wagner, Mass Incarceration: The Whole Pie 2019, *Prison Policy Initiative*, March 19, 2019, available at: www.prisonpolicy.org/reports/pie2019.html.

6 Criminal Justice Facts, *The Sentencing Project*, available at: www.sentencingproject.org/criminal-justice-facts/.

7 See Racial Disparity, *The Sentencing Project*, available at: www.sentencingproject.org/issues/racial-disparity/.

8 Criminal Justice Facts, *The Sentencing Project*, available at: www.sentencingproject.org/criminal-justice-facts/.

9 Throughout this book, "England" will be used as shorthand for England and Wales, which share the same legal system. Scotland and Northern Ireland each have their own distinct systems.

10 President Barack Obama, The White House, Remarks by the President at the NAACP Conference, July 14, 2015, available at: https://obamawhitehouse.archives.gov/the-press-office/2015/07/14/remarks-president-naacp-conference.

11 Michelle Alexander, *The New Jim Crow: Mass Incarceration in the Age of Colorblindness* (New York: The New Press, 2012), 6.

12 Sawyer and Wagner, Mass Incarceration.

13 John F. Pfaff, *Locked In: The True Causes of Mass Incarceration and How to Achieve Real Reform* (New York: Basic Books, 2017), 45.

14 Ibid., 32–33.

15 John Gramlich, 5 Facts about Crime in the U.S., Pew Research Center, October 17, 2019, available at: www.pewresearch.org/fact-tank/2019/10/17/facts-about-crime-in-the-u-s/.

16 Morris Hoffman, A Judge on the Injustice of America's Extreme Prison Sentences, *Wall Street Journal*, February 9, 2019, available at: www.wsj.com/articles/a-judge-on-the-injustice-of-americas-extreme-prison-sentences-11549557185.

17 Pfaff, *Locked In,* 52–55.

18 Sawyer and Wagner, Mass Incarceration.

2

THE RISKS OF CONSTITUTIONAL RULE-MAKING

Today, in the United States, there is hardly an aspect of the criminal process that has not been impacted by a long series of Supreme Court decisions that we sometimes refer to as the "criminal procedure revolution." Most citizens will be familiar with the most famous of these cases: *Gideon* v. *Wainwright*[1] on the right to counsel; *Mapp* v. *Ohio*[2] announcing an exclusionary rule for Fourth Amendment violations; and *Miranda* v. *Arizona*[3] setting out the warnings that must be administered to arrestees prior to questioning in a police station. But there are dozens more on issues that range from the way police may or may not approach a suspect on the street, the way in which the Constitution impacts jury selection, the way scientific tests must be introduced at trial so as to satisfy the confrontation clause, the balance between freedom of the press and the protection of a defendant's right to a fair trial, whether the public may be removed from the courtroom when a young victim testifies, the right of an indigent defendant to trial transcripts for an appeal, and so on.

Most of these decisions involve delicate balances among competing values. For example, if the police enter a home to make an arrest for a crime or in response to a 911 call, what should they be permitted to do to ensure their personal safety? Can they quickly look in adjoining rooms or look upstairs if they are in a house to see if others are present? Might this only be proper if the police are in hot pursuit of someone for a violent crime or should this be permitted routinely as a matter of officer safety in a domestic violence situation?

The Importance of the Constitution in Our Federal System

In most other countries, many of these questions would be handled through statutes or rules of procedure that would be proposed by legislative committees or commissions that would include judges, police officials, and others experienced in the particular issues. Often proposed rules would be published and feedback sought from the public as well as from those who would be directly affected by the rules.

But in the United States, because of our federal system, the Supreme Court has taken on the task of balancing the competing values in order to establish the rules that govern the investigation and prosecution of criminal cases throughout the country. One by one, the rights in the Bill of Rights, which were adopted as protections for citizens against federal power, have been held applicable to the states through the due process clause of the Fourteenth Amendment.

This has the advantage of providing a certain basic uniformity in the criminal process throughout the country because so many of the central features of our criminal justice system today are controlled by Supreme Court precedent.

This book will challenge some of the things the Court has done and will show that these affect our incarceration situation. In criticizing a series of Supreme Court decisions and linking them to our mass incarceration problem, this is not meant to shift responsibility for our situation away from other actors in our criminal justice system, such as legislators, prosecutors, judges, and law enforcement officers. The book will talk about these other actors and the consequences of their policies, statutes, and enforcement decisions.

But the role of the Supreme Court in our incarceration situation has not been part of the conversation on mass incarceration. This is understandable because it is painful. Most American lawyers were educated on a steady diet of cases from the criminal procedure revolution—cases where the Court acted decisively to try to remedy problems that often politicians would not face up to. Many of the earliest decisions were handed down in the middle of the civil rights era when southern states were often strongly resistant to integration and their criminal justice systems provided unequal justice for black citizens accused of crime.

The Court's opinions were powerful and often quite beautiful in explaining the values behind their decisions. To go back today, decades later, and suggest that some of these decisions were unwise and turned out to have unforeseen consequences will be disturbing.

There is today a mood in the country that is ready for some reforms of the system, especially in the area of sentencing. As mentioned in Chapter 1, high-population states like California, New York, and New Jersey have passed major reforms lowering sentences for many nonviolent crimes and even removing criminal sanctions completely for some drug offenses.

But if we are to lower our incarceration rate to a rate anywhere close to its historic levels or even get to half the present rate, we have to look at all aspects of our system, including elements of the criminal procedure revolution. We have a trial system that is dying out and we have a public that does not have strong trust in our criminal justice system. The Court's work has to be included in any evaluation of the system.

The author must acknowledge that many of the Court's decisions seemed sensible to him when they were handed down. But as the author gained experience as a federal prosecutor and later when the author began to study other Western systems of criminal justice, he came to see shortcomings in these decisions. Making sweeping constitutional rulings that will affect what happens in police stations and courthouses throughout the country was heady stuff. But it was always going to be highly risky. This chapter will consider some of serious risks the Court faces when it makes sweeping procedural rulings that are to apply to every criminal investigation, every trial, and every post-conviction appeal.

The Limitation of the Single Case Before the Court

When criminal cases go to the Supreme Court, the Court knows what happened to this particular defendant and what the lower court rulings were. Litigation is meant to sort out the facts of the case and determine who did what to whom and why. But when the Court is making constitutional rulings that will apply across the country, the narrow focus of traditional litigation is a problem.[4]

The case before the Court may be dramatic but the Court will often not know with precision: (a) how often this problem comes up; (b) how serious it is (compared to the case up for review) when it does arise; and (c) whether the problem occurs only in a few states or many.

The Court will, of course, have two argumentative briefs in front of it and may have some amicus briefs from others—but they are written from a partisan perspective. These briefs will vary in quality and they are not written with the goal of painting a complete picture of the issue. Indeed, the lawyers writing the briefs may have no idea exactly how often the problem before the Court comes up.

Obviously, there will be cases where the Court is simply deciding whether the ruling in the case below was correct, for example, was the confession voluntary or was the officer justified in stopping the suspect. But when the Court is making a more sweeping ruling, especially one that requires additional hearings, the limits of the case are a risk. The Court may be adding significant expense for a problem that may often be not serious.

The Court's Lack of Expertise

When a legislative body (or an administrative agency) is considering adopting a certain rule, the body can commission neutral studies of the issue or hold public hearings where experts of all stripes can give their opinions and be questioned about those opinions. It can gather the expertise that individual legislators do not possess.

The Court itself also possesses limited expertise on many of the issues it faces. Some justices have typically been chosen from one of the federal appellate benches or they may even have been a federal trial judge. But how many have been state court judges or spent any time in misdemeanor courtrooms? How many have been public defenders or prosecutors? How many have trial experience? Or are familiar with the private defense bar?

They, of course, have a bevy of smart young law clerks at their disposal. They can research any legal issue to find cases going back to the start of the republic but they themselves have no or very little experience in the field.

Many years ago, I had two former police officers in one of my criminal procedure classes and they were invaluable because they knew things that were not obvious if you have not been in the field. For example, I assumed that once an arrestee was handcuffed, the officers were pretty safe, but it turns out that there are people who are difficult to handcuff and who can slip out of handcuffs. There are also some people who can get their handcuffed hands from behind their backs to the front of their bodies, at which point, in a patrol car, the handcuffs can become weapons.

There are lots of questions where the Court simply lacks expertise. This is fine for important moral and political issues that come to the Court that help define our society—separate but equal is not equal, one person one vote. But when you are making rules about the questioning of suspects and where such questioning should take place, the Court lacks expertise on these issues.

Sometimes the lack of expertise or even a certain naivety shows itself in their opinions. In *Miranda* v. *Arizona*,[5] where the Court announced that the Fifth Amendment requires a right to counsel for arrestees prior to questioning at a police station, the opinion states:

> If the accused decides to talk to his interrogators, the assistance of counsel can mitigate the dangers of untrustworthiness.... The presence of a lawyer can also help to guarantee that the accused gives a fully accurate statement to the police....[6]

You are a public defender and are called to the police station to assist someone arrested for a serious assault and the arrestee says, "I want to confess. I did it." You have not looked at any police reports because they have not been written. You do not know the evidence, you do not know the arrestee, but you are going to help the arrestee make a fully accurate statement to the police? It is not going to happen. The lawyer will always say,

> Don't say anything. I need to study the evidence in the case and we can decide together what to do. A full confession may be appropriate but not at this time. It may be appropriate after I talk to the prosecutor, but don't say anything right now.

Another example of the Court's naivety occurs in a series of cases involving lineups. In *United States* v. *Wade*,[7] the Court was worried, with good cause, about the high risk of convicting innocent defendants if lineups are suggestive and unfair. The Court in *United States* v. *Wade* quoted an article stating that: "'the influence of improper suggestion at lineups upon identifying witnesses probably accounts for more miscarriages of justice that any other single factor—perhaps it is responsible for more such errors than all other factors combined.'"[8]

The Court worried, with good cause, that once a witness has picked out the accused at a lineup, the witness is unlikely to change their identification at trial. It is very difficult for a witness to sort out whether the witness is making the identification based on memories of the crime or whether the witness is actually making the identification because of the suggestive lineup. Thus, said the Court, "for all practical purposes," the issue of identity is determined at a lineup, not at trial:

> The trial which might determine the defendant's fate may well not be in the courtroom but at the pretrial confrontation, with the State aligned against the accused, the witness the sole jury, and the accused unprotected against the overreaching, intentional or unintentional, and with little or no effective appeal from the judgment rendered by the witness—"that's the man."[9]

So the Court's solution? To protect a suspect from the harms of a suggestive post-indictment lineup, the Court declared that such a lineup was a critical stage for Sixth Amendment purposes requiring the right to counsel at such a lineup.

The problems to which suggestive lineup procedures lead are serious and real. But the Court's remedy was naïve in the extreme because defense lawyers do not want to help the police ensure that a lineup is fair. It is an awkward position in which to put a defense lawyer. They do not want to improve the lineup or give their imprimatur to a lineup that will lead to their client's conviction. And if the lawyer says nothing but only observes? Still a damning position for the lawyer (an officer who administered the lineup testifying at trial: "I asked counsel three times if there were suggestions to improve the lineup and counsel said nothing").

Also, if counsel is present simply to observe a lineup without saying anything and they see unfairness in a lineup, how will they bring this out in court at trial? By withdrawing and testifying themselves?

The problem of suggestive lineups is serious but the Court's solution—extending the right to counsel to lineups—is confused, naïve, and expensive. There are many other ways of insuring a lineup is fair such as by recording the lineup including recording what is said to witnesses before the lineup and after the lineup or by making sure where possible that the lineup is administered "double blind" meaning that neither the witness nor the administrator of the lineup is aware of who the suspect is or even if the suspect is in the lineup. But insisting that fair trials require counsel at a lineup is not a good solution to the problem.

The Inability to Obtain Feedback on Proposed Rules, Requirements, or Standards

The previous example shows another problem with adding rules and procedures by constitutional fiat: the inability of obtaining feedback on possible rules. An agency or a legislative body can seek comments on possible rules. Perhaps the rule the Court is thinking of will solve the problem, but perhaps it is too narrow or too broad for the particular problem. Or the rule may impact courts or police officers in rural counties in a way that differs markedly from the way it would impact courts and police forces in large cities.

Making the draft of a statute or a proposed regulation available for comment will often improve the proposal as there may be possible negative impacts that can now be brought to the attention of the drafters which could be limited or avoided in later versions.

Another way to think of the problem is to contrast a legislature's approach to a problem with that of the Court. Legislation is much more about alternatives for solving a problem. Legislators have to consider factors such as the likely effectiveness of various proposals, whether a moderate remedy might suffice, and, of course, the costs of a proposal.

Constitutional decisions are generally not concerned with costs. They are about the constitutional right of citizens and if a right needs to be protected, there is no issue of costs; the federal government and the states have a duty to protect that right from being violated.

But at some point, any criminal justice system runs into cost issues. If a ruling makes trials more expensive or makes certain sorts of investigations much more difficult, there will be costs to that ruling. Legislatures can better assess the costs of rules and, if the cost will be significant, they can perhaps find a less expensive alternative or perhaps secure savings elsewhere.

The Court's Limited Options for Reform

Relating to the issue of costs is the limited arsenal of Supreme Court options for solving a particular problem. It does not have the range of legislative options that might be available to limit the particular problems. It cannot, for example, draft statutes or rules of procedure that might prevent abuses or trial problems from occurring in the first place. The lineup problem is an example. It really calls for a fairly sophisticated reform measure that would include: the number of the people in the lineup; the requirement of an administrator with no prior knowledge of whom the suspect might be; a rule about the relative similarity of those in the lineup; what should be said to the witness before the lineup; a mandate on the use of video equipment and where the equipment should be placed; the way in which statements should be taken from a witness after the lineup and preserved; and so on. The rule may also have to include exceptions from some of the restrictions if a lineup has to be conducted quickly for some reason (such as the delicate health of a witness).

The problem is that the Court cannot do such comprehensive legislation under the guise of a constitutional ruling as it has to draw with a broad brush and it would be hard to see how due process demands many of these very sensible lineup precautions. Good lineup procedures could foreclose many later problems.

There are other areas where a rule of criminal procedure or a statute might be able to keep a problem from occurring. Consider jury selection, for example. In many cases involving black defendants, the prosecution is trying to remove as many black prospective jurors as it can, using peremptory challenges. (Obviously, it can happen the other way around with the defense striking black jurors if the crime victim is black.) Peremptory challenges are, of course, those challenges for which a prosecutor or a defense attorney need not give an explanation.

One way to limit the problem would be to cut back on the number of peremptory challenges, so it would be much harder for a lawyer to direct the challenges to jurors of a certain race or gender. There are challenges for cause with which lawyers can remove jurors who are likely to favor one side or the other, so why do lawyers need eight, ten, or sometimes even twenty peremptory challenges in a routine criminal case? What if the number of peremptory challenges was reduced to three or two in routine cases? Peremptory challenges could still serve their function as a back-up to challenges for cause, but it would be much harder to remove systematically all the jurors of a certain race or gender. It would also help ensure a broader cross-section of citizens of juries even apart from race or gender. (Right now, it is fine for a prosecutor or a defense attorney to use a raft of peremptories to remove all veterans, all college-educated jurors, all jurors with children, and so on.) We talk a good game about a jury as being a cross-section of society but we honor it in the breach.

But limiting peremptories really is a legislative solution—there might have to be exceptions that would permit a few more peremptories in certain types of cases or perhaps if peremptory challenges were sharply limited, the standard for a challenge for cause might need to be expanded.

But sensible as a rule limiting peremptories might be, the Court cannot dictate rules like this. So instead, the issue for the Court was: (a) whether to make peremptories less "peremptory"; or (b) whether to abolish by constitutional fiat all peremptory challenges; or (c) do nothing about the abuse of peremptories.

In *Batson* v. *Kentucky*,[10] the Court chose option (a) which requires a delicate hearing into whether a lawyer used a challenge to remove a juror *solely* on the basis of race. This is not an easy task where challenges are labeled "peremptory" and lawyers can remove jurors for any reason except *solely* on the basis of race. Our trial tradition allows lawyers to question prospective jurors and aren't there always reasons a lawyer can find for supporting a challenge that will mask a challenge on the basis of race—too old, too young, sloppy appearance, lack of eye contact, casual demeanor, too educated, and so on?

Batson v. *Kentucky* was unusual in that the issue of barring peremptory challenges on the basis of race had been percolating in state courts and lower federal courts for several years and, in addition, the Supreme Court had hinted, in a case out of New York denying certiorari, that it was thinking of doing something about peremptory challenges based on race.[11]

In response to the Court's hint, federal trial judges urged the Court not to go down the road of requiring trial judges to ferret out motives for individual peremptory challenges. One argued:

> Even assuming the existence of a clear theoretical line regarding what types of peremptory challenges are legal, enormous difficulties would arise from any attempt to implement such a rule in practice.... A great deal of time, effort and expense would be necessary to attempt to determine whether any given peremptory challenge is legal. Any such determination would entail the extremely difficult task of assessing the internal motives of attorneys.... Rather than introduce such a rule, it would be infinitely preferable if the entire system of peremptory challenges were abolished.[12]

Another judge warned that "[t]he transactional costs involved in litigating whether the reasons are 'pretextual' will be vast and the reliability of the results uncertain."[13]

A third judge stated that while a rule barring peremptory challenges solely on the basis of race would be "well-intentioned" such a rule "raises innumerable practical difficulties that outweigh its usefulness."[14]

Now, two decades later, the failures of *Batson* v. *Kentucky* are well documented. In a concurring opinion in which he argues for abolishing peremptory challenges because of the failure of *Batson* v. *Kentucky*, Justice Breyer cites a number of articles and studies on the ineffectiveness of *Batson* v. *Kentucky*.[15]

But if the present *Batson* v. *Kentucky* regime is costly in drawing out jury selection while benefiting few prospective jurors, the abolition of peremptory challenge presents costs that are unknown—what will this do to trial verdicts? How often will there be hung juries and are there certain jurisdictions or certain types of cases in which there will be more hung juries? These are costs that are difficult to calculate. Hung jury rates presently vary around the country with the rate being 5 percent very typically but sometimes going up to 15 percent or 20 percent in some cities.

The point here is not to argue for or against peremptory challenges, rather it is to show not only the power of Supreme Court decisions but also the risks. Abolishing peremptory challenges is a no-go in most legislatures where trial lawyers have a lot of influence. They are a trial lawyer's security blanket, and jury selection is much emphasized in the United States. The Court, however, can do it in one swift move. But, again, what are the costs?

Tackling Issues in Isolation from Other Issues

The problem for the Court in trying to solve the misuse of peremptory challenges is that it can only deal with peremptory challenges in isolation from other issues. One legislative compromise, that might have been attractive at the time *Batson* v. *Kentucky* was being decided, might have been to abolish peremptory challenges but to permit nonunanimous verdicts.[16] England abolished peremptory challenges, however, judges may accept a nonunanimous verdict of 10–2 after two hours of deliberation.

There are many reasons to object to this proposal—will it lead to false convictions? Why the numbers 10 and 2?

The point here is not the merits of this specific proposal but the way in which issues can be tied together to reach something of a compromise. If this were a legislative proposal, it might be that a state would set up a pilot project to see how this works with less serious crimes in a certain county. How much time does it save? What percentage of cases end in verdicts that are unanimous or non-unanimous?

Unfortunately, the Court does not have the ability of stepping back and seeing how different pieces of the system are working together. In constitutional litigation, the Court's focus is narrowly tied to one issue.

The Language of Constitutional Decisions

When the Court announces a decision imposing a rule that must be followed by police, prosecutors, or judges in every police station or every courthouse in the country, the Court has to be strong and sweeping in the language it uses to announce the rule. The Court has to find the procedure to be demanded by the Constitution and to be obvious. It cannot say things like "This was the best proposal on which we were able to get a majority to agree" or "We think this decision is supported by common law history but there is some evidence that raises a doubt." Instead, it must insist that the particular constitutional provision on which it is basing its ruling "demands no less." What this means is that the Court tends to oversell its ruling and strongly commit to a rule or a standard that may not work out. At the same time, the Court will often tend to denigrate the rule it is striking down and replacing. There will often be sound practical reasons why a state does something one way, but they will be dismissed as clearly insufficient to support the state procedure.

Writing in Constitutional Stone

One of the obvious differences between legislation and constitutional decision-making is the permanence of constitutional rules. With constitutional decisions, the Court is saying, "This is what this clause of an amendment means in this sort of situation. If you want to change it, you need to change the Constitution." Generally, we are stuck with what the Court has done because it is not easy for the Court to say, "Gosh, this really didn't work well at all so we need to rethink that decision."

Of course, sometimes the Court does retreat and effectively reverse itself but when it does so, it is not very elegant. Mentioned above was the Court's decision to protect suspects from unfair and suggestive lineups, by requiring defense counsel at lineups and how awkward that use of counsel is for assuring the accuracy of lineups.

Five years later, the Court effectively overruled the earlier case by limiting the right to counsel to lineups after the defendant has been charged.[17] But lineups almost always occur before a suspect is charged with a crime. The police want to make sure they have the right person and will want to put the arrestee in a lineup immediately when memories of witnesses are fresh. And prosecutors are not going to charge someone with a crime, especially a serious crime, if they don't know whether the witnesses can actually identify the suspect as the one who committed the crime.

The upshot is that the Constitution demands that counsel be present to make sure lineups are fair in order to prevent serious miscarriages of justice—except for the vast majority of lineups. The Court effectively gutted the prior opinion without having to say, "Asking counsel to ensure the fairness of lineups was a bad idea."

Another problem with Court decisions as they age is that there can be social changes or technological changes that make older decisions seem badly outdated or even retrograde. An example of social change passing the Court by is *Globe Newspaper Co. v. Superior Court*,[18] in which the Court dealt with a Massachusetts statute which barred the press and public from the courtroom when a victim under the age of eighteen testified in a sexual offense trial. There was a transcript available so the hearing was not "secret" but it allowed the victim to testify in a little less public way as the public gallery would be empty.

The Court struck down this statute and made the bar to removing the public very high. A trial judge needs to hold a hearing and make findings sufficient to justify closure. The state's interest in closure "must be a weighty one." The Court went on:

> Whereas in the present case, the State attempts to deny the right of access in order to inhibit the disclosure of sensitive information, it must be shown that the denial is necessitated by a compelling governmental interest, and is narrowly tailored to serve that interest.[19]

The Court's test is confused and vague. First of all, it is not "the disclosure of sensitive information" that the rule is trying to control; the transcript is available. It is about giving some privacy to the victim in how they testify.

And what findings does the Court contemplate in order to support removing the public? A twelve-year-old victim is going to testify about being raped at knifepoint and what the defendant did to intimate parts of their body or what sex acts they were made to perform? Or a victim of child pornography is going to testify about what sex acts they were made to perform as the acts were recorded for distribution on the Internet? Would either of these scenarios be sufficient to close the hearing?

It may be that the Massachusetts rule is too broad—perhaps it should be limited to victims under sixteen or maybe a representative of the press should be allowed to stay in the courtroom. (Today, a compromise might be a video feed into a different courtroom that the press and public could watch.) But there needs to be clarity on an issue like this. Without clear guidance, prosecutors are going to be reluctant to move to remove the public when there is the risk of a second trial if the ruling might be reversed.

Globe Newspaper Co. v. Superior Court is an old case that is outdated at this point—it was decided thirty-eight years ago. The treatment of sexual assault victims has changed in many ways. At one point in the case, the Court notes that "the press is not denied access to the transcript … thus the statute cannot prevent the press from publishing the substance of that testimony, as well as the victim's identity."[20] This statement confounds three distinct issues. The way in which young victims should be allowed to give their testimony, the substance of that testimony, and the identity of sexual assault victims.

On the identity issue, most countries shield the identity of sexual assault victims of any age from publication. England, for example, gives victims of sexual assault lifelong anonymity from publication of their names by the press or even by members of the public on social media.[21] In Canada, a judge may make an order restricting publication or transmission in any way of a victim under eighteen's identity.[22]

But identity of the victim is not what the Massachusetts statute was about. Nor was the statute intended to keep the victims' testimony hidden or private. There was a transcript available. The only issue was whether to give young victims a small measure of privacy as they explain the attack.

Later in this book, the author will discuss the victims' movement, which was in its nascent stages in 1982. Today, the movement is a force to be reckoned with on criminal justice issues as they affect victims. One suspects that *Globe Newspaper Co.* v. *Superior Court* would not come out the same way today. But, at a minimum, the Court would treat the issue with much greater understanding.

The Supreme Court and the Law of Unintended Consequences

Any government action, no matter how well intended, may have consequences that overwhelm or even undercut the benefits that the law sought to achieve. This phenomenon is what economists refer to as "the law of unintended consequences." The law of unintended consequences is usually traced back to the legal philosopher John Locke in 1691, who argued against a proposal in Parliament by mandating that the market rate of 6 percent interest be lowered to a maximum rate of 4 percent.[23] The proposal was intended to stimulate a stagnant economy by making cheaper money available to new businesses or businesses wanting to expand.

But Locke argued that it would have the opposite effect: those with money would find other investments for their money rather than settle for an under-market return. Or, having the money others need, they would find ways around the law to get their 6 percent and those schemes would make things worse for borrowers, not better.

Today if you plug "the law of unintended consequences" into a search engine, you will find numerous articles on federal ethanol legislation designed to reduce fuel costs, cut greenhouse emissions, and cut dependence on foreign oil.[24] The articles detail the horrific environmental consequences—not just nationally but internationally—when a major grain exporter is encouraged to devote more and more of its corn production to ethanol.

The Supreme Court is not immune from the law of unintended consequences and, for the reasons mentioned above, such as the Court's limited data on issues before it, the risks of something turning out wrong are greater than they are for legislation. This is where we are today. The Court took major risks in issuing sweeping rulings that were intended to improve our criminal justice system but, looking back with 20–20 hindsight, it was a high-risk endeavor and the "criminal procedure revolution" contributed to our present incarceration problem. The Court took the protections in the Bill of Rights and applied them to the states in the same way they were to be applied in the federal system. The result is a series of powerful protections that exist in theory while the reality is something different.

The next chapter, Chapter 3, will discuss the problems in taking protections that apply against the federal government in criminal cases and applying them in the same way to the states.

Notes

1 See *Gideon* v. *Wainwright*, 372 U.S. 335 (1963).
2 See *Mapp* v. *Ohio*, 367 U.S. 643 (1961).
3 See *Miranda* v. *Arizona*, 384 U.S. 436 (1966).
4 A book that was very helpful in my thinking on the issues in this chapter was Donald L. Horowitz, *The Courts and Social Policy* (Washington, DC: Brookings Institute, 1977). In the book, Horowitz takes four different Supreme Court cases, including *Mapp* v. *Ohio*, and shows the difficulties the Court has in finding and applying data relevant to the decisions, and in understanding and predicting the effects of decisions.

 5 See *Miranda v. Arizona*, 384 U.S. 436 (1966).
 6 See *Miranda v. Arizona*, 384 U.S. at 470.
 7 See *United States v. Wade*, 388 U.S. 218 (1967).
 8 See *United States v. Wade*, 388 U.S. at 229 (quoting Patrick M. Wall, *Eye-Witness Identification in Criminal Cases* (Springfield, IL: C.C. Thomas, 1965, 26)).
 9 See *United States v. Wade*, 388 U.S. at 235–236.
10 See *Batson v. Kentucky*, 476 U.S. 79 (1986).
11 See *McCray v. United States*, 461 U.S. 961 (1983).
12 See *King v. County of Nassau*, 581 F. Supp. 493, 501–502 (E.D.N.Y. 1984).
13 See *Roman v. Abrams*, 608 F. Supp. 1433, 1440 (S.D.N.Y.), rev'd, 822 F.2d 214 (2dCir. 1987).
14 See *Schrebier v. Salamack*, 629 F. Supp. 1433, 1440 (S.D.N.Y. 1985), aff'd, 822 F.2d 214.
15 See *Miller-El v. Dretke*, 545 U.S. 231, 266–269 (2005) (Breyer, J. concurring).
16 The Court has since taken this option off the table because it recently ruled in *Ramos v. Louisiana*, 590 U.S. (2020) that the Sixth Amendment requires unanimous verdicts. At the time of the decisions in *Ramos v. Louisiana*, only Oregon permitted nonunanimous jury verdicts.
17 See *Kirby v. Illinois*, 406 U.S. 682 (1972).
18 See *Globe Newspaper Co. v. Superior Court*, 457 U.S. 596 (1982).
19 Ibid., 606–607.
20 Ibid., 610.
21 See Gemma Mullin and Richard Wheatstone, Know the Law, What are UK Anonymity Rights for Rape Cases and Why are Victims' Names Kept Secret, *Sun*, July 11, 2017, available at: www.thesun.co.uk/news/1923580/uk-anonymity-rape-sex-offence-cases/.
22 See Section 486.4(1), *Order Restricting Publication*, Martin's Criminal Code 2018.
23 Roger Woolhouse, *Locke: A Biography* (Cambridge: Cambridge University Press, 2007), 290–291.
24 See, for example, James M. Griffin and Mauricio Cifunetes Soto, The Unintended Consequences of America's Ethanol Policy, *Houston Chronicle*, May 4, 2012, available at: www.chron.com/opinion/outlook/article/The-unintended-consequences-of-America-s-ethanol-3535969.php; and Cinnamon Stillwell, Fuel or Folly: Ethanol and the Law of Unintended Consequences, *SFGATE*, April 2, 2008, available at: www.sfgate.com/politics/article/Fuel-or-folly-Ethanol-and-the-law-of-2533126.php.

3

THE FEDERAL SYSTEM, STATE SYSTEMS, AND *MIRANDA V. ARIZONA*

The Bill of Rights—the first ten amendments of the Constitution—was enacted to protect citizens against the power of the federal government. In the so-called "criminal procedure revolution," which began during the Warren Court, the Court used the due process clause of the Fourteenth Amendment to impose almost all of the protections of the Bill of Rights on the states. Thus, the protection against unreasonable searches and seizures, the right to counsel, the right to jury trials, the confrontation clause, the protection against compulsory self-incrimination, and so on were eventually made applicable against the states. Today, all of the rights in the Bill of Rights, with one exception, are applied against the states—the lone exception being indictment by grand jury, which the Court has never applied to the states.

In application, these rights are to be applied in the same way in state courts as they are in federal courts. The one concession to the states has been the size of juries: while federal juries must be composed of twelve jurors, the states are permitted to have juries of as few as six.

Cases in the Federal System

The problem in treating the federal system and state systems as nearly identical is that they are very different in resources, in the number of cases, in the type of crimes, and in the sorts of defenses that are often raised. Just the volume of cases alone suggests caution in adding complexity to the pre-trial or trial stage because the impact will be quite different in the federal system compared to state systems.

The starting point is that the federal system is a limited jurisdiction. Bank robbery is a federal crime because banks are federally insured, but the vast majority of robberies—of convenience stores, of fast-food franchises, of retail stores, and of citizens on the street—are the responsibility of the states. Rape, burglary, larceny, and other common major crimes are primarily state cases.

While the federal system has fewer routine crimes to investigate and prosecute, it has many complicated crimes to handle that would be beyond the competency of most state prosecutors to investigate and bring to trial. For example, insider-trading cases, Ponzi schemes, price-fixing, tax frauds, and major environmental crimes are just a few of the cases that will almost always end up in federal courts rather than state courts. One reason these sorts of cases end up in federal court is that the federal system has tremendous resources that are rarely available to state prosecutors. There are large federal agencies such as the Internal Revenue Service, Customs, the Environmental Protection Agency, and the Security Exchange Commission that have investigators, computer experts, accountants, forensic scientists, and the like to carry out sophisticated investigations that may spill across state lines or even international borders. If an investigation begins in California but it later turns out the crime has tentacles in Florida, that is not a problem for federal agencies as they have agents all around the country and they are used to working together.

In addition, federal prosecutors have investigative powers and resources that most prosecutors do not have. In major cities, there are grand juries sitting every day that can be used to carry out lengthy investigations. These grand juries can force the production of thousands of pages of documents and computer files from banks, corporations, phone companies, and the like, and they have the experts to comb through those documents to see how they relate to their investigations.

To an extent that is not possible for state prosecutors, federal prosecutors choose their defendants. If a federal investigation does not work out, they will not prosecute the case. They will move on to another case. Federal prosecutors tend to be conservative and the system allows them to be selective on the cases they file. When they bring charges against defendants, the cases are strong or they will not be filed.

If someone steals a Mercedes in Phoenix and drives it to Los Angeles, that is a federal crime as state borders were crossed, but federal prosecutors will not prosecute that case. A "one-car case," in prosecutor-speak, in federal court? Unlikely. They will decline to prosecute.

But if it is a car ring where thieves are targeting late model cars, moving them interstate to a "chop shop," and selling the parts to unscrupulous repair shops, the federal prosecutors would definitely be interested. But someone has to handle that one-car case and proving the defendant stole the car or knew it was stolen can be much trickier than proving the case against a multi-defendant car ring (where defendants will line up to offer to cooperate).

Cases in State Systems

The states are in a very different situation when it comes to choosing cases—they cannot choose their serious cases in the same way. When someone calls 911 because of a shooting, it is not the FBI that has to go out and try to sort out what has happened or what is still happening. If a store has been burgled or if someone has been sexually assaulted, the police cannot just decide not to pursue the crime and hand it over to someone else.

This raises another important distinction between the federal model and the state model, namely, the very different nature and volume of federal and state crimes. For all practical purposes, the federal courts do not handle violent crime. Of course, this is painting with a broad brush as there are violent crimes committed against federal officials, or committed in national parks, or on tribal lands. None of us can forget the domestic terrorist attack against the federal building in Oklahoma City, which took the lives of 168 victims. However, violent crimes are not common in federal courts. In 2018, the entire federal system handled 2,735 violent offenses. That may seem like a lot but the city of Los Angeles alone that year—a year in which violent crime was down—prosecuted 27,246 violent offenses.

It is not just the number of violent offenses in state courts that distinguishes state systems from the federal system, but the nature of violent offenses as well: state courts have a very high level of interpersonal crimes which would rarely surface in federal court.

Whether it is murder, sexual assault, domestic abuse, battery, or even burglary, a very high percentage of these cases involve victims where the suspect has had a prior relationship with the victim.

These cases are often messy. Why would a young person come home and put a bullet through the back of their father's head? Or why would a burglar break into the house of a former co-worker … or an ex-spouse? Why did the assailant pull out a knife outside a bar and stab a patron with whom the assailant had been drinking earlier? There are lots of reasons for crimes. There are stories here and they deserve to be told and listened to. When many of these cases come to trial, they are not like the television dramas of courtroom trials. Morris Hoffman, a trial judge in Denver, who has presided over hundreds of trials, once told me, "Most trials are not who-dun-its with prosecutors saying this was the perpetrator and the defense claiming innocence. They are about the moral guilt of the defendant." Sometimes that will mean the comparative moral guilt of the defendant versus the victim.

You do not see these interpersonal cases often in federal court. Compared to state cases, federal cases are strong; they are usually major in importance and they are clean. The acquittal rate in state courts should always be much higher than in federal courts.

Another distinguishing feature of state systems, especially in large western states, is the fact that some counties are very rural. While most violent crime occurs in urban areas with sophisticated police departments and knowledgeable judges, serious crime can happen in a remote and rural county. The judges in those counties—or often the only judge in the county—may not have a law degree and the police officer called to the scene will have received some basic training, but may lack any experience with a serious crime. If the county is poor, salaries for the prosecutor and police will be lower than in urban counties, making it difficult sometimes to attract applicants to those positions and difficult to retain such personnel.

Many years ago, the then Chief Justice of the Colorado Supreme Court told me that some of the most difficult criminal procedure issues came to the court from rural counties. This should not be surprising. Officers—and judges—in those counties do not have the training, the experience, and the resources when a terrible crime suddenly happens in their county.

One final difference between the federal system and state systems is the very different role misdemeanor cases play in state systems compared to the federal system (misdemeanors are those crimes punishable by up to a year in prison).

For all practical purposes, the federal system does not have misdemeanor cases. Perhaps some traffic violations on federal lands or minor crimes in national parks, but they don't have the flood of minor crimes that deluge criminal courts in major cities—shoplifting, petty theft, turnstile jumping, prostitution, drunk driving, simple assaults, and so on. Misdemeanors are a minor inconvenience in federal courts, while in state systems, 75–80 percent of criminal cases are misdemeanors.

These cases often go under the radar when the topic is mass incarceration because many are dismissed over time and when defendants do plead guilty, they are usually put on probation or given a short sentence in a local jail. However, misdemeanors play an important role in incarceration. In the words of the Prison Policy Initiative, misdemeanors are "incarceration's front door" because they lead to more serious problems down the road.[1] Even an arrest that ends in a dismissal of all charges can have a serious impact. If it means a day or two in jail, the arrestee may be fired from their job or lose hourly income that is needed for their family.

Pleading guilty and being put on probation keeps the offender out of jail, but probation too often has incarcerative effects as the tight restrictions put on offenders sets them up for failure. Probation tends to look for slip-ups and mistakes by the person on probation, instead of providing the sorts of support that would help the offender avoid future problems with the law.

Previously, it was mentioned that more than ten million offenders pass through misdemeanor courts each year in the United States. Many will have their cases dismissed, but the effects of that volume of citizens marked with even just an arrest has an impact on incarceration rates.

Miranda v. *Arizona* in the Federal and State Systems

When you understand the differences between the federal system and state systems, it is easy to see why the Court was taking a major risk in applying the provisions in the Bill of Rights to the states in the same way that they would apply in the federal system. The types of cases differ, the resources differ, and, especially, the number of cases differ radically between the federal and state systems. When the Court adds an additional hearing to the criminal process, the effect on the federal system is likely to be slight. To use an analogy, federal cases are like large battleships—destroyers, aircraft carriers, and the like. You can throw thirty-foot waves of procedure at them and they will be largely unaffected. But state cases are far more varied. Their fleets consist of trawlers, dinghies, motorboats, and lots of rowboats. If you throw a thirty-foot wave at that fleet, the results will not be pretty.

One of the Supreme Court decisions that impacts the federal system only slightly but state systems in a major way is *Miranda* v. *Arizona*,[2] one of the most famous cases of the Warren Court era. Four cases were joined in *Miranda* v. *Arizona* for the Court's review and in three of the four cases, the suspect under arrest had been given warnings by the police before questioning, but they were not the four warnings that the Court announced must be given to arrestees before questioning or any incriminating statements must be suppressed. The four famous warnings are: you have the right to remain silent, any statements you make may be used as evidence against you, you have the right to an attorney, and, if you cannot afford an attorney, one will be appointed for you.

Over the years, there have been many cases in the aftermath of the decision on issues such as whether the arrestee must expressly waive their rights,[3] whether the police can approach the arrestee who asserted their right to remain silent to re-interrogate them,[4] what constitutes questioning an arrestee,[5] whether an arrestee should be told that there is a lawyer hired by their family outside waiting to assist them,[6] and so on.

Miranda v. *Arizona* is deeply concerned with police pressure, especially police trickery, being used to entice suspects to answer questions. Relying heavily on a "how to get suspects to confess" manual by Fred Inbau and John Reid,[7] the Court enumerates some of the trickery police are told to use in the book: the good cop/bad cop routine in questioning, claiming falsely to have incriminating evidence against the suspect, implied promises of leniency for confessing, and so on.

The problem with *Miranda* v. *Arizona* is that it went too far and gave arrestees the right to determine whether *any* questions could be put to them after arrest. This is not so important for the federal system due to the nature of their cases and also the timing of their arrests. The federal investigators and prosecutors will do their investigation first and confront the suspect with the evidence, sometimes in a grand jury setting, as the investigation goes along. Federal crimes do not usually demand an immediate arrest.

State cases are very different because the timing of an arrest is often not in the hands of the police and the arrest will often occur prior to the investigation. Assume police are called by two neighbors who heard a shout from the apartment above them followed by what sounded like a gunshot. They then went to the window and saw a man run from the building. They described him as a white male of average height with long hair, wearing jeans and an Oakland Raiders jersey. The police arrive, enter the apartment, and find a woman on the floor dead from a shot to the head. A handgun is lying on the ground next to the body. Homicide detectives are called to the scene, while a radio call is put out seeking a white male fitting the description given by the neighbors.

A person fitting that description is spotted by an officer in a patrol car a half-mile from the shooting scene walking hurriedly along the sidewalk. The detectives tell the officer to place the suspect under arrest and bring him to the station for questioning.

At the station, the detective gives the arrestee his *Miranda* v. *Arizona* warnings and he asks for an attorney. A public defender arrives shortly. The attorney and the arrestee state that there will be no questioning of the suspect. (This scenario of the arrival of a lawyer to assist in the interrogation room is a bit of a fiction as the police know that there will be no questioning of the suspect once a lawyer is on the scene, so no lawyer will be called to the station.)

The Start of Adversary Criminal Proceedings?

At that point, shortly after the arrest of the suspect, access to the suspect for questioning is at an end. Why should that be so, given the need to figure out what happened that caused the death of the person in the apartment? The Court in *Miranda* v. *Arizona* had an explanation:

> … when the individual is first subjected to police interrogation while in custody at the station or otherwise deprived of his freedom of action in any significant way, it is at this point that our adversary system of criminal proceeding commences, distinguishing itself from the inquisitorial system recognized in some countries.[8]

This is a very unusual view of what an adversary system is: it kicks in when the investigation has barely started and before any charges have been filed? It looks like a homicide perhaps, but we do not know who pulled the trigger or why it happened. Sure, the fact that the arrestee ran from the apartment (apparently) is suspicious, but maybe there are other innocent reasons why the arrestee did not want to be there when the police arrived. We are not sure whose gun was left at the scene, if there are fingerprints on the gun, and what the relationship might be between the arrestee and the deceased.

This is not to deny the concerns the Court had with questioning suspects at the police station or to say that counsel should not be provided. However, the conceptualization of questioning itself as somehow wrong or suspect, which seems to be behind the Court's thinking, is naïve when it comes to investigations.

If one were writing a manual for criminal investigators, wouldn't it make sense to say: investigators should interview anyone with information about the crime; accurate records should be made of such interviews; and investigators should return to witnesses if further investigation raises other questions that witnesses might answer?

It would be a strange manual that said interview everyone who can further the investigation except do not talk to anyone who may be or definitely is a suspect. This is exactly the opposite of what most would think to be reasonable—you should definitely talk to the suspect to see what their account of the matter is and to see if perhaps there are innocent explanations for what has happened or explanations that are mitigating. Those explanations should be fully investigated as well.

That there is an arrest complicates things—arrests are frightening, police trickery and police coercion is a serious problem, and an arrestee should have legal advice going forward. But if, in the famous words of Justice Robert Jackson, Chief United States Prosecutor at the Nuremberg Trials and Supreme Court justice—"… any lawyer worth his salt will tell the suspect in no uncertain terms, to make no statement to the police under any circumstances"[9]—why should we allow questioning at all in the police station?

The legal advice to an arrestee is that simple in the United States because there is no legal reason to give any assistance to the police in their investigation. Thus, the magic words in Supreme Court *Miranda* v. *Arizona* doctrine are: "I want a lawyer." At that point, no lawyer will likely be called as it is a formality—like oil and water, questioning a suspect and a lawyer do not mix.

The balance is different in many other countries, for both common law or civil law, where questioning and a lawyer do blend together.

In England, there is, first of all, a preference that questioning of a suspect (or a key witnesses) takes place at a police station, where all "interview rooms," as they are described in English statutes, have recording systems, and there are precise procedures on the use of such recording devices. The use of the word "interview" rather than the pejorative word "interrogation" to describe what should happen in these rooms is important. The questioning of witnesses and suspects are "interviews" and the English system prefers that statements be obtained in an interview room rather than having an officer testify to what was said on the street after an arrest or what was said in a patrol car. The door of the interview room will have a sign noting that it is a "Taped Interview Room" and the recording machine will be visible on the table. There are set protocols for what is said at the start of the interview, during breaks, and at the end of the interview. There is also a protocol for securing the recording medium to protect against tampering.

The big difference is that an arrestee does not need to answer questions but the arrestee cannot stop questioning. The police have a right to question. Lawyers (solicitors) are available to assist and advise the arrestee, but they cannot prevent questions being put to the arrestee.

The warnings given to an arrestee are somewhat similar to *Miranda* v. *Arizona* warnings, but also warn a suspect that there are consequences to not answering questions. The warnings given are the following:

> You do not have to say anything. But it may harm your defence if you do not mention when questioned something which you later rely on in court. Anything you do say may be given in evidence.[10]

What this tells a suspect is that if the suspect withholds an explanation or excuse for the crime or any factor that might be alleged in the suspect's defense and the suspect brings this up at trial for the first time, the suspect will be cross-examined on the fact that the suspect failed to mention this when questioned. If a suspect has a defense for the crime or any explanation that might lower the degree of the crime, the suspect needs to bring it up during the questioning.

Miranda v. *Arizona*'s Problems

What *Miranda* v. *Arizona* does is to draw a line between sophisticated and unsophisticated arrestees. Those who are legally sophisticated—perhaps by prior contact with the law or by having access to lawyers previously in other matters—will always insist on an attorney. *Miranda* v. *Arizona* draws some fine lines that the sophisticated will know. One such line is that between saying "I want a lawyer" or saying "I do not want to answer questions." The former bars any questioning until the demand for a lawyer is met[11] while the latter may permit the police to try to get the arrestee to answer questions after a break between the first and second attempts.[12]

For a Court that was committed to providing equal justice to all defendants, rich or poor, *Miranda* v. *Arizona* has to be a disappointment. Many academics bemoan the fact that a fairly high percentage of arrestees, especially poor arrestees, waive their *Miranda* v. *Arizona* rights and answer questions to their detriment. They are puzzled by this and tend to attribute it to the way the warnings are administered. Some of that is true.

But academics often miss the most obvious reason why arrestees waive their rights and that is a common-sense understanding that the police are doing *what they should be doing*. You should expect that the police would want to ask questions of a suspect. This is what should happen in a good investigation—talk to anyone with information about the crime. The fact that there was an arrest does not change this.

I once asked a criminal defense lawyer from Australia why he permitted his client to answer questions from a police officer about a criminal matter when the lawyer was present. He replied, "Because the police are pretty good blokes and they are doing their job. My job is to protect my client from unfair questioning, false statements about the case, undue pressure, and the like."

There is also a cultural tension that figures into citizens answering police questions. Sometimes when arrestees, particularly immigrants, are brought to court to appear in front of a judge for bail purposes, the arrestee will start to blurt out an apology for what they have done. There are moral reasons why some of our citizens feel they should own up for what they did and admit their mistake. Academics, trained to "think like lawyers," often miss this pressure on suspects to answer questions.

Miranda v. *Arizona*'s Consequences for the Investigation and the Trial

If there is no access to the suspect after arrest, it makes the investigation more time-consuming. It would be nice to ask the arrestee directly, "Were you at the apartment [in question] when the shot was fired?" If the arrestee admits to being there, it makes a lineup unnecessary. Similarly, a detective will want to know, "What is your relationship with the deceased?" The police will want to know if they were friends, enemies, business partners, lovers, etc. They may be able to get this information from other sources but again a statement from the suspect will narrow their focus of inquiry.

The investigation will continue, of course, and the police might wish to go back to the suspect as additional information is obtained. Perhaps the gun is shown to belong to the suspect. Perhaps the police have evidence that the suspect was in debt to the deceased. Perhaps there was a romantic relationship between the suspect and the deceased. However, going back to the arrestee with new developments is not possible. There is a very narrow window for questioning an arrestee—the period from arrest and before the arrestee is brought into court for bail purposes. Once in court, the Sixth Amendment right to counsel attaches and no defense lawyer will allow the police access to their client for questioning.

In other countries, a suspect or even an important witness may be brought to the police station for questioning on two or three occasions as evidence develops and before arrest. The Supreme Court does not like moving the suspect around and to bring a suspect to the station for questioning— unless the suspect volunteers to go to the station—requires that the suspect be arrested.[13] In turn, that means that the investigators will usually get only one chance to question the suspect.

The federal system is different. With grand jury subpoenas, the investigators can bring suspects or witnesses in front of the grand jury several times as an investigation proceeds.

The above is not meant to deny the need for an attorney during questioning, however, to mark an arrest as being the beginning of the adversary process would not be accurate. There is no charge filed against the arrestee and should not be; there is a big difference between arresting someone on probable cause and proving guilt of a crime beyond a reasonable doubt. At the time of arrest, in this hypothetical example, there are enormous gaps in this case and no prosecutor would want to file charges until the prosecutor knows exactly who fired the shot in question and why the shot was fired. And even if it is clear from the evidence that the suspect fired the shot—it may be hard to convince a jury to convict without being able to explain the motive for the act.

If arrest marks the start of the adversary process, one wonders why any questioning of an arrestee is allowed? Why this strange compromise?

Just as the investigation is more cumbersome without some access to the suspect during the investigation, if there is a trial, the trial would be more time-consuming and complicated. Without access to the suspect during the investigation, the prosecutor cannot be sure what the defense will be and a prosecutor may need to be ready for what is sometimes referred to as an "ambush defense." Perhaps in our hypothetical, as the last witness at trial, the defendant will insist it was self-defense. Perhaps the defense will be that the victim shot herself after he broke off the relationship. Perhaps the defense will be that the victim shot herself as she claimed to have cancer or the onset of dementia (and he wanted to stop her). Perhaps he will have an alibi—he had been in a bar and had just left it to take the bus home when the police arrested him.

At the trial, the defendant will be the last witness and will have heard all of the prosecution's evidence. Whatever the prosecution's evidence—that the defendant bought a "throw away" gun a week before the shooting, that the defendant was indebted to the victim, that they had been lovers, etc., a sophisticated defendant will have an explanation.

Because there is no access to sophisticated defendants after arrest, it is hard to know what the issues are and what the issues will not be at trials in the United States. There is no mechanism for compelling a defendant to explain the nature of the defense in detail and no way to simplify the trial by asking the defendant on what factual matters do you take issue with the prosecutor and on what issues are you in agreement. If the defendant concedes he was present in the apartment, the prosecutor may not need as many witnesses on identity. If the defendant does not dispute that the gun belonged to him, it can also make the trial shorter.

Regarding the defense, the prosecution has to try to anticipate what the defense will be. The prosecution might be able to anticipate and rebut most defenses easily enough but the timing of the defense makes it harder, as it takes time to gather evidence on what may be a new issue in the case that was not anticipated. The defense will also have had the autopsy report, the ballistics report, and so on, and can use items in the evidence to buttress their defense or avoid contradicting such evidence.

The obvious question—can the prosecutor simply bring out the fact that the suspect invoked his *Miranda* v. *Arizona* rights and refused to say anything to the police when arrested? The Supreme Court and lower courts have struggled with this issue. The Court has said it would be unfair to tell the suspect that they have a right to remain silent and then use that silence against the defendant at trial.[14]

Some defenses are easy to anticipate—self-defense or accident—but some cannot be anticipated in detail, such as an alibi. Suppose, for example, the defendant testifies that he couldn't have done the shooting because he was drinking beer by himself at Joe's Bar just before he was arrested.

The timing of an alibi is problematic because it comes up at the end of trial, when the judge and jury want to be done with the case. To solve this problem, the federal system and many state systems have come up with a "solution" that is a testament to the problems *Miranda* v. *Arizona* raises for reliable trials. There are in place "notice of alibi" rules that, upon request of the prosecution, require the defense to give the specifications of the time and place where the defendant claims to have been at the time of the crime as well as a list of witnesses who will support the alibi.

In turn, the Court has ruled that to be constitutional, the prosecution after investigating the alibi, must give to the defense the names of witnesses who will be called to rebut the alibi.[15] This sounds fair—both sides exchanging information for and against the alibi—however, it is not a fair rule. To understand the oddity of the rule, assume that the prosecution has developed evidence that destroys the alibi completely—video recording showing the defendant was not in the bar.

Evidence of a false alibi is powerful evidence of guilt so one would expect that the prosecution would want to use it as evidence in their direct case but many alibi rules don't permit this. In fact, the rules vest complete control over the alibi defense in the defendant and if the defendant "withdraws" the alibi, the prosecution cannot use the notice of alibi against the defendant. The federal rule states: "Evidence of an intention to rely on an alibi defense, later withdrawn, … is not … admissible against the person who gave notice of alibi."[16] In short, the false alibi is to be ignored and treated as if it did not exist.

This is gamesmanship that undervalues truth. Because notice of alibi rules, like the federal rule, allows defendants to "try out" an alibi defense without penalty, some prosecutors choose not to avail themselves of notice of alibi rules. (The rules are triggered by a *request by the prosecution* for alibi information.) Their theory is that the alibi will not be strong or else the defendant would have avoided prosecution altogether. What is more, if the alibi can be shown to be false, they do not want to let the defendant withdraw the alibi defense with impunity. They would rather take their chances and delay the trial for a day to investigate the alibi because if they can show the defendant could not have been where they claimed to be, it is devastating for the defense.

As suggested above, if a suspect in England has a defense, the suspect must offer it to an officer during questioning or risk impeachment at trial with the fact that this defense was not brought forward in a timely fashion when the suspect was asked about the crime.

In addition, the prosecution and defense, preparing for a case in Crown Court—the jury trial court—have to disclose the nature of their respective cases including witnesses in advance of trial.[17] In response to prosecution disclosure, defendants must fill out a Defence Statement form that indicates the nature of the defense, why the defense disagrees with the prosecution, and what the particular matters of fact are on which the defense relies.[18] If it is an alibi defense, they must provide the names and addresses of alibi witnesses and, if not known, any information that might help identify or locate that witness.

When each side outlines their evidence and their specific disagreements, it is easier to predict the length of the trial and which witnesses will be needed as well as those who will not be needed. The adversary battle will take place at trial once the issues have been narrowed down and clarified.

The United States takes a different view: the adversary battle begins at arrest and can be won at that point without a trial. Both sides jockey for position—in federal cases, the prosecution tries to share as little of its information with the defense as possible and, as we have seen, the defense does not have to cooperate with the investigation, much less indicate those issues on which it agrees with the prosecution and those matters of fact on which it disagrees.

Miranda v. *Arizona* and Mass Incarceration

To criticize *Miranda* v. *Arizona* and its progeny may seem unrelated to mass incarceration but without some access to the suspect, the investigation becomes harder and more time-consuming, and trials—if there is to be one—become more expensive and more taxing on the participants. Trial avoidance is a consequence.

Chapter 4 turns to the phenomenon of the vanishing trial in the United States. *Miranda* v. *Arizona* did not cause the vanishing trial but it is a factor. As the Court built a system that became increasingly complicated and also undervalued truth, the goal for prosecutors and judges was to find ways to avoid trials. That is an unfortunate consequence, as a strong criminal justice system needs trials to keep the system honest.

Thus, *Miranda* v. *Arizona* today is becoming increasingly less relevant because there will be no trial for the overwhelming majority of defendants. Prosecutors do not want trials—nor do judges and defense lawyers. Instead, the system puts pressures on defendants to plead guilty, sometimes using pressures that are far greater than those the Court worried about in *Miranda* v. *Arizona*.

Notes

1 Wendy Sawyer and Peter Wagner, Mass Incarceration: The Whole Pie 2019, *Prison Policy Initiative*, March 19, 2019, available at: www.prisonpolicy.org/reports/pie2019.html.
2 384 U.S. 436 (1966).
3 See *North Caroline* v. *Butler*, 441 U.S. 369 (1979).
4 See *Michigan* v. *Mosley*, 423 U.S. 96 (1975).
5 See *Rhode Island* v. *Innis*, 446 U.S. 291 (1980).
6 See *Moran* v. *Burbine*, 475 U.S. 412 (1986).
7 Fred E. Inbau and John E. Reid, *Criminal Interrogation and Confessions* (Baltimore, MD: Williams and Wilkins Co., 1962).
8 See *Miranda* v. *Arizona*, 384 U.S. 436 (1966) at 477.
9 See *Watts* v. *Indiana*, 338 U.S. 49 (1949), 59 (Jackson, J. concurring in part and dissenting in part).

10 A full explanation of the use of recordings, the warnings to be given, the way in which questioning should take place, the length of questioning sessions, the way in which a tape or CD of the interview should be preserved, and so on is available at the UK Government's website, Interviewing Suspects, Health and Safety Executive: www.hse.gov.uk/enforce/enforcementguide/investigation/witness-questioning.htm#sigstate.

11 See *Edwards* v. *Arizona*, 451 U.S. 477 (1981).

12 See *Michigan* v. *Mosley*, 423 U.S. 96 (1975).

13 See *Dunaway* v. *New York*, 442 U.S. 200 (1979).

14 See *Doyle* v. *Ohio*, 426 U.S. 610 (1976).

15 See *Wardius* v. *Oregon*, 412 U.S. 470 (1973).

16 See Rule 12.1(f) *Notice of an Alibi Defense*, Federal Rules of Criminal Procedure, available at: www.federalrulesofcriminalprocedure.org/title-iv/rule-12–1-notice-of-an-alibi-defense/.

17 See generally, The Criminal Procedure and Investigations Act 1996, available at: www.legislation.gov.uk/ukpga/1996/25/section/5.

18 The Defence Statement form is available at: www.justice.gov.uk/courts/procedure-rules/criminal/docs/october-2015/dis001-eng.pdf.

4

THE VANISHING TRIAL AND MASS INCARCERATION

The Vanishing Trial

In 2004, the American Bar Association Section on Litigation, alarmed by the decline in trials in U.S. courtrooms, financed a major project appropriately titled "The Vanishing Trial," which studied the phenomenon from many different angles.[1] More than 400 pages of articles were published in the *Journal of Empirical Legal Studies*. The data of the decline of trials were shocking, leading to the phenomenon that is generally referred to by the title of the ABA study as "the vanishing trial."

The phenomenon affects both civil and criminal trials. In the civil area, however, there are several ways to resolve cases short of trial that allow the parties to present their side of the issues while sparing them the enormous strains and costs of a full-blown trial. There is, for example, mediation in which a mediator, often an experienced lawyer or judge, tries to help the parties resolve their dispute. The mediator does not take a position on the issues but tries to open lines of communication between the parties to help them reach a settlement they can each accept.

There is also arbitration, where typically three arbitrators take on a judicial role: they hear evidence, rule on issues raised in the process, and make a binding decision on the merits of the dispute.

Finally, there is the possibility of a private trial before a retired judge or even a private jury trial in front of a retired judge. These sorts of private trials can be conducted quickly—rather than waiting for a public trial on a civil docket and they will be less expensive than a full-blown trial in a public court. Also, the verdicts in these private trials can be kept private and help the losing party avoid collateral lawsuits, which is a benefit that has troubling aspects.

In the criminal area, however, there is no informal alternative that would allow a single disputed issue to be resolved other than plea bargaining. There is nothing wrong with plea bargaining per se and many defendants prefer to plead guilty, accept a reduced sentence, and avoid conviction on strong evidence, however, the percentage of cases being plea bargained has gone up to the point that trials have become a rarity. In the 1970s, 80 percent of our convictions came from plea bargaining.[2] Today, the plea-bargaining rate is 95 percent or higher for those charged with felonies (crimes punishable by more than one year in prison).[3] In the federal system, the plea-bargaining rate is 98 percent.

If you add misdemeanors to the mix, the number of convictions from trials is miniscule. For example, in researching an article in *The Atlantic* in 2017 titled, "Innocence Is Irrelevant," the author, Emily Yoffe, went to Davidson County in Tennessee, which includes Nashville. The public defender's office in that county handled 24,900 felonies and misdemeanors of which eighty-six went to trial.[4] That is a plea-bargaining rate of a small fraction of 1 percent.

We are at the point where trials are bordering on extinction. If one compares the number of trials that were conducted in the early 1960s with the number of trials that take place in the same jurisdiction today, though the number of judges has expanded significantly, there are fewer trials in absolute numbers taking place today than took place fifty years ago.

Our federal system, once a model for the states in the way things should be done, is a sad example of the decline in criminal trials. The ABA's report on the vanishing trial found that although the number of federal judges had doubled between 1962 and 2002, the absolute number of criminal trials declined by 30 percent over that same period.[5] More recent statistics show that the decline has accelerated.[6]

The ABA report showed a similar decline in state systems in the absolute number of criminal trials and a declining percentage of cases resolved by trials.[7]

On top of the scarcity of trials, there is the worry that we are not trying the right cases—the close cases where defendants have a colorable defense. One warning sign is the decline in the number of acquittals in many jurisdictions. Professor Ronald Wright has looked at the federal system where acquittals are disappearing and he concludes that the drop in the number of acquittals over the last thirty years raises serious doubts about the quality of justice being dispensed.[8]

In Chapter 3, it was explained that many state cases involve the moral guilt of the defendant—there are reasons why the defendants did what they did that make the crime understandable even if not excusable. These are cases where the defendant's explanation deserves to be heard.

Trials have always functioned to give defendants a break when the defendant's action was understandable and the defendant poses no danger of reoffending. Sometimes juries functioned to buffer the defendant from a harsh penalty. In the nineteenth century, for example, when many crimes carried the death penalty, juries might return a verdict declaring that the amount of the property involved in a theft was "less than 12 pence."[9] This reduced the crime sufficiently to allow a thief to avoid the gallows.

This came to be known as "pious perjury" on the part of the jury. The term "pious perjury" is traced to William Blackstone's mid-eighteenth-century treatise, where he described the practice which violated the jurors' oaths—and was therefore perjurious—but it was pious in its intent of sparing the life of the defendant.[10] Both the nullification of criminal charges through false acquittals and pious perjury to understate crimes were widespread in eighteenth-century England.[11]

Juries also had other ways of obtaining a result that better squared with their sense of fairness. Used both in England and Ireland until the middle of the twentieth century, juries would sometimes attach "riders" to their verdicts—a brief piece of information or commentary—that explained the jury's reasoning, or perhaps what troubled them about the case, or frequently asked the judge to seek the commutation of the death sentence from the king, or even the exercise of clemency to pardon the offender.[12] Judges also would sometimes seek royal clemency for an offender, where the judge felt the jury's verdict of conviction was wrong or too harsh in result for this offender.

Juries today—if given an opportunity—may do similar things to spare a defendant the full brunt of the law. People can be pressured into committing a crime by a parent, or a spouse, or a friend. A jury may return a reduced verdict in such circumstances or may even acquit if the defendant was only peripherally involved.

One suspects that these are the cases that are not being tried but instead, we are trying cases where no plea bargain is possible because the defendant is going to get a lengthy sentence no matter what, or because there are other reasons why the defendant simply cannot afford a conviction.

There are many reasons asserted for the decline in criminal trials in both federal and state courts, such as the shift in sentencing power from judges to prosecutors, the growth of high mandatory minimums, and the passage of harsh laws, which will be discussed in the following chapters. Before we get to these topics, however, we need to understand why trials are important in keeping an incarceration rate in check.

The Effects of Trials on Charging

In criminal cases, we tend to think of the investigating officer and the prosecutor as working together and being "on the same side." That is probably a fair assessment when a case is at the trial stage but in every country with a strong trial system, there is considerable tension between the police and the prosecuting authority when it comes to deciding which cases to pursue. This is true whether the person filing the charges is referred to as "the Crown" (Canada), the "state's attorney" (Norway), the "Crown prosecutor" (England), or the "procurator fiscal" (Scotland).

There is tension over the filing of charges because the police and prosecutors have different perspectives on charging. The police want the cases they have worked on and solved ("cleared" in police terminology) to be prosecuted. They know who committed the crime and want to see their work rewarded: the perpetrator tried, convicted, and punished.

In contrast, prosecutors only want to prosecute strong cases, that is, those cases where they can confidently prove guilt beyond a reasonable doubt, which is not an easy standard. This will be particularly the case with felonies. It may be that the person the police want prosecuted has done similar things in the past, but the prosecutor may doubt the admissibility of these prior acts. Or, in some cases, the trial may present the jury with two different accounts of the incident—a claimed assault, for example, where the defendant claims self-defense. Even though the prosecutor finds the testimony of the victim completely convincing, they may choose not to prosecute without additional evidence corroborating the victim's account. Proof beyond a reasonable doubt is a high standard and it should force prosecutors to be selective in choosing those cases that they will pursue.

In understanding the messiness of criminal cases, it is worth remembering that many criminal cases in state courts involve defendants and victims that have had a prior relationship of some sort. What looks like a burglary under the law may look quite different to a jury, who understands that the victim owed money to the defendant and had refused to repay the loan, or that the victim had taken some valuable items from the defendant at a prior point.

Similarly, an assault case may look strong at first glance—the defendant assaulted the victim as the victim exited a bar late at night—but it may turn out to be not such a sympathetic case for prosecution when the prosecutor learns that the victim had been taunting the defendant with racial epithets in the bar and had resisted calls to stop from the victim and others.

Who knows what a jury might do in these situations? These are not cases with a legal defense but they are cases that deserve a trial if charges are filed. Perhaps the jury will acquit or perhaps it will return a lesser verdict than the facts alone would dictate as a purely legal matter.

Prosecutors will look for a way out of cases like these—perhaps restitution with a plea to a minor offense or perhaps deferring prosecution if the arrestee promises no further problems with the law for a set period of time.

Sometimes, cases are not sympathetic at all and the prosecutor would like to see the wrongdoer convicted of a crime but the prosecutor knows there is a major weakness in the case. Often, it will be the *mens rea* element that is a problem—proving, for example, that the individual intended a certain result or that the individual knew the property was stolen. These are cases that do not plea bargain if trial is a realistic option because defense attorneys can see the problems with the cases. They know they have a good shot at an acquittal.

This is, of course, a generalization as there are serious crimes, such as homicides, rapes, and serious assaults where prosecutors will be under pressure to file charges even though the case has some problems. While many routine criminal cases—burglaries, possessions of stolen goods, simple assaults, and thefts—will not be prosecuted if they are not very strong cases. Prosecutors do not want to prepare and devote a week of trial time only to see the jury return a "not guilty" verdict. There are plenty of other stronger cases to pursue.

Resources, in any criminal justice system, are always limited and the prospect of a trial forces prosecutors to make some choices about the cases that they will pursue. As suggested, they will choose stronger cases over weaker cases, but there will also need to be choices made about the crimes on which the office will focus. Maybe the office will prosecute one or two cases of a certain crime as a way of sending out a message that the conduct is a crime, but they will not pursue every such crime that the police send their way.

There is a similar healthy tension between judges and prosecutors over charging. Judges do not want to take a week of trial time hearing a case that has an obvious weakness and they will not be pleased with a prosecutor who forces them to do so. They also do not want to tie up their courtroom with handling trials for minor crimes when there are more serious cases that deserve their attention.

This puts added pressure on prosecutors to be careful in charging and to look for alternatives that would avoid a trial, such as perhaps charging the crime at the misdemeanor level, giving the defendant a plea bargain that understates the actual crime, or giving the defendant a deferred sentence in which the defendant pleads guilty but is not sentenced and will not be sentenced, if the defendant commits no additional crime for a set period of time, such as one or two years, depending on the state statutes.

What is true in the case of felonies is equally true of misdemeanors. When there is the possibility of a trial, even a very simple one-hour trial, prosecutors have to make some hard choices. What minor anti-social behaviors will the office pursue and which will it avoid charging? Which behaviors might the office seek to handle outside of the criminal process?

It may be that a prosecutorial office will decide that arrest is sufficient punishment for certain minor crimes and that these crimes will not be taken any further. Or a prosecutorial office might decide that all first-time shoplifters will be offered a deferred sentence, which would allow the offender to avoid having a conviction on their record if they do not reoffend for a fixed period of time. Perhaps some anti-social behaviors can be handled simply by giving the offender a ticket punishable by a small fine and thus take that behavior out of the criminal justice system. Or prosecutors might join forces with social workers or therapists to find ways to deal with some anti-social behaviors rather than handling them as criminal matters.

These are not easy choices for prosecutors and politicians in large cities as some anti-social behaviors affect the quality of urban life. Much has been written about "turnstile jumping" in major cities and what should be done about an offense that has become increasingly common but washing vast numbers of citizens through our criminal justice system is not an ideal solution either. Thus, once trials are no longer a possibility and prosecutors can force defendants to plea bargain, misdemeanor courts in large cities become mills for churning out conviction after conviction in literally three minutes or less. Writers for the *Wall Street Journal* visited misdemeanor courts around the country and found the same pattern in court after court—defendants being forced to plead guilty one after another in three minutes or less. The article begins with this powerful line:

> For the millions of Americans charged each year with misdemeanor crimes, justice can be blindingly swift.[13]

In short, strong trial systems force prosecutors to screen cases carefully in deciding which cases to pursue to trial. Strong trial systems also force prosecutors to make set priorities to differentiate the crimes that the office will pursue and those they will handle in other ways. In the drug area, for example, an office may decide its general rule will be to not prosecute drug possession cases unless the amount of drugs is above a certain amount. Often, these are informal office policies known to the prosecutors and the defense lawyers, but are not advertised to the public. What is more, they are not written in stone and exceptions will be made for bad actors. But strong trial systems impose a discipline in charging that dissipates once defendants cannot take the risk of a trial.

Today, trials in the United States are not an option for defendants. This is, in part, because prosecutors have ways to force the defendant to accept a plea bargain, such as the availability of charges with high mandatory minimum sentences. Once the healthy tension between the police and prosecutors over charging disappears, prosecutors can charge many more crimes—crimes that would be too expensive to justify a full trial or crimes that would be hard to prove beyond a reasonable doubt at trial. This is, unfortunately, our situation in the United States and it contributes mightily to our high incarceration rate.

To understand what is happening, we need to return to John Pfaff's conclusions on mass incarceration and his analysis of the data from 1994 to 2008. Arrests for violent, property, and non-marijuana drug crimes fell steadily over those years, but the numbers in our prisons did not fall because the number of felony cases filed by prosecutors rose significantly. In short, the key actor in prison growth has been the prosecutor. Pfaff concludes his analysis of the causes of prison growth by saying that, by pushing up admissions, prosecutors have been the ones who are responsible for the overall prison growth:

> The primary driver of incarceration is increased prosecutorial toughness when it comes to charging people, not longer prison sentences. Stopping prosecutors from sending people to prison would be far more effective in cutting incarceration rates than reducing the amount of time prisoners spend in prison once they are there—and this fact points to a very different set of reforms than those generally proposed.[14]

There are some commentators on our incarceration problem who insist that prosecutors became more hardened in the period when our incarceration rate climbed to historic heights. It may be that prosecutors were "kinder and gentler" in the 1950s and 1960s—who really knows? But what this chapter (and this book) is trying to show is that there were structural reasons why prosecutors could be tougher and could send more people to prison. One of them was a trial system that is failing.

The Attributes of Strong Trial Systems

I have used the term "strong trial system" to describe the way such a system impacts charging and helps keep cases out from being prosecuted. But what is a strong trial system?

There is no perfect trial system and when you look at other countries with much lower incarceration rates than the United States, you see quite a variety of systems: some countries use no lay persons at their trials; some use mixed panels of citizens along with professional judges; and some use juries only for serious cases. But even among those countries which use juries, the size of the jury can vary—a jury of twelve jurors is common but some systems have juries of ten (Norway) or even fifteen jurors (Scotland).

The United States is strongly committed to unanimous verdicts (until recently, when the Supreme Court ruled that jury verdicts must be unanimous, Oregon was the lone outlier in allowing verdicts of 11–1),[15] but some countries accept verdicts of 8–2 (Norway), 10–2 (England), 11–1 (Australia), and even 8–7 (Scotland).

But whatever the differences among national trial systems, a strong trial system needs three attributes:

(1) it must have fair procedures;
(2) it must produce reliable verdicts in which the public can have confidence; and
(3) it must make efficient use of its resources.

Fair procedures are obviously basic to any system—the system needs to have procedures that allow relevant evidence to be gathered, to be admitted at trial, and to be tested. Thus, if a system does not permit indigent defendants access to scientific experts or if a system allows prosecutors to keep from the defense evidence that would be helpful to the defendant's case, we would not consider those procedures fair.

But fair procedures are insufficient if the factfinders cannot be trusted to understand the evidence and reach verdicts in which we have confidence. Perfection in convicting the guilty and acquitting the innocent is not attainable in any system, but we hope that miscarriages of justice are rare and can be rectified.

Finally, trial systems need to be efficient to be strong. This is, of course, a relative concept; there will be trials that may turn on complex issues such as major fraud cases that may take many weeks to complete. But whatever procedure a country adopts for its trials, one would hope that it makes efficient use of what will always be limited resources.

These issues are obviously related. If you have fair procedures but they are extremely complicated, that may impact the system's efficiency. If trials are lengthy, that may impact reliability as factfinders may have trouble remembering and putting together information gained over several days, or weeks, or sometimes months.

So how strong is the trial system in the United States? And if it is strong, why do we avoid using it?

The Supreme Court's Lack of Confidence in Our Trial System

On many criminal justice issues, we take our lead from the Supreme Court and the Court is nervous about our trial system. A case that demonstrates that lack of confidence is a Warren Court decision, *Anders v. California*,[16] that essentially requires full appellate review of all trials.

In *Anders v. California*, an attorney appointed to file an appeal after trial for an indigent defendant in a marijuana possession case had sought to withdraw from filing the appeal because, after examining the record and consulting with the client, the attorney believed the appeal had "no merit" and so indicated in a letter to the court. The lawyer indicated, however, that Anders wished to file a brief in his own behalf. Anders asked for a different attorney to be appointed which was denied, so Anders filed a brief pro se and a reply brief to the state's response. The appellate court affirmed Anders' conviction.

Several years later, Anders filed a writ of habeas corpus that claimed he was unconstitutionally incarcerated because he had been denied his Sixth Amendment right to counsel on appeal. The California courts denied the writ, but the United States Supreme Court concluded that the procedure that had been followed after Anders' trial had not been adequate to protect the defendant's right to counsel.

In Anders' case, the Court disapproved of the way the attorney had been permitted to withdraw by simply sending a letter to the court stating the appeal had "no merit." Instead, the Supreme Court outlined a more stringent framework for "no merit" cases: first, if after a conscientious review of the record, the lawyer determines that any appeal would be "wholly frivolous," the lawyer must so advise the appellate court by letter; second, the lawyer must accompany the letter with a brief referring to anything in the trial record that might support an appeal and showing why it was meritless; third, a copy of the brief—now usually referred to as an *Anders* brief—must be furnished to the defendant with sufficient time to allow the defendant to raise issues of the defendant's choosing; and, fourth, the appellate court must make a full examination of all of the proceedings to see if "the case is wholly frivolous."

There are many problems with *Anders v. California* but, first of all, notice the picture of criminal trials the Court has painted—they must be examined closely because there may be errors hidden in the reeds. In order to do this, it is obvious that there needs to be a transcript provided for the full trial. A transcript for a day of trial can vary depending on the jurisdiction, but a ball-park figure is $900 for each day of trial. Notice that a transcript is always required for appeals so that the attorney can scrutinize it for error.

The second problem with that opinion is the way the Court avoids any discussion of the ethical issue that the appellate lawyer for *Anders v. California* faced. In theory, any lawyer—whether their client is rich or poor—should not "assert ... an issue ... unless there is a basis in law and fact for doing so that is not frivolous...."[17] Here was an opportunity to speak about this ethical issue as there is a tension between a lawyer's duty to the client and a lawyer's duty to the court and the administration of justice.

Between the lawyer's duty to the client and the lawyer's ethical obligation to courts, the Supreme Court clearly wants attorneys to pursue an appeal. The implication of the opinion is that wealthy defendants will always find attorneys willing to file an appeal for them, ethics notwithstanding, so indigent defendants should get equal treatment. There is not an ounce of sympathy for the lawyer who wrote the "no merit" letter.

The third problem with *Anders* v. *California* is that the procedure the Court sets out is unworkable and raises additional problems. The idea of asking an attorney in an *Anders* brief to point out any possible errors and then explain why they are frivolous puts the attorney in the position of arguing against the client. Then, if the attorney files an *Anders* brief, the appellate court is supposed to make an independent review of the entire record to see if it can find additional possible errors. If it finds such an error, the appellate court must appoint counsel to file a brief. Then, having found a possible error on the defendant's behalf and having ordered an attorney to brief the issue, the appellate court is supposed to step back into its judicial role to rule on the issue the court itself has raised.

Anders v. *California* is a mess in state courts. Many have simply caved in and, to avoid the awkwardness of the procedure the Court required, have simply said to lawyers, "Don't worry about the ethics issue, counsel, just file a brief raising the frivolous issue or issues." But some have adopted their own procedures for handling the problem that occurred in *Anders* v. *California*, taking the position that it is the highest court of the state—not the United States Supreme Court—that determines the ethical practice of lawyers in that state.[18]

Putting aside the procedural problems *Anders* v. *California* created, what is important for our topic is the picture of trials that is assumed in the Court's reasoning. If you look hard at the transcript of trials, there may be an appellate issue. In effect, the Supreme Court is not confident in our trial system and prefers that all cases be reviewed on appeal.

The Court's Distrust of Trial Judges

There are serious costs to mandating appellate review of every non-frivolous issue in a criminal case. Obviously, requiring a transcript, the appointment of counsel for indigent defendants, the preparation of a brief (and the cost of an opposing brief from the state), and the time of appellate courts to review and decide the case is expensive. *Anders* v. *California* was a possession of marijuana case. How complicated can that case have been? If there was a serious search or arrest issue, it would stand out and obviously be reviewed on appeal. But the Court wants transcripts scrutinized for any possible issue that is not, in the Court's unforgettable words, "wholly frivolous."

There is another major cost to mandatory appellate review of criminal convictions and the Court's insistence that the trial record be closely examined for any possible error—it suggests a lack of confidence in trial judges to deliver fair trials and an overconfidence in the ability of appellate courts to correct "errors."

Consider a basic issue in jury selection: should this prospective juror be removed for cause? Imagine a sexual assault trial and the last prospective juror called into the jury box states that they were the victim of sexual assault several years earlier. The judge questions the prospective juror for a few minutes, delves into the issue of whether this person could be fair to the defendant, and comes away concluding that the juror could be fair. The defense has no more peremptory challenges, so this person stays on the jury that convicts the defendant. On appeal, the failure of the judge to remove this juror for cause is raised as an error requiring reversal and a new trial.

In sports, this is what is called a "judgment call." Many judgment calls in sports occur where opposing players are in close contact and are battling for position. In football, holding calls; in basketball, blocking calls; and in soccer, interference calls. Most judgment calls are not reviewable because it is understood that these matters need to be left in the hands of referees. Review would not settle the merits of the call but simply express another judgment call.

But some judgment calls in sports are reviewed because multiple angles and slow-motion video help reviewers to see what happened more clearly than the referee could see in real time. In our legal system, appellate courts are in a *worse* position than a trial judge to review many judgment calls. How can an appellate court with only a transcript of what was said second-guess the judge on the refusal of a challenge for cause, when the appellate court never had a chance to hear the tone or the cadence of the juror's answers, never had a chance to make eye-contact with the juror, and never saw the body language of the juror as they answered questions?

This is but one of many, many decisions at trial that are judgment calls on which reasonable judges can disagree. One of the most common is the decision to allow or not allow certain evidence to be heard because the probative value of the evidence outweighs or is outweighed by its prejudicial value. And to be really fair, you would have to see how the judge ruled on evidentiary issues for the opposing side. Like players on opposing teams in a basketball game, lawyers in a trial adjust to the judge. As long as the judge applies the rules the same way to both parties, lawyers will adjust.

Our legal system has difficulty accepting that some decisions by state actors are basically judgment calls on which reasonable people and reasonable judges will differ. Instead of accepting the limits of appellate review, the Court in a decision like *Anders* v. *California* puts tremendous pressure on review of judgment calls and the results are often embarrassing as appellate judges disagree with each other over decisions that none of them are well positioned to review.

On top of the difficulty of reviewing judgment calls on appeal, the United States has a special problem that is not as common in other countries—many appellate judges in the United States have never been trial judges and thus, do not fully appreciate the difficulties of ruling quickly without appellate briefs or research memos. They also might not understand what it is like to have several balls in the air as a judge tries to balance concerns for jurors and for witnesses, while keeping the trial moving along.

In insisting on appeals from all trial convictions, the Court is confident that appellate courts are well positioned to evaluate errors. But in any national system that uses juries for serious cases, it is not easy to evaluate errors. There is a reason that a right to appeal a criminal conviction is not in the Bill of Rights; jury trials that result in a one-word verdict are difficult to review.

European trials are different as the presiding judge will draft a full explanation of the bases for the conviction in a document which explains how legal issues were handled, how conflicts between witnesses were resolved, and why the particular sentence was imposed. Appellate review is one of the basic protections of defendants in continental criminal procedure and it fits their trial system.

In contrast, with jury trials, there is no way to get "inside" the jury's verdict. Assume that a trial judge lost their temper with a defense lawyer in front of the jury in a three-week trial. (In the United States, baiting a judge into error is fair game for defense lawyers unfortunately.) How can we know if this outburst was a harmless error or not? Perhaps the first thing the jury said during deliberations was that "the judge clearly didn't think much of the defense case by the way she shouted at the defense attorney"? How can we know that the error was "harmless beyond a reasonable doubt," which is the standard the Court requires for reviews of trial errors?

Is an appellate court going to reverse a three-week trial where the evidence was strong because of an outburst by the judge? Not likely. But in declaring errors such as this "harmless beyond a reasonable doubt," the system becomes by degrees less honest.

In effect, the Supreme Court has mandated appellate review—there must be a transcript and *Anders* v. *California* requires scrutiny of the transcript for any possible error other than ones that are "wholly frivolous." Even then, there must be a brief filed.

Other common law criminal justice systems are far more grudging on appeals after jury trials. In Canada,[19] England,[20] and Australia,[21] for example, the defense must request permission to appeal and have the issue reviewed before a transcript is ordered and the case is briefed for a full appellate review. The preliminary review will be done by a judge (or judges), who is or has been a trial judge. There are exceptions to this screening requirement for appeals, if, for example, the issue is solely a legal issue or if the judge who handled the trial certifies an issue that should be reviewed. For the vast majority of trial errors, however, the defense needs to get permission to appeal.

In addition to being cautious in allowing appeals, other common law countries do not try to guess whether the error might have affected the jury—an impossible task. Instead, what they ask is whether there is a danger that the conviction is "unsafe" or a possible "miscarriage of justice."

Shouldn't that have been the issue on appeal in *Anders* v. *California*? Is there something about Anders' conviction for possession of marijuana that suggests a miscarriage of justice?

The Supreme Court's aggressive approach to appellate review undercuts the authority of trial judges. Compared to judges in other common law systems, trial judges in the United States are extremely passive. American judges will be reluctant to cut off a meandering line of questioning by a defense attorney that might avoid the necessity of recalling the witness on the next day. They will also refrain from asking a clarifying question of a prosecution witness whose testimony is confusing. Ask a clarifying question of a prosecution witness whose testimony is confusing? If there is a conviction, a judge will have these actions reviewed. Even if the conviction is not reversed, who wants to be second-guessed by a panel of judges who may not have been trial judges? The lesson of *Anders* v. *California* is that passivity at trial is the safest option.

This is in sharp contrast to judges in other common law countries where judges ask clarifying questions all the time. They will also try to weave the facts of the case into jury instructions so jurors can better understand how the law relates to the factual issues. Sometimes judges in other common law countries even put a legal instruction into their own words.

Our appellate system discourages these things. A judge who does any of these things is courting rebuke and possible reversal. Better to stay passive, ask no questions, and read form instruction after form instruction that has been vetted for use in books of acceptable jury instructions.

Anders v. *California*'s aggressive approach to appellate review of trial rulings takes a toll on trial judges. In an article in the *New York Review of Books*, titled "Why Innocent People Plead Guilty," Jed Rakoff, a federal judge in New York City, notes that judges taking guilty pleas are supposed to question defendants about the facts of the case to make sure the defendant is really guilty of the crime in question. He goes on to explain that this does not happen because, "…in practice, most judges, happy for their own reasons to avoid a time-consuming trial will barely question the defendant…."[22] Why are trial judges happy to avoid trials?

This question is complicated to answer. These are judges used to making important rulings on issues such as the interpretation of a statute, the legality of an agency decision, the adequacy of an administrative procedure, even the constitutionality of an executive action. Judges know that these decisions will be reviewed and that is completely understandable. At some point, there has to be a final decision on these issues. But review of everyday trial decisions is of a very different nature. It is demeaning.

Many years ago, I spoke at a judicial conference for judges of the Ninth Circuit Court of Appeal. (The Ninth Circuit is the large circuit that includes the states along the west coast from Washington to Arizona as well as Alaska and Hawaii.) In the course of my talk, I explained how judges in countries sharing the common law tradition—excepting those in the United States—always summarize the evidence for the jury at the end of the trial as part of the jury instructions. For this reason, they take notes during the trial and ask clarifying questions, as they need to be sure of the testimony.

In the discussion that followed, I asked at one point why federal judges, who had the power to summarize the evidence, did not do so. The judges began talking among themselves and then one judge summarized the conversation in this way:

> Probably it makes sense to summarize the evidence in complicated cases, perhaps more importantly in civil cases than in criminal cases. But it is just one more appellate issue.

I recall this judge's comment years later because it summarized so clearly the position in which our appellate system puts trial judges. Here was a room full of highly talented judges at the pinnacle of the profession, but the system prefers that these judges be far more passive than judges in other common law countries.

Chapter 5 will discuss another way in which the Supreme Court has evidenced a distrust of trial judges in requiring jury trials for all felonies and misdemeanors to protect defendants from possibly "biased" and "compliant" judges.

In fairness to the Court, we have a complicated system for choosing judges that is different from other countries. Many judges in the United States run for election to the position in partisan elections; judges in many states are appointed initially, but can be voted out of office; still other judges—such as federal judges—enjoy lifetime appointments.

There are, no doubt, some poor judges on the bench, but this is probably true in many national systems. However, treating all judges as suspect is no solution. What the Court has done in *Anders v. California*, through its insistence on reviewing minor issues that have little to do with the justice of the conviction, is discourage judges from controlling trials and from taking steps to assist juries to reach fair and accurate verdicts.

Is this chapter claiming that *Anders* v. *California* is responsible for the vanishing criminal trial? Not at all but when you put *Anders* v. *California* together with *Miranda* v. *Arizona* and the lack of access to suspects to learn even what their defense is, when you put *Anders* v. *California* together with the lack of authority granted trial to judges to close hearings to protect fair trials, when you put *Anders* v. *California* together with ethics rules that undervalue an advocate's duty to the court, and when you add hearing after hearing to the criminal process, you start to have a system that is hugely expensive, very stressful, and unreliable.

Every common law country is worried about the cost and the reliability of jury trials as the law gets more and more complicated. It has been suggested in England that, to keep trials alive in that country, judges have to be more aggressive in narrowing issues and in forcing parties to agree on documents or issues of fact.[23] New Zealand has gone in a different direction: it has given trial judges the authority to deny a jury trial to defendants in cases, except for very serious crimes, that will take more than twenty days where the judge determines that the defendant's right to a jury trial is outweighed by the likelihood that potential jurors will be not able to perform their duties effectively.[24]

The alternative in the United States is simply to avoid jury trials.

Notes

1 See Marc Galanter, The Vanishing Trial: An Examination of Trials and Related Matters in Federal and State Courts, *Journal of Empirical Legal Studies* 1(3) (2004): 459–460.

2 See William J. Stuntz, *The Collapse of American Criminal Law* (Cambridge, MA: Harvard University Press, 2011), 209.

3 The Bureau of Justice Statistics in a report in 2013 found a plea-bargaining rate of 95 percent among felony defendants in the 75 largest counties in the United States. See Brian A. Reaves, Felony Defendants in Large Urban Counties 2009, *Bureau of Justice Statistics*, December 20, 2013, available at: www.bjs.gov/index.cfm?ty=pbdetail&iid=4845

4 See Emily Yoffe, Innocence Is Irrelevant, *The Atlantic*, September 2017, available at: www.theatlantic.com/magazine/archive/2017/09/innocence-is-irrelevant/534171/.

5 See Galanter, The Vanishing Trial, 493.

6 See Robert J. Conrad and Katy L. Clements, The Vanishing Criminal Jury Trial: From Trial Judges to Sentencing Judges, *George Washington Law Review* 86(1) (2018): 132–133.

7 See Galanter, The Vanishing Trial, 510–513.

8 See Ronald F. Wright, Trial Distortion and the End of Innocence in Federal Criminal Justice, *University of Pennsylvania Law Review* 154 (2005), 79.

9 See John H. Langbein, *The Origins of the Adversary Criminal Trial* (Oxford: Oxford University Press, 2003), 58.

10 William Blackstone, *Commentaries on the Law of England* (Oxford: Clarendon Press, 1765–1769), Vol. 4, 239.

11 See Peter King, *Crime Justice, and Discretion in England 1740–1820* (Oxford: Oxford University Press, 2000). King determined that around one-seventh of those indicted for property crimes in the major courts of Essex between 1740 and 1805 had the indictments dismissed as "not found" by the grand jury. The jury trial then acquitted almost a third of the remainder and brought in pious perjury verdicts in a further 10 percent.

12 See Mark Coen and Niamh Howlin, The Jury Speaks: Jury Riders in the Nineteenth and Twentieth Centuries, *American Journal of Legal History* 58(4) (2018): 505–534.

13 See John R. Emshwiller and Gary Fields, Justice Is Swift As Petty Crimes Clog Courts, *Wall Street Journal*, November 13, 2014, available at: www.wsj.com/articles/justice-is-swift-as-petty-crimes-clog-courts-1417404782

14 John F. Pfaff, *Locked In: The True Causes of Mass Incarceration and How To Achieve Real Reform* (New York: Basic Books, 2017), 6.

15 See to *Ramos* v. *Louisiana*, ___U.S.___ (2020).

16 See *Anders* v. *California*, 386 U.S. 738 (1967).

17 American Bar Association, Model Rules of Professional Conduct, Rule 3.1 (dealing with the role of the lawyer as Advocate), available at: www.americanbar.org/groups/professional_responsibility/publications/model_rules_of_professional_conduct/rule_3_1_meritorious_claims_contentions/.

18 On the struggle in the states to comply with *Anders* v. *California*, see Martha C. Warner, *Anders* in the Fifty States: Some Appellants' Equal Protection Is More Equal Than Others, *Florida State University Law Review* 23(3) (1996): 625–687.

19 See Section 675, *Martin's Criminal Code, 2018* (Canada) (certificate of appeal must be granted to file an appeal on a mixed issue of fact and law).

20 The procedure for gaining permission to appeal a Crown Court conviction is set out on the government website at: www.gov.uk/appeal-against-sentence-conviction/crown-court-verdict and the form that must be completed to gain permission is available at: www.justice.gov.uk/courts/procedure-rules/criminal/forms#part39.

21 Australia's criminal appellate system is modeled after the English system. See generally Catherine Penhallurick, The Proviso in Criminal Appeals, *Melbourne University Law Review* 27(3) (2003): 800–818.

22 Jed Rakoff, Why Innocent People Plead Guilty, *New York Review of Books*, November 20, 2014, available at: www.nybooks.com/articles/2014/11/20/why-innocent-people-plead-guilty/.

23 One of the classic books on advocacy in England is Richard Du Cann's, *The Art of the Advocate*. In the conclusions of the book, he worries about the future of jury trials and argues that the position of trial judges needs to be strengthened (as it has in fraud cases) to force disclosure of each side's case and to force

agreement on facts and on documents so as to simplify the case for trial. See Richard Du Cann, *The Art of the Advocate: An Incisive Examination of the Role of the Advocate in Today's Legal System* (London: Penguin Books, 1993), 224–226.

24 New Zealand allows a judge to order a trial to a judge instead of a jury if the trial is likely to take more than twenty days and the judge determines that the defendant's right to a jury trial is outweighed by the likelihood that potential jurors will be not able to perform their duties effectively. This section does not apply to those serious crimes that carry a possible sentence of more than fourteen years in prison. See Section 102, Criminal Procedure Act 2011 (New Zealand), available at: www.legislation.govt.nz/act/public/2011/0081/latest/DLM3360166.html.

5

MUST FAIR TRIALS ALWAYS BE JURY TRIALS?

One of the major differences between the United States and other common law countries is the extent to which the United States is committed to jury trials as the way to decide criminal cases. Criminal trials for very serious cases, such as homicide or rape, will require a jury trial in any common law country but less serious criminal charges—for example, assaults, thefts, or burglaries—do not require a jury trial, as will be explained later in this chapter.

The United States takes a different approach: all criminal charges confer on the defendant the right to a jury trial, except for those offenses deemed "petty" offenses, which are those minor crimes limited to sentences of less than six months. The two main cases are *Duncan* v. *Louisiana*,[1] decided in 1968, announcing the right to jury trial for felony cases and *Baldwin* v. *New York*,[2] decided two years later, which extended the right to misdemeanor cases.

Duncan v. *Louisiana*: Jury Trials and Felony Cases

The first case to address the right of a defendant to a jury trial was *Duncan* v. *Louisiana*, which is a fascinating and historic case for many reasons. It is, of course, an iconic case of the civil rights era, which stands as a tribute to the courage of Gary Duncan and his family, who chose to fight a baseless assault charge instead of pleading guilty. It is also a testament to the courage of his lawyers, who stepped up to fight for Duncan in a hostile community. So, in addition to its legal significance, it is historically important. It provides a snapshot of the mistreatment blacks suffered in the battle for civil rights and the resistance they faced from parts of the legal establishment.

Gary Duncan was a nineteen-year-old black man charged with battery in Plaquemines Parish, a staunchly segregationist parish located fifty miles south of New Orleans.[3] Duncan's two twelve-year-old cousins had broken the color barrier at a school in the parish that had previously been reserved for white students only. The two boys had been assaulted, threatened, and harassed at their new school.

The battery charge stemmed from an incident in which Duncan and his two cousins were involved in a confrontation with four white teenage boys. Duncan had stopped his car and was trying to defuse the situation by getting his cousins into his car and away from the white teenagers. In the process, Duncan "touched" or "slapped" (depending on whose account one believed) one of the white teenagers on the elbow leading to the battery charge.

Duncan refused to plead guilty and, worried that no local attorney would be willing to defend him, Duncan's family turned to the Lawyers Constitutional Defense Committee, which litigated civil rights cases in Mississippi, Alabama, and Louisiana. Richard Sobol, a lawyer on leave from a Washington, DC law firm, and Robert F. Collins, who later to become the first African-American U.S. District Judge, agreed to take the case.

At the start of trial, Duncan's lawyers filed a motion seeking a jury trial based on the Sixth and Fourteenth Amendments. The motion was denied and the trial went ahead in front of the local judge, who was a pawn of the political machine. Despite sharply differing accounts of what had happened between the black and white witnesses, the judge found Duncan guilty of simple battery and sentenced him to sixty days, a harsh sentence for simple battery.

The issue of the applicability of the right to a jury trial to the states eventually made it to the Supreme Court.

One might think that, given the bias against Duncan, this would be an easy case for the Court but it was not easy. For one thing, Justice White, in his majority opinion, could look down the road and see what lies ahead—there are hundreds of cases taking place every day in courts of limited jurisdictions throughout the country where defendants are tried in front of a single judge. If the Court imposes jury trials on the states, does this mean that all trials without juries are unfair? Also, Justice White was fully aware of the fact that many Western countries with strong criminal justice systems—Denmark, Sweden, and the Netherlands, for example—do not use juries and, of course, Louisiana has a strong French influence on its legal system and France does not use juries. (Some of these countries use lay people to decide cases but they sit and decide along with professional judges.)

Justice White noted, however, that countries which do not use juries for serious cases have other protections in place that do not exist in Louisiana.[4] That is certainly true: European countries will typically have a panel of judges (not a single judge), the trial will conclude with a reasoned verdict that explains how the verdict was reached and why the particular sentence was imposed, and an appellate court in an important case will often re-examine some of the evidence to make sure the verdict or sentence was correct. Louisiana had none of these protections.

Looking at the United States, White noted that "in most places," the fact that more trials for "serious offenses" are to juries than to a court alone suggests jury trials are "very likely" serving the "intended purpose of making judicial or prosecutorial unfairness less likely."[5]

But does a minor battery like the one charged against Duncan in which he received a sentence of six months qualify as a "serious offense"? Serious offenses in most countries would constitute crimes such as murder, aggravated assault, rape, and treason.

The Court answered this question by noting that in forty-nine of the fifty states crimes tried to a judge alone were punishable by no more than a year in jail. Since battery in Louisiana was punishable by up to two years in prison, the Court ruled it was a serious crime requiring a jury under the Sixth Amendment. (Typically, short sentences of up to a year are served in a local county jail, while those sentenced to more than one year will be sent to one of the state prisons.)

It left to another day to draw the precise line that would separate "serious crimes" requiring a jury and "petty offenses" where no jury would be required.

The decision in *Duncan* v. *Louisiana* shows many of the limitations the Court faces in using the Constitution to solve difficult criminal justice problems. There are ways to involve laypersons in a criminal justice system that do not involve the full federal jury trial model. Scotland, for centuries, has used justices of the peace to handle minor criminal cases. Justices of the peace are laypersons who receive no pay for their work and who handle 75 percent of criminal cases in Scotland. Their sentencing authority is limited to six months in jail.

England's use of lay people as "magistrates" to handle the great bulk of criminal cases (except for very serious crimes) will be discussed shortly.

But the Court cannot reach an alternative way of involving laypersons in a minor trial by a constitutional decision, so instead it ended up requiring jury trials for even a rather minor offense.

While it was a victory for Duncan and also provided a strong endorsement of jury trials, the aftermath of the decision was sobering. The Louisiana legislature quickly amended its simple battery statute to make the crime now punishable by no more than six months imprisonment—battery became a petty offense triable by a judge alone. Thus, the same trial judge who had convicted Duncan was still on the bench and he would be deciding battery cases without a jury and could sentence defendants to the same sentence he had given Duncan—sixty days in jail.

Reflections on the Evolution of Jury Trials

Duncan v. *Louisiana's* insistence that the right to a jury trial must be afforded defendants in serious criminal cases is sound, but a minor battery is not a serious criminal case. Drawing the line at any crime where a possible sentence might be up to two years upon conviction is very expensive and jury trials in the United States are far more expensive than in other countries.

If you look at the history of jury trials, they were not the time-consuming, multi-day events of today. They were very efficient. John Langbein has done research on jury trials at the Old Bailey in the period from 1675–1835.[6] ("Old Bailey" is the affectionate name for the Central Criminal Court in the City of London, which today is still the London venue for jury trials for very serious criminal cases such as murder, rape, or treason.) He describes a report of a two-day session in which two juries disposed of thirty-two cases in two days. Cases were put to juries one after another in batches of three or four cases and each jury deliberated only three or four times each day, returning verdicts for each of the cases in that batch.

Some of the speed of trials has to do with the fact that most cases involved defendants caught in the act—there were no police agencies to carry out investigations. Trials were about guilt, but in days when felonies were capital offenses, trials were about the sentence as well. Also, many jurors were veterans of previous trial sessions. They had done this before so they knew their role. And, finally, because there were only a few crimes, judges' instructions were minimal. There was also no jury selection, no opening statements, and—no lawyers.

Even early in the twentieth century in the United States, jury trials were not multi-day events. Juries sometimes returned two, three, or even four verdicts in a single day.[7]

But today, jury trials have evolved into complicated proceedings and they are more complicated in the United States than in other common law countries. Chapter 4 discussed the way appellate review was effectively mandated for any issues that are not "wholly frivolous." This is expensive and other countries are more grudging on appellate review.

In addition, many issues that are within the sound discretion of the trial judge in other countries, such as closing a hearing to protect a defendant's right to a fair trial or closing a hearing in a sexual assault trial for the testimony of a young victim, are not committed to the discretion of the trial judge in the United States. Instead, there must be a hearing on the issue of closure, with findings of fact, possible interlocutory appeal if the press takes issue with closure, and appellate review if there is a conviction.

Finally, jury selection is much more heavily emphasized in the United States. In England, there are no peremptory challenges. In Canada, there are peremptory challenges but lawyers cannot question prospective jurors.

Most states in the United States give lawyers five, ten, or even twenty peremptory challenges in routine felony cases and extensive questioning of prospective jurors about their reading preferences, their television viewing preferences, and so on, is permitted. Sometimes jurors must fill out extensive questionnaires in advance so lawyers have even more information about which to question jurors. It is not unknown in a high-publicity case for a defense lawyer to have investigators drive by the home of prospective jurors to see if they can garner useful information from the state of the home or the neighborhood.

In 1983, a *New York Times* article cited a study showing that jury selection in New York state was then averaging 12.7 hours of trial time and consumed 40 percent of the trial itself.[8] Jury selection can be even more time-consuming today, as that article was published in the pre-*Batson* v. *Kentucky* era and now courts need to rule on whether a lawyer is challenging jurors "solely" on the basis of race or gender. (The difficulties that *Batson* v. *Kentucky* presents for trial judges were discussed in Chapter 2.)

Jury trials have strengths and they are a part of the common law tradition—but they have weaknesses, too. For one thing, they have become very expensive (and more expensive in the United States than in other common law countries).

Having come down very strongly in *Duncan* v. *Louisiana* in favor of jury trials as an essential part of the U.S. system of justice but refusing to draw the line indicating which crimes required jury trial, the Court could not leave the line undrawn for long. Courts that handle misdemeanor cases—those crimes punishable by up to a year in jail—have large volumes of these minor criminal cases and needed clarity on what the Constitution demands.

Baldwin v. *New York*

In 1970, in *Baldwin* v. *New York*, the Court set out to resolve the constitutionality of trials without juries in misdemeanor cases.

The case arose because New York City did not provide jury trials to defendants charged with misdemeanors and Robert Baldwin, who had been charged with "jostling"—a pickpocketing offense—had been convicted without a jury and sentenced to a year in jail.

New York City presented a stark contrast to Plaquemines Parish, Louisiana, the venue of Gary Duncan's disgraceful trial. The district attorney's office for New York County in the late 1960s had long been considered one of the finest prosecutorial offices in the country. Prosecutors in that office, including Thomas Dewey, Frank Hogan, and later Robert Morgenthau, not only handled the sort of high-volume crimes that plague any major city, but they undertook important investigations of political corruption, organized crime, and white-collar crime.[9]

The Legal Aid Society in the city, one of the first legal institutions in the country dedicated to representing indigent clients, was equally respected for the quality of its work in both civil and criminal cases. It traces its roots back to 1876.[10]

Finally, the New York City Bar Association had a long history of taking aggressive positions in reports, studies, and amicus briefs against injustice, not just locally but nationally and even internationally.[11]

The plurality opinion, again by Justice White, viewed New York City as an outlier in denying jury trials to those charged with misdemeanors. Justice White noted that since *Duncan* v. *Louisiana*, the other two states, Louisiana and New Jersey, that had at one time allowed convictions for misdemeanors without jury trial had changed their laws to provide jury trials. White also noted that even other cities in New York State—such as Buffalo and Albany—provided jury trials in misdemeanor cases.

Against this background, White concluded that "this near-uniform judgment of the Nation" required that the line for requiring jury trials be extended to offenses carrying a possible sentence of more than six months.[12]

White's opinion made New York City seem grudging and unfair for not following the rest of the state and other big cities in granting jury trials in misdemeanor cases, but New York City was in a very different situation from other cities in New York, and may well have been in a very different position from cities like Chicago or Los Angeles. To understand the special nature of criminal courts in New York City, one only has to reflect on the fact that the New York City Criminal Court, which handles misdemeanors had, at the time of *Baldwin* v. *New York*, a caseload docket that was thirty-nine times greater than that of Buffalo, New York's second largest city.

The Court was clearly in a hurry to draw a line and, in the process, to force New York City to extend the right to a jury trial to misdemeanor defendants. The dissent questioned just how "near-uniform" the judgment on jury trials was as it pointed to three states—Maryland, North Carolina, and Pennsylvania—that did not provide jury trials for misdemeanors or minor felonies as freely as White's opinion might suggest.[13]

Like so many Supreme Court decisions on criminal procedure issues, there is no statistical analysis comparing New York City to other major U.S. cities. One would have liked to have seen a comparison of misdemeanor caseloads in New York City compared to other large cities, the number of trials in each city, and the plea-bargaining rate to see if those cities were providing anywhere near the number of misdemeanor trials that New York City provided. It might have been the case that New York City gave many more defendants a chance to put on a defense at trial, whereas other cities offered jury trials in theory but not nearly the percentage in practice as New York City.

Another distinction between New York City and other large cities was the right of misdemeanor defendants in New York City to ask for a trial in front of a panel of three judges. Justice Harlan noted in dissent in *Baldwin* v. *New York* that the *American Bar Association Project on Standards for Criminal Justice, Trial by Jury* had suggested this might be a sound compromise where jury trials are not permitted or are waived.[14]

In many Western countries with strong legal systems, a panel of judges is commonplace at criminal trials. But the Court tossed this protection aside quickly stating only that it is necessary to interpose "between the accused and his accuser the common-sense judgment of a group of laymen ... who ... are less likely to function or appear to function as but another arm of the Government that has proceeded against him."[15]

Applying the Federal Model to Misdemeanors

This is an instance where applying the federal model to states does not work. As mentioned earlier, the federal courts basically do not have misdemeanors when compared to the state systems. But misdemeanors represent the overwhelming majority of state cases—some 75 or 80 percent of their caseloads are misdemeanors and the volume of such cases is staggering. The federal system does not have to deal with simple assaults, thefts of services, shoplifting, purse snatching, and the many other crimes that flood into misdemeanor courts every. To apply the federal jury trial model to these cases is like using an Indy racing car to go to the corner store—it is excessively expensive and too impractical for such a task. It is not meant for those sorts of cases.

Were the trials before judges in New York City unfair? Justice Harlan's dissent states that the President of the Legal Aid Society in a speech at a judicial conference in 1968 reported that, in 1967, 49 percent of the Society's clients who were tried in New York City were acquitted.[16] This suggests that judges were doing what they should in the cases before them.

Baldwin v. *New York*'s Effect on Charging

A major cost of *Baldwin* v. *New York* is the effect it has on charging. If the trial will be the same and a prosecutor would strongly prefer not to spend a week at trial, there are advantages in charging at the felony level and upping the risk of conviction for the defendant. Chapter 1 cited John Pfaff's work in exposing the myths surrounding our incarceration rate and his efforts to find the actual causes of its rise. His conclusion on the causes is important for understanding the forces that pushed our incarceration rate so high. He concludes that the single biggest factor in the rise of our incarceration rate is the willingness of prosecutors to file felony charges.[17]

Part of this willingness was explained earlier—the vanishing trial makes it easy to file even cases with a weakness, as defendants will not be able to run the risk of trial.

But another influence on deciding to charge at the felony level is the influence of *Baldwin* v. *New York*. If you want a plea bargain, you charge as high as you can ethically and bargain down. *Baldwin* v. *New York* gives you no reason to charge at the misdemeanor level and offers advantages to charging high.

This contrasts sharply with other national systems where there are strong incentives for both the prosecution and the defense in keeping charges low, if possible. Both England and Canada show the advantages in having two trial models—the jury trial model for very serious crimes and a simpler trial model for less serious felonies and misdemeanors.

Many criminal cases can be charged at either level. If an arrestee defendant took a swing at a victim with a beer bottle in a bar fight that might be disorderly conduct, but it could also be assault with intent to injure, or perhaps even assault with a deadly weapon, depending on state statutes. If you would accept a plea to disorderly conduct, it makes sense in a plea-bargaining system to charge assault with intent to injure and then bargain down to disorderly conduct.

Much the same can be said of theft. If theft under $1,000 is a misdemeanor, a prosecutor will charge a computer thief with theft over $1,000. There is no leverage in charging only at the misdemeanor level. A prosecutor would want the defendant to worry about the stain of a felony conviction on their record as well as any mandatory sentence that might follow a conviction of felony theft.

The incentives in the United States are to charge as high as is ethically possible. The next sections explain how the incentives run the other way for prosecuting authorities in England and Canada.

England's Two Trial Models

In *Duncan* v. *Louisiana*, the Supreme Court traced jury trials back to the Magna Carta and quoted Blackstone for the proposition that a defendant's criminal conviction must be by "the unanimous suffrage of twelve of his equals and neighbours, indifferently chosen and superior to all suspicion."[18] But while jury trials have a long history in England going back to early common law, the Court's history of trials in England was truncated and limited. The reality is that for two centuries or more England has had two criminal courts, only one of which hears jury trials.

The two trial courts in England are the magistrates' court and Crown Court. Crown Court is the one Americans are likely to know from television and movies because it is quite dramatic with judges and barristers wearing white wigs, dickey collars, and robes appropriate to their position and seniority. It is a setting that is quite theatrical.

Criminal trials in Crown Court are always jury trials and all the most serious criminal cases— murders, rapes, etc.—will end up in Crown Court. But only 3 percent of criminal cases end up in Crown Court.[19] The real workhorse of the English criminal justice system is the system of magistrates' courts, where all criminal cases are initially filed and where most are resolved by plea bargaining, dismissal of charges, or trial.[20]

There are two types of judges hearing trials in magistrates' courts, lay magistrates and district judges. Lay magistrates are citizens without formal legal training, who go through an appointment process and, if chosen, are appointed by the Lord Chancellor. The lay magistrates receive no pay (other than expenses) and will often have other employment but they must be available to sit as a magistrate for at least twenty-six half-day sessions a year. They usually sit in panels of three and are assisted on points of law by a solicitor or barrister.

There are approximately 16,000 lay magistrates in England and Wales and they have been called the backbone of the English criminal justice system. One way to think of lay magistrates is to picture them as analogous to citizens appointed to a planning board or a school board in a small U.S. city. They are respected members of the community with the desire and the time to serve the community in which they live. They are appointed for a two-year term, but may be reappointed.

District judges sit in magistrates' courts in the larger cities in England, where the volume of cases is very high. District judges are trained in the law, work full time in magistrates' courts, and are paid (hence their former title as "stipendiary magistrates" to distinguish them from lay magistrates). Often, in large cities, both lay magistrates and district court judges hear cases, but district judges tend to work more quickly because of their experience and training.

Minor criminal cases—petty offenses and misdemeanors—will always be heard in magistrates' courts. What is interesting from a comparative perspective is the way felonies are handled. As mentioned above, serious felonies such as rape or murder must be sent to Crown Court if there is to be a trial and it will be, as mentioned above, a jury trial. However, there is a category of felonies, often referred to as "hybrid" offenses or "either-way" offenses, such as theft, assault, and burglary, which can be tried in either a magistrates' court or Crown Court.[21] The defendant can insist on trial by jury in these either-way offenses but not many make that choice due to the limited sentencing authority possessed by magistrates or district judges, which is six months in prison (or one year for more than one charge) for such felonies.

The limited sentencing authority in magistrates' courts is key to understanding why so few cases are tried in Crown Court. It is strongly to the advantage of the prosecuting authority—the Crown Prosecution Service—to have cases tried in magistrates' courts, if at all possible, as it is much cheaper and trials will be much quicker. Similar advantages accrue to defendants as well—they are assured of a rather lenient sentence: six months or a year if there are multiple charges.

This is only a thumbnail sketch[22] but the purpose is not to suggest England as an exact model to be followed in detail, but simply to show the way having two distinct trial models provides incentives to keep charges low and keep trials simple, if possible.

Canada is another example—different from England—but again the incentives are to keep the charges low, if possible.

Canada's Two Trial Models

Canada, like England, has two different trial courts: provincial courts and superior courts. Provincial courts handle all the minor offenses as well as the vast majority of the less serious felonies. Offenses tried in the provincial courts are always tried by a judge.

Jury trials only take place in superior courts. If a defendant is to be tried in the superior court, the defendant may waive a jury or not.

The key distinction between provincial courts and superior courts is the limited sentencing authority of judges in the provincial courts compared to superior court judges. Judges in the provincial courts—for most offenses—may only impose a sentence of imprisonment of six months. There is a general statement in the Canadian Criminal Code setting out this limit on sentences after a "summary trial"—meaning no indictment and no jury trial.[23] Many minor crimes—for example, littering, prostitution, and public indecency—are set out by statute as summary offenses and they will be handled in a provincial court. These summary offenses are roughly equivalent to misdemeanors in the United States.[24]

When it comes to more serious crimes, there are three types of what Canada refers to as "indictable offenses." The least serious, such a betting or bookmaking, which can be punished by up to two years in prison, must be tried in a provincial court, unless for some extraordinary reason the judge decides otherwise. At the other end of the spectrum are a tiny number of very serious crimes that must always be tried in a superior court including murder, treason, and piracy. The great bulk of indictable offenses may be tried in either a provincial court to a judge or a superior court with the right to a jury.

In some of these mid-range offenses, the choice is up to the prosecutor and many statutes provide quite different penalties if the conviction takes place in superior court as compared to a summary conviction for the same offense. Thus, for example, possession of drugs carries a penalty of up to seven years upon conviction after indictment, but only six months for a summary conviction (or up to one year if there was a previous conviction).[25]

There is also another category of mid-level indictable offenses where the choice of the forum for trial belongs to the defendant. These are sometimes referred to as "hybrid" offenses that may be tried in either a provincial court or a superior court at the option of the defendant. One example is theft under $5,000.[26]

But these different categories of indictable offenses and the related differences over whether the prosecutor or the defendant can choose the mode of trial are not as important in practice as they might appear because there are strong incentives for both the prosecutor and the defendant to opt for trial in a provincial court, if possible. This is reflected in the fact that only a tiny percentage of criminal cases—approximately 2 percent—are tried in a superior court.[27] The reason for this is that both prosecutors and defendants benefit from a trial in a provincial court.

The main benefits are similar to those in England when a trial takes place in magistrates' court compared to Crown Court. Prosecutors in Canada get a much shorter trial because it is not a jury trial. It is the same evidence as would be presented to a jury but it goes much more quickly to a professional judge. Where a trial might take a couple of hours in a provincial court, it might take a week if tried to a jury in a superior court.

Defendants also benefit from trials in provincial courts. Clearly, the big advantage is the limited sentencing authority of provincial court judges. Defendants are assured of a rather lenient sentence after trial in a provincial court compared to what they might receive in a superior court.

There are other important benefits for defendants when the trial takes place in a provincial court. Defendants who have a summary conviction are often spared the collateral consequences such as deportation or loss of residency status.[28] It is also easier to get a conviction "suspended" after conviction of a summary offense, which removes the conviction from the general database on convictions, so that they can apply for employment with a clean record. A defendant may apply to have their conviction suspended after five years, while they must wait ten years to apply for suspension after conviction of an indictable offense.[29]

Obviously, the Canadian government wants cases handled in provincial courts if possible, and the sentencing authority has been raised for certain crimes to try to keep those crimes in a provincial court. While the sentencing authority of provincial court judges is six months for most offenses, as mentioned above, this limit has been raised to eighteen months for some more serious, high-volume crimes, including assault with a weapon, uttering a threat to cause death or bodily harm, causing bodily harm, and sexual assault. Thus, for example, the sexual assault statute sets out two different penalties depending on the court that is chosen for trial. If the trial takes place in a superior court, the maximum sentence is ten years, while it is only eighteen months if the trial takes place in provincial court.[30]

What Canada wanted to accomplish by increasing the sentencing authority of provincial judges for these crimes, many of which would seem to require a sentence in excess of six months, is to convince prosecutors to try those crimes in a provincial court, if possible.

The way the two courts function in Canada is similar to the way the two different courts function in England. By having two trial models for misdemeanors and most felonies, the pressure in charging or choosing a type of trial is strongly downward.

The Additional Costs of *Baldwin* v. *New York*

The effects of *Baldwin* v. *New York* on charging have been mentioned, but there are several other costs to the decision.

First of all, the elimination of trials for misdemeanors robs the system of an important training ground for prosecutors, defense lawyers, and judges. Lawyers who were in the Manhattan District Attorney's Office or worked for the Legal Aid Society prior to *Baldwin* v. *New York* had tried many simple cases of all types "on the fly." It gave them experience and training that cannot be easily be duplicated outside courtrooms.

When you are trying cases with little preparation, you get used to listening and adjusting to what is said in the courtroom. Perhaps the police officer's testimony is a bit different than it appeared in the police report or perhaps the defendant's testimony varies from what they told the police. Prosecutors and defense lawyers learn valuable lessons when these things occur.

Second, by insisting on jury trials for minor cases, we lost a very different kind of advocacy from what you will find in federal courts or state courts when serious crimes are being tried. If a victim on the stand in a nonjury misdemeanor trial varies from their statement in the police report and the defendant is acquitted, that is fine. "Next case, please." If a judge gives a defendant a break because there are sympathetic reasons why they committed a minor crime, the prosecutor will understand that sometimes justice does not fit the written law exactly. "Next case, please."

But if these cases are going to be conceptualized like felony cases, you are asking for a very different style of advocacy with pre-trial hearings, careful rehearsing of witnesses, a day or more of jury selection for a one-hour case, and so on. Prosecutors, judges, and *especially* defendants cannot afford this much time devoted to a misdemeanor case. For indigent defendants, it means days off work, waiting in crowded courtrooms for a trial that may or may not happen that day, the costs of transportation to and from the court, possible daycare complications, and other difficulties.

By way of illustration, consider what happened to a cohort of fifty-four marijuana possession cases in the period from March 2011 through March 2012 in the Bronx that the public defenders in that borough—the Bronx Defenders—and their clients wished to take to trial. The defenders thought these were winnable cases and the defendants in this cohort had no prior criminal record.

The title of a report put out by the Bronx Defenders, "No Day in Court," sums up what happened.[31] Even though the defendants wanted to challenge the charges against them, not a single suppression hearing was ever completed and, eventually, the majority of the defendants were simply worn down by the process and accepted conditional release agreements or pleas to disorderly conduct charges.

Thirty percent of the cases were eventually dismissed outright, but those defendants paid a price as it took on average five court appearances and 270 days to get those dismissals. The report explains the toll the process exacted on defendants as they were required to return to the courthouse again and again to await hearings that rarely took place:

> After making it into the courthouse, they must wait, sometimes for hours, in crowded courtrooms, where judges frequently hear in excess of 100 cases a day, before having their cases called. And because prosecutors rarely reveal whether they will state "ready" for hearings and trial until the case is called on the record, the wait is colored by anxiety and uncertainty.
>
> Beyond the physical and psychological toll exacted by these delays, each postponement brings with it the potential for another missed day of work, lost wages, school absence,

rescheduled medical appointment, financial hardship, or childcare emergency. Clients must pay for transportation to and from court.

Repeated absences from work strain relationships with current employers, and potential employers are less likely to hire clients when a background check reveals a pending criminal case. Clients working in the public sector or in jobs requiring state-issued licenses—such as security guards, home health aides, or cab drivers—are especially vulnerable, as an open case may lead to an immediate suspension without pay and, ultimately, termination.[32]

It is fair to put some of the blame on the prosecutors and judges for "No Day in Court." It is also fair to see what happened as revealing serious problems with the speedy trial statute in New York. However, a large share of the blame is due to the Court's naivety in expanding the right to jury trial to minor criminal cases.

Another cost of *Baldwin* v. *New York* is the impact of the case on the private practice of criminal defense. Imagine that you are a private defense attorney. You have a varied clientele—some drunk driving cases, some drug cases, some simple assault cases, some burglary cases, some prostitution cases, and so on. You have a good reputation and clients seek you out if they can pay for your services but these clients don't have a lot of money. Maybe they can pool monies from their family to pay your retainer, and have you look at the police reports and advise on a plea. But they cannot afford your services for three or four days of trial, to say nothing about the work you would have to do outside the courtroom preparing witnesses, suggesting jury instructions, and so on. If the trial were a quick one—an hour win or lose—that is doable and affordable, but a full-blown jury trial?

Final Thoughts on *Duncan–Baldwin*

Many countries are going in the opposite direction of *Duncan* v. *Louisiana* and *Baldwin* v. *New York*. As mentioned above, Canada has tried to make trials in the lower court possible even for somewhat serious felonies such as assault with a weapon and some sexual assaults.

Jury trials have strengths but they have weaknesses, too. Is it better to have more trials but simpler trials or to offer elaborate trials but grant them to fewer defendants? We have taken the latter route.

At the time *Baldwin* v. *New York* was decided in 1970, it was estimated that a judge in the New York City Criminal Court handling misdemeanors could hear perhaps two jury trials a week but could handle somewhere between fifteen and twenty-five nonjury trials in a week. That large discrepancy in the costs of jury trials versus nonjury trials is probably much greater today.

The impact of *Baldwin* v. *New York* on the availability of trials is dramatic. In 1967, the year prior to the decision in *Baldwin* v. *New York*, there were 5,701 trials in the Criminal Court of New York City. In 2014, the Criminal Court of New York City, which had 100 judges at that time, handled 252,741 misdemeanor cases. Of those, only 580 went to trial (175 were jury trials).

Imagine a world in which even twenty of those 100 judges heard fifteen trials to the court each week for perhaps forty weeks each year. The number of trials would be 12,000.

Many lawyers and judges will complain that the system needs more resources so that it can do more trials. Frankly, this is wrong—the system has plenty of resources. It is how it chooses to use those resources that is the problem. New York City does not need to wash 250,000 citizens through its misdemeanor courts each year and a realistic possibility of contesting some of those arrests would force the City to seek other ways of handling minor antisocial behaviors.

It would also improve policing, as testimony about improper police actions by certain officers, or a certain precinct, or testimony about an improper police tactic was brought out in case after case. It is too easy today to hide these issues in a system where, as the saying goes, "the process is the punishment."[33] If you want to challenge an arrest or defend yourself from a charge you think wrong or unfair in an urban misdemeanor court, the system will make you pay heavily.

In a wonderful book, *Misdemeanorland*, Issa Kohler-Hausmann takes an in-depth look at misdemeanor courts in New York City and she shows how these courts have become tools for the social control of vast numbers of our citizens.[34] She demonstrates that the adjudicative model, in which courts try to determine if a defendant is guilty or not, is no longer the way these courts function. Instead, she explains, these courts operate under a managerial model which imposes a period of control over those passing through them.[35] One of the techniques to test and exert control over defendants is the "procedural hassle," described in the excerpt from "No Day in Court" above. Another effective technique of social control, which Kohler-Hausmann describes, is the conditional dismissal of a case which is set for dismissal after a set period of time—perhaps six months or a year—*if* the defendant is not rearrested.

New York City was a special jurisdiction during the period Kohler-Hausmann studied misdemeanor courts because the policy of the police was to vigorously enforce the law, even laws for minor infractions, in the belief that it would head off more serious crime and provide order in public spaces for law-abiding citizens.[36] This policing policy is sometimes referred to as Broken Windows policing, the idea being that one broken window invites others to break windows if the first broken window is not repaired.

One of the factors that makes the managerial model possible, according to Kohler-Hausmann, is the "near structural impossibility of a formal adversarial operational model in lower criminal courts."[37] *Misdemeanorland* focuses on the operations of a set of misdemeanor criminal courts in a single city under a particular policing policy.

But as criminal trials vanish in our felony system and large numbers of citizens churn in and out of our prisons each year, is it time to worry that felony courts are moving away from the adjudicative model to the managerial model?

Notes

1. See *Duncan v. Louisiana*, 391 U.S. 145 (1968).
2. See *Baldwin v. New York*, 399 U.S. 66 (1970).
3. The story of *Duncan v. Louisiana* is beautifully told by Nancy King; see Nancy J. King, How Bigotry in the Bayou Led to the Federal Regulation of Juries, in Carol S. Steiker (Ed.), *Criminal Procedure Stories: An In-Depth Look at Leading Criminal Procedure Cases* (New York: Foundation Press, 2006), 261.
4. See *Duncan v. Louisiana*, 391 U.S. at 149 n. 14.
5. See *Duncan v. Louisiana*, 391 U.S. at 158.
6. See John H. Langbein, Shaping the Eighteenth-Century Criminal Trial: A View from the Ryder Sources, *University of Chicago Law Review* 50(1)(1983), 115.
7. See Lawrence Friedman, The Day Before Trials Vanished, *Journal of Empirical Legal Studies* 1(3) (2004), 692 (citing Arthur Train, *The Prisoner At the Bar: Sidelights on the Administration of Criminal Justice* [New York: Charles Scribner's Sons, 1906], 159).
8. See Marcia Chambers, Issue and Debate: Who Should Pick Jurors, Attorneys or the Judge, *New York Times*, June 13, 1983, available at: www.nytimes.com/1983/06/13/nyregion/issue-and-debate-who-should-pick-jurors-attorneys-or-the-judge.html.

 9 Frank Hogan, the District Attorney in New York City for more than thirty years, was known as "Mr. Integrity." *See* Chip Brown, Cyrus Vance, Jr.'s "Moneyball" Approach to Crime, *New York Times*, December 3, 2014, available at www.nytimes.com/2014/12/07/magazine/cyrus-vance-jrs-moneyball-approach-to-crime.html.

10 See The History of the Legal Aid Society, available at: www.legal-aid.org/en/las/aboutus/ourhistory.aspx.

11 On the history of the New York City Bar Association, see generally, About the New York City Bar Association, available at: www.nycbar.org/about-us/overview-about-us.

12 See *Baldwin* v. *New York*, 399 U.S. at 72.

13 See *Baldwin* v. *New York*, 399 U.S. 117, 139 (Harlan, J. dissenting).

14 See *Baldwin* v. *New York*, 399 U.S. at 136.

15 See *Baldwin* v. *New York*, 399 U.S. at 126.

16 See *Baldwin* v. *New York*, 399 U.S. at 136, n. 16.

17 John F. Pfaff, *Locked In: The True Causes of Mass Incarceration and How To Achieve Real Reform* (New York: Basic Books, 2017), 6.

18 See *Duncan* v. *Louisiana*, 391 U.S. at 151–152.

19 See Tyler Marshall, Lay Magistrates Rule in 97% of English, Welsh Criminal Cases, *LA Times*, December 20, 1985, available at: http://articles.latimes.com/1985–12–20/news/mn-5008_1_criminal-cases.

20 See generally, Herbert M. Kritzer, Courts, Justice, and Politics in England, in Herbert Jacob, Erhard Blankenburg, Herbert M. Kritzer, Doris Marie Provine, Joseph Sanders (Eds.), *Courts, Law, and Politics in Comparative Perspective* (New Haven, CT: Yale University Press, 1996), 103; A.T.H. Smith, England and Wales in Christine Van den Wyngaert (Ed.), *Criminal Procedure Systems in the European Community* (1993), 73 and 77.

21 See Kritzer, Courts, Justice, and Politics in England, 103, n. 20.

22 Among other issues not discussed is the ability of magistrates to send a case to Crown Court if they feel the sentence limit in magistrates' court is not sufficient for the crime. See Kritzer, Courts, Justice, and Politics in England, 103, n. 20.

23 S. 787(1) of the Criminal Code of Canada states: "Unless otherwise provided by law, everyone who is convicted of an offense punishable by summary conviction is liable to … a term of imprisonment not exceeding six months …" *Martin's Annual Criminal Code of Canada* (Toronto: Thomson Reuters, 2018).

24 See Lori Hausegger, Matthew Hennigar, and Troy Riddell, *Canadian Courts: Law, Politics, and Process* (Don Mills, ON: Oxford University Press, 2009), 35.

25 See S. 4(3), Controlled Drugs and Substances Act, in *Martin's Criminal Code of Canada* (2018).

26 See Hausegger et al., *Canadian Courts*, 36, n. 24.

27 See Cheryl Marie Webster and Anthony N. Doob, Superior Courts in the Twenty-First Century: An Historical Anachronism? in Peter H. Russell (Ed.), *Canada's Trial Courts: Two Tiers or One?* (Toronto: University of Toronto Press, 2007), 57 and 62.

28 Thus, for example, a permanent resident in Canada will not be required to leave unless convicted of a crime with a possible sentence in excess of ten years or unless given a sentence in excess of six months. See Section 36 (1)(a), *Immigration and Refugee Protection Act 2001*, available at: http://laws-lois.justice.gc.ca/eng/acts/I-2.5/.

29 See Parole Board of Canada, *Record Suspension Guide* 1 (2014), available at: http://pbc-clcc.gc.ca/prdons/pardoninstr-eng.pdf.

30 See S. 271, *Martin's Criminal Code of Canada* (2018).

31 The Bronx Defenders, No Day in Court, available at: www.bronxdefenders.org/wp-content/uploads/2013/05/No-Day-in-Court-A-Report-by-The-Bronx-Defenders-May-2013.pdf.

32 Ibid.

33 The phrase is attributed to Malcolm Feeley, a law professor who has written extensively on misdemeanor courts; see Malcolm M. Feeley, *The Process Is the Punishment: Handling Cases in a Lower Criminal Court* (New York: Russell Sage Foundation, 1979).

34 Issa Kohler-Hausmann, *Misdemeanorland: Criminal Courts and Social Control in an Age of Broken Windows Policy* (Princeton, NJ: Princeton University Press, 2018).

35 Ibid., 71–75.

36 Ibid., 25–30.

37 Ibid., 75.

6

THE SHIFT FROM INDETERMINATE SENTENCES TO DETERMINATE SENTENCES

The previous chapters have described the way trials have vanished in both our federal system and state systems in favor of plea bargaining. Plea bargaining and sentencing deserve more specific treatment and the next chapters will focus on those topics.

Some background on the way sentencing power has evolved over the past decades is necessary to understand how we ended up with fixed sentencing ranges for most crimes, high mandatory minimums for some, and some particularly harsh laws for repeat offenders. These changes in sentencing laws shifted considerable power to prosecutors as they obtained more control over sentences by the way they charged crimes or even by the way they described crimes for sentencing purposes.

This chapter will discuss a confluence of factors that came together to change the nature of sentencing in the United States—usually in ways that increased the harshness of criminal statutes. Among these were:

(1) a shift away from rehabilitation as the dominant theory of sentencing;
(2) the increasing pressures on state legislators in the wake of crime;
(3) the exploitation of the fear of crime by politicians;
(4) the backlash against Supreme Court decisions; and
(5) the emergence of a powerful victims' movement.

From Rehabilitation to Retribution, Deterrence, and Incapacitation

In the 1950s and 1960s, rehabilitation was emphasized as the proper function of sentencing and other purposes, such as retribution for the crime committed, were thought to be regressive. Indeed, Franklin Zimring and Gordon Hawkins, two noted criminologists reported that for most of the twentieth century—up to the mid-1970s—the concept of rehabilitation "dominated penal policy and practice by acclamation and largely without dissent."[1] For example, in its report on "The Challenge of Crime in a Free Society," the 1967 President's Commission on Law Enforcement and Administration of Justice was optimistic that experimental programs and new techniques of treatment could reform offenders.[2]

Some states were so committed to rehabilitation that they did not give defendants specific terms of years in sending them to prison but instead gave them indeterminate sentences with the understanding that offenders would be evaluated and treated at the prison, and then released to the community when they had been rehabilitated. In effect, the sentence was really to be determined by experts in the prison system. Prison officials were optimistic about what could be established through reform in prisons. Parole boards also played an important role in the rehabilitation, as they could offer prisoners a chance for early release if the board found progress toward rehabilitation.

This was a forward-looking view of sentencing that aimed to fit the sentence to the offender and the offender's future. The aim was to change the attitude, the character, and, hopefully, the behavior of the offender.

But, in the late 1970s, scholars began to argue against rehabilitation as a basis for sentencing as increasing skepticism about the prospects for reforming people emerged. Scholars such as Norval Morris, the dean at the University of Chicago Law School at the time, argued that forcing prisoners to participate in treatment programs that they did not really want in order to show they had been "rehabilitated" was unlikely to benefit such prisoners and it would also undercut the effectiveness of such programs for inmates who sincerely wanted the treatment program. It was better for every offender going to prison to know on the first day exactly when they would be released.[3]

Morris and many others had become pessimistic about the ability of experts to rehabilitate people. It was buttressed by data suggesting that rehabilitative efforts achieved very little in terms of reducing recidivism.

The thinking on rehabilitation had changed so dramatically that by 1979, Francis Allen, a professor at Michigan Law School, could report:

> In a remarkably short time a new orthodoxy has been established asserting the rehabilitative objectives are largely unattainable and that rehabilitative programs and research are dubious and misdirected.[4]

What would replace rehabilitation as that goal became discredited? The rejection of rehabilitation as the goal of sentencing made room for the other three goals often put forward as proper sentencing objectives: retribution, deterrence, and incapacitation.

This move away from rehabilitation pushed sentences higher. To understand this, one only has to consider that rehabilitation programs are usually relatively short in duration. In addition, a judge might conclude that the best program for the offender could be made available to the offender without the need for a prison sentence. If an offender had to be sent to prison, the rehabilitative focus suggested a short stay to reform offenders by showing them the results they have brought on themselves.

Finally, even if an offender was sent to prison for a term of years when rehabilitation was in vogue, it was understood that the offender would not serve anywhere close to the full sentence, but could be released after as little as one-third of the sentence if offenders behaved themselves and showed good progress in various prison programs.

Rehabilitation falling out of favor opened the door to harsher sentencing laws. Incapacitation is based on the view that the offender needs to be incarcerated to prevent them from continuing to commit crimes. Three-strikes laws—often mandating a life sentence—are an example of incapacitation taken to extreme. There are many problems with such laws. Although it has been shown over and over that we cannot accurately predict who will continue to commit violent crime and who will not, statutes aimed at incapacitation became acceptable and more common. Criminologist Michael Tonry, writing in 2019, is fairly devastating in his assessment of the problems predicting dangerousness:

> Predictions of dangerousness are more often wrong than right, use information they shouldn't, and disproportionately damage minority offenders. Forty years ago, two-thirds of people predicted to be violent were not. For every two "true positives," there were four "false positives." Contemporary technology is little better: at best, three false positives for every two true positives. The best-informed specialists say that accuracy topped out a decade ago; further improvement is unlikely. All prediction instruments use ethically unjustifiable information. Most include variables such as youth and gender that are as unjust as race or eye color would be. No one can justly be blamed for being blue-eyed, young, male, or dark-skinned. All prediction instruments incorporate socioeconomic status variables that cause black, other minority, and disadvantaged offenders to be treated more harshly than white and privileged offenders. All use criminal history variables that are inflated for black and other minority offenders by deliberate and implicit bias, racially disparate practices, profiling, and drug law enforcement that targets minority individuals and neighborhoods.[5]

Despite this research, the Court has upheld harsh sentences after a nonviolent third felony so these statutes have a strong foothold in the United States at this point in time. In *Ewing* v. *California*, the Court upheld a sentence of twenty-five years to life for a defendant whose third felony was the theft of three golf clubs from a pro shop in El Segundo, California.[6] (Chapter 8 will return to *Ewing* v. *California* to explain the Court's struggles over the issue of whether the protection against cruel and unusual punishments should apply to extremely long sentences.)

Deterrence as a sentencing goal also pushed sentences higher. If a state is trying to deter a certain crime, it may choose a stiff, mandatory sentence to make it clear to citizens tempted to commit such a crime that the consequences will be severe. Mandatory sentences for sales of drugs, for example, became more and more common. Most readers will, no doubt, be familiar with the Congressional law passed in 1986 as citizens became alarmed by news accounts of a growing "crack" cocaine epidemic. The statute created a 100–1 disparity in the punishment of crack cocaine as compared to cocaine in powder form. (This had a strong disparate racial impact, since those selling and using crack are overwhelmingly black.)[7]

Finally, retribution does not demand as severe a sentence as deterrence or incapacitation, but it will also tend to push sentences higher as rehabilitation fades as a goal. Retribution insists that the offender pay a proportionate penalty for the crime. Thus, if the offender has good chances for rehabilitation through a unique local program, retribution might demand that the offender receive a prison sentence nonetheless, even though it would not advance rehabilitation or might even make recidivism more likely.

Pressures on State Legislators
"To Do Something About Crime X"

The loss of faith in rehabilitation opened up many options for states in enacting criminal laws aimed at goals such as deterrence and incapacitation. These are dangerous concepts on which to base criminal statutes as it is hard to know whether a certain term of years deters or who among a class of offenders is certain to offend again. But states showed no hesitancy and waves of statutes with harsh mandatory minimum sentences began to sweep the country.

The earliest and best known of the statutes evincing a new "tough on crime" mentality were the infamous Rockefeller Drug Laws passed in 1973 that featured, among other provisions, a fifteen-year mandatory prison sentence to anyone distributing even a relatively small amount of narcotics. Michigan followed suit with its own version, the so-called "650-Lifer Law", which imposed a mandatory life sentence without parole for possession of 650 grams of heroin or cocaine. Eventually, other states put in place their own quantity-based mandatory sentence laws for drugs.

Drugs, however, were only a part of the broad expansion of mandatory minimum laws. If you carried a firearm in the commission of a serious felony, if you committed an assault in a detention facility, if you robbed a person above a certain age (or below a certain age), and so on, there would be an additional term of years added to the sentence for the original crime and a judge had no power to go below the "mandatory" term in sentencing.

The Michigan 650-Lifer Law is also evidence of another trend in sentencing that is unique to the United States: visiting life without the possibility of parole on offenders. Life without parole (LWOP) is a very dramatic sentence, especially when the person is young. It was rare for a state to have such a law on its books in the early 1970s, but today almost every state has sentences mandating life LWOP upon conviction. Usually, LWOP is limited to homicide, but as the Michigan law shows, it was sometimes imposed for other offenses as well.

Even when restricted to homicide, it is a brutal sentence. There are offenders who one day kill a parent or a spouse after years of abuse; it is a terrible crime—and the earlier abuse is not a defense—but life without any chance of parole is disproportionate to these crimes and such a bleak sentence, as it gives a person no hope of release even after decades as a model prisoner.

In addition to the passage of extremely harsh sentences such as LWOP, the harshness of punishments for more routine crimes also increased as states moved to "truth in sentencing." As mentioned above, everyone in the system understood in the era of rehabilitation that an offender given a ten-year sentence would not serve even the majority of that sentence if the offender behaved appropriately in prison and took advantage of prison programs. But in the "truth-in-sentencing" era, "earned" reductions in a sentence were taken away entirely or greatly reduced. In addition, the authority of parole boards to reduce sentences was greatly limited. Many states abolished parole altogether or reduced eligibility for parole to those convicted of certain crimes. The goal of "truth in sentencing" was to assure the public that two years or five years in prison meant very close to two years or five years of time in prison.

Once laws increasing punishments or mandating a certain minimum are in place in one state, it is hard for other states to resist enacting such laws in their own state. When, for example, a state has put into place a stiff mandatory minimum sentence for those who sell drugs near a school, legislators in other states will have a tough time explaining to voters why they have not enacted the same law, which is needed "to protect our children."

Harsh laws that threaten LWOP or very high mandatory minimums are, thankfully, more bark than bite in terms of the actual sentences defendants receive because prosecutors in the United States have broad charging discretion and they often do not charge offenders with statutes mandating brutal mandatory sentences. They are rightly hesitant to visit a brutally long sentence on most offenders. Legislators know this and it gives them an excuse to enact harsh laws. They can show—rather dramatically—to voters that they "did something about crime X," but know that the statute will be used only sparingly.

However, harsh sentences affect our incarceration rate even when they are not imposed on many defendants; they are powerful weapons for prosecutors to use to force defendants to accept plea bargains. Statutes with harsh mandatory minimums are a factor in the rise of the plea-bargaining rate in most states from around 80 percent in the 1970s to the present rates in most states of 97 or 98 percent.

We are in a period now where many states are rethinking harsh statutes and there have been major reforms. For example, the Rockefeller Drug Laws in New York and the 650-Lifer Law in Michigan were effectively repealed by doing away with the mandatory sentence provisions. Three-strikes laws have also been modified in some states to limit the three felonies to serious violent crimes. And Congress has repealed the 100–1 disparity in sentencing for crack as compared to powder cocaine.

And yet there are still many determinate sentencing laws with high mandatory minimums that give prosecutors considerable control over sentencing if they charge those offenses and this helps prosecutors force defendants to accept plea bargains that avoid those laws. And while we are in a period where there is room for sentencing reform and we have seen reforms, especially in the drug area, the mood can swing in the opposite direction if public emotion and anger is stoked by politicians or if a horrific crime occurs.

The Exploitation of Fear of Crime by Politicians

The United States is different from other countries in that we elect most of our judges and prosecutors. Some of the elections are nonpolitical—merely asking the voters if the judge should be retained—but some are completely political with candidates of different parties vying for the same position and promising voters they will be tough on offenders or that they will end frivolous lawsuits. There have been attempts to change this from time to time—usually aimed at taking state supreme courts out of the political arena—but these attempts always fail. American populism is strong.

When crime is on the rise, politicians will play to that concern and try to paint the opposing candidate as one who is "soft on crime." The most famous example occurred in the presidential campaign between George H.W. Bush and Michael Dukakis.[8] Dukakis was at one time governor of Massachusetts and during his tenure there was a prison program—which had been in effect from a time prior to his becoming governor—that granted prisoners occasional weekend furloughs from prison to spend time at home in order to help them with the transition when they would eventually be released.

The program had run well without incident for several years, but there had been one tragic failure when a prisoner serving a sentence for murder, Willie Horton, had not returned from such a furlough and had fled to Maryland, where he went on a crime spree during which he had kidnapped a young couple, pistol-whipped and stabbed the man, and raped his girlfriend. The Bush campaign took this incident and ran powerful and highly effective racially inflammatory advertisements—using the arrest photo of Horton, who was black—that tied the incident to Dukakis. The advertisements offered this contrast: "Bush supports the death penalty for first-degree murderers. Dukakis not only opposes the death penalty, he allowed first-degree murderers to have weekend passes from prison. One was Willie Horton, who … fled, kidnapping a young couple …"[9]

This was a powerful advertisement that turned many people against Dukakis and helped swing the election to Bush, who had been trailing in the polls until this advertisement was released.

Besides the race-baiting nature of the advertisement, it feeds into fear that ordinary citizens are likely to be raped or murdered by strangers. And fear is a very bad basis on which to base crime policies.

There is rarely any political advantage for politicians in being seen as "soft on crime" and politicians are loath to get in front of legislative proposals that are harsh and unwise. An enormous firestorm of controversary followed the decision of a California judge to give a Stanford student only a six-month sentence for sexually assaulting an intoxicated Stanford student. The California legislature quickly amended their sexual assault statutes to require a mandatory minimum that would prevent a sentence such as the student had been given. When the law came to Governor Jerry Brown's desk, he expressed the politically correct response that he was "normally opposed to mandatory minimum sentences," but he nonetheless signed the law.[10]

The Backlash Against Supreme Court Decisions

Some of the increasing harshness of criminal statutes in the United States is part of a backlash against Supreme Court decisions. Perhaps the most dramatic "rejection" of Supreme Court decisions concerned the death penalty. In *Furman* v. *Georgia* in 1972, the Court basically halted executions after it ruled that the death penalty under the Georgia statute was unconstitutional in the way it was applied as it provided insufficient protection against death sentences that were imposed arbitrarily and discriminately.[11] Because the protections the Court wanted were not in place in any state, the death penalty was put on hold.

Two of the justices, Justices Brennan and Marshall, would have gone farther and ruled that the death penalty is a violation of the Eighth Amendment proscription against cruel and unusual punishment. Though the death penalty has a long history in the United States and is contemplated in the Constitution, they felt that the sentence had become incompatible with the "evolving standards of decency" of our contemporary society. Very quickly thirty-four states adopted new death penalty statutes that addressed the flaws revealed in *Furman* v. *Georgia*.

This swift move to reinstall a death penalty reflected in part a more general concern about what the Court had been doing with criminal procedure. Many decisions of the Supreme Court also came under attack shortly after they were handed down. *Miranda* v. *Arizona*, for example, was immediately attacked by many in the law enforcement community, who saw it as a decision "protecting the guilty." Similarly, *Mapp* v. *Ohio* (excluding evidence if the police made an illegal arrest or an illegal search) was similarly attacked. These decisions were central campaign issues in Richard Nixon's 1968 campaign for the presidency. There were legislative attempts in Congress at various times to limit these decisions but changing decisions that are based on the Constitution is not easy.

So, what can citizens do when they feel that the Court has gone too far? They can recall judges, not on the federal level as they have lifetime appointments, but they can recall judges at the state level. In 1986, three justices on the California Supreme Court, including the Chief Justice Rose Bird, were recalled in a highly partisan attack on their pattern of refusing to uphold death penalty sentences. The advertisements seeking the recall featured the children of murder victims in some of the cases that these three justices had voted to reverse. Bird's recall passed easily with 67 percent of the voters supporting the recall.

Mention was made above of the controversary that followed a six-month sentence for a Stanford student convicted of sexual assault, which led to the passage of mandatory minimums for sexual assault. The sentence had been recommended by probation and the student's conviction mandated a lifetime of sex offender registration but the judge who imposed the sentence was recalled from office. Sixty percent of California voters voted for the recall.[12]

The more obvious way in which citizens express frustration with our criminal justice system is through legislation that makes criminal penalties harsher and harsher. In many states, especially in the west, legislative ballot initiatives are permitted and, with a sufficient number of signatures, harsh criminal statutes can be put in place without the need for legislative action. One of the early states to adopt a three-strikes law (and the first state to describe the law using the baseball analogy) was Washington, which put the issue to voters in 1993. It passed with 72 percent of the voters supporting the proposed law. Many states quickly followed suit.[13]

Other laws pushed by citizens in the wake of perceived failures of the criminal justice system are described in the next section, which deals with the crime victims' movement.

The Crime Victims' Movement

In the 1960s, when the Supreme Court was handing down many decisions that constitute the foundation of the criminal procedure revolution, the Court's conceptualization of criminal cases was simplistic. On one side was the defendant and on the other side was "the State." In a two-sided world, it is easy to enforce rules between the parties—if one side errs, we punish that side to the benefit of the "other side." But the world of criminal trials is no longer two-sided. As explained in Chapter 2 on the risks of making procedural rules using the Constitution, one of the risks is evolving societal values and one value that has emerged over the last four decades is the need to do more for victims of crime.

In the earliest days of criminal trials, victims once played a central role—they brought criminal cases themselves. There were no prosecutors or defense lawyers in the courtrooms, or even organized police forces.[14] But gradually their role diminished to the point that they were limited to being spectators at trials—assuming they were not sequestered from attending—or possible witnesses, but only if the prosecutor needed their testimony.

Starting in the 1970s, a powerful victims' movement emerged in the United States based on the premise that the criminal justice equation failed to take into account the stake that victims, or the family of victims, have in criminal cases. Victims are not "the State," and have nothing to do with the police, but at the same time, they have a stake in the outcome of the criminal case that is quite different from the prosecutor or the police. They care deeply about *this particular case* because the case is about them and what happened to them, or to their family, or their friends.

The victims' movement is not a U.S. movement; rather, it is an international movement. Many countries that have trial systems not based on the adversary model now give victims, usually victims of serious crimes, a right to participate in criminal trials, sometimes on a rather equal basis with the defense. Many victims such as those who have lost a family member due to murder do not choose to participate at trials, but it is common for rape victims or victims of domestic abuse to choose to participate at trial. Counsel will be appointed in such cases if the victim cannot afford to hire an attorney.[15]

International bodies have also recognized that criminal justice systems have not done enough for crime victims. The United Nations General Assembly in 1985 adopted the Declaration of Basic Principles of Justice for Victims of Crime and Abuse of Power.[16]

Even the International Criminal Court, which only began functioning in 2002, has had to grant victims of genocide and crimes against humanity a right to participate in trials of these horrific crimes.[17] The International Criminal Court is designed for cases that, even with adequate resources, present enormous logistical difficulties to which victim participation will add another layer of complexity. The recognition that victims of horrific crimes should have a right to some level of participation—a right not granted victims at previous international criminal tribunals: the International Criminal Tribunal for the former Yugoslavia (ITCY) and the International Criminal Tribunal for Rwanda (ITCR)—suggests how much the treatment of victims has changed over the last few decades and how it continues to evolve.

It is not easy to know exactly what victims are seeking and sometimes they cannot explain it precisely. One statement that encapsulates the frustration victims feel in criminal justice systems is a statement from a woman whose four sons were murdered in a rural Indiana farmhouse. She described interviews with the county prosecutor:

> … I was treated with kindness and respect, but I soon began to feel like another piece of evidence…. When I asked about my rights and the rights of our four sons, I was told that as a victim I had no particular rights.[18]

Notice that this was not a criticism of the prosecutor, but of the way the system treats victims. That they were treated as "a piece of evidence" is a common refrain of crime victims. This was a one of the criticisms levied against the international tribunals for the former Yugoslavia and for Rwanda. Victims felt they were being used solely as witnesses for the prosecution. They wanted to be listened to and be allowed to tell their story.

In U.S. courts, a trial procedure that sees victims simply as witnesses is a particular frustration for victims of serious crimes. It is easier in European courts for victims to talk about the crime and its impact because all witnesses (including defendants) are encouraged to give their accounts in narrative form before questions are put to them. It is not unusual to hear a rape victim speak for twenty minutes or more, giving a full account of what happened including what they were thinking, what they were frightened about, what they did immediately after the crime, and how the crime affected them then and now.

But in common law courts, victims are in a frustrating position. They take a stern oath to "tell the truth, the whole truth, and nothing but the truth." But the system doesn't allow a victim to tell the whole truth. They are required to answer very specific questions and are not permitted to stray outside the limits of those questions. As for the impact of the crime, our trial system does not want to hear about that at the trial. The victim may get a chance to explain the impact of the crime but that will occur at sentencing if there is a conviction.

In the United States, understanding how to accommodate the interest of victims in our criminal justice system has not been easy. Over the last thirty years, every state has passed either statutes or constitutional amendments insisting that victims be kept informed of the progress of the case, be notified of important court hearings, and be consulted about possible plea bargains.

Today, it is a rare prosecutor in a serious criminal case that does not keep the victim apprised of the progress of the case or does not consult the victim about a possible plea bargain.

Nevertheless, the battle for stronger victims' rights continues. Some of the earlier victims' right legislation is unenforceable and so there is now pressure to revise the first-generation of victims' legislation to strengthen certain victims' rights. For example, the Crime Victims Act of 2004 passed by Congress barred the exclusion of crime victims from any hearing unless there was "clear and convincing evidence" that their testimony would be "materially altered" by attending. This seemed a step in the right direction. It was sometimes a defense tactic for the defense to subpoena the victim as a defense witness to keep the victim out of the courtroom for much of the trial. They would never call the victim as a witness. This would be more difficult under the federal act and the rule of criminal procedure, Rule 60(2), that was adopted to put into effect the requirement of a strong showing in order to sequester the victim.

Today, victims are pushing for changes in the law to give them the right to stay in the courtroom throughout the trial as a matter of right. Some state constitutions have now been changed to give victims the right to attend any hearing—just like the defendant—with no power given to a judge to order their sequestration.[19] Similar changes are occurring to strengthen other victims' rights such as the right to be heard at relevant proceedings or the right to a proceeding free from unreasonable delay.[20]

The Supreme Court and Crime Victims

Given the emergence of the victims' movement, many Supreme Court opinions seem dated at this point as there is no consideration of the impact of its decisions on victims of crime. *Mapp* v. *Ohio* dealt with an outrageous search of Dollree Mapp's apartment, where the police—who were supposed to be looking for a crime suspect—went through Mapp's belongings to find obscene materials.[21]

But what happens when the police are too lazy to get a warrant in a murder investigation where two people were beaten to death? Who is really being punished if reliable evidence is excluded? Victims are never mentioned in the opinion.

The Court was concerned obviously, in *Mapp* v. *Ohio*, with the way the police were treating citizens on the streets, particularly the indigent and racial minorities. It was and still is a very serious problem. But where do victims fit in the balance?

In *Faretta* v. *California*, the Court said that defendants had the right to represent themselves in criminal trials.[22] Faretta was charged with grand theft. But what should happen in a vicious child abuse case or a rape case, where defendants want to represent themselves and cross-examine the victims? Is this the way to treat victims?

Chapter 2 explained the way the Court in *Globe Newspaper Co.* v. *Superior Court* struck down a state statute, which permitted trial judges to empty the public gallery at a sexual assault trial when a victim under eighteen testified. The Court had trouble understanding even what the statute was trying to do and ruled that there would have to be a hearing and a strong case made for closing the hearing to the public. The Court's grudging approach is in sharp contrast to other countries.

Similarly, courts in other countries protect the identity of sexual assault victims and forbid publication of anything that could identify them to the public. In an internet world, this is important as publication has global and permanent effects. But how would this square with the Court's dim view of prior restraints on the press under the First Amendment?

States have ways to get around some of these problems—in *Faretta* v. *California*, perhaps erecting screens to shield victims from their abusers. But *Faretta* v. *California* is typical of so many earlier Supreme Court opinions—a sweeping announcement boldly expanding rights but leaving the hard issues for the states to figure out. In doing so, states have to argue against the constitutional decision.

One issue with which the Court has struggled is the admissibility of victim impact information at sentencing. This can be a very emotional and moving testimony. But what exactly is its relevance in sentencing? If a defendant in a robbery shot and killed a bystander who happened to be a pillar of the community and the single parent of three young children, should the defendant receive a harsher penalty than if the bystander happened to be a homeless person with no family and no roots in the community?

In 1987, in *Booth* v. *Maryland*, a death penalty case, the prosecution introduced evidence of the impact that the murders of an elderly couple had on the children and grandchildren of the victims as well as evidence of the wonderful qualities of the two victims and how they would be missed.[23]

The Supreme Court ruled that the introduction of a victim impact statement at a capital sentencing violated the Eighth Amendment. The Court stated that the information in a victim impact statement is irrelevant to the issue of punishment and it creates an unacceptable risk that the death penalty would be imposed in an arbitrary and capricious manner.

The Court followed that up two years later in another death penalty case, *South Carolina* v. *Gathers*, reversing the death penalty of a defendant where the prosecution had read from a religious tract the victim had carried with him and emphasized the victim's personal qualities in his summation to the jury.[24]

Two years later, the Court reversed itself on the issue of victim impact statements in capital cases. In 1991, in *Payne* v. *Tennessee*, the Court ruled that victim impact evidence was admissible and relevant to a jury's sentencing decision in a capital case.[25] (The victim impact statement included very powerful statements from a three-year old, who was also stabbed but had survived the knife attack that killed his mother and two-year-old sister.)

The Court's flip-flop on victim impact statements is symptomatic of the struggle to understand where victims fit in a criminal justice system in which defendants, the press, and even the public have been given very powerful constitutional rights, which are usually stronger than in other countries.

Many of the above criticisms of Court decisions are made with 20–20 hindsight. When cases like *Mapp* v. *Ohio* and *Faretta* v. *California* were decided, there was no National Organization for Victim Assistance, an organization that was not founded until 1975, and today often files amicus briefs in courts in support of better treatment for victims of crime in the criminal justice system;[26] nor was there a National Center for Victims of Crime that lobbies on behalf of victims and offers training programs for law enforcement, victim service providers, and policymakers;[27] nor was there a separate office set up in the Justice Department, the Office for Victims of Crime,[28] that is directed to improving the way victims are treated in the system. That is the risk of rule-making by constitutional decisions. Society evolves and the victims' movement is one such change that has impacted trials in most Western countries.

Today, victims have power and they know how to use it. They can put tremendous pressure on judges and they can push for harsher laws that affect our incarceration rate.

Consider a few examples of the latter power. In New York, "Jenna's Law" was passed in 1998 after the murder of Jenna Grieshaber by a parolee released early. (The speaker of the assembly—a powerful position in New York's government—tried to keep Jenna's law from reaching the floor of the assembly for a vote. But he caved quickly after intense pressure from the public and other members of the assembly.) The law established determinate sentences for those convicted of violent crimes and required that offenders serve at least six-sevenths of their sentence before being eligible for parole, and then required those released to undergo at least eighteen months of parole supervision.[29]

In Florida, a statute, known informally as "Jessica's Law" was passed in the wake of the brutal murder of nine-year-old Jessica Lunsford, who was kidnapped by a paroled sex offender, held for a weekend where she was repeatedly raped, and finally murdered by being buried alive. The statute—widely copied in other states—requires that offenders who commit sexual assault on a victim under twelve serve at least twenty-five years in prison to be followed by lifetime electronic monitoring as well as lifetime parole supervision.[30]

One final example is the three-strikes law passed in California in the wake of the horrific murder of twelve-year-old Polly Klaas, who was kidnapped from her home and later found strangled to death. Her father was part of the movement to enact the law through a statewide referendum. The law mandated a life sentence to anyone convicted of *any* felony, who had two prior convictions for a serious crime. (This statute was extremely broad and it led to instances of defendants getting life sentences where the third felony was stealing a slice of pizza or shoplifting five videotapes.) The proposed referendum was put into a statute and passed quickly by the legislature and signed by the governor because the politicians knew the law would easily be adopted by referendum in any event.[31]

The passage of harsh laws in the aftermath of horrific crimes is a very poor way to make criminal justice policy. These statutes oversimplify the problems and they are often passed without any attempt to take advantage of what we know about criminal actors and their likelihood of reoffending.

The Court must bear a measure of responsibility for such laws because many Court decisions suggest that criminal procedure issues are easy when they are not. The victims' movement reminds us that our two-sided adversary process is a structure for testing evidence, but is not the reflection of a metaphysical reality; criminal cases are often multi-sided.

The public is receptive to reform of our criminal laws at the moment and there have been major reforms in our drug laws in many states. However, lowering our incarceration rate substantially will require rethinking how we treat those convicted of violent crimes and property crimes. A strong victims' movement may be prove a barrier to such reforms.

Notes

1 Franklin E. Zimring and Gordon Hawkins, *Incapacitation: Penal Confinement and the Restraint of Crime* (Oxford: Oxford University Press, 1995), 7.

2 The Challenge of Crime in a Free Society: A Report by the President's Commission on Law Enforcement and Administration of Justice (Washington, DC: United States Government Printing Office, 1967), 7.

3 See Norval Morris, *The Future of Imprisonment* (Chicago, IL: University of Chicago Press, 1974).

4 Francis Allen, *The Decline of the Rehabilitative Ideal: Penal Policy and Social Purpose* (New Haven, CT: Yale University Press, 1981), 33–34.

5 Michael Tonry, Predictions of Dangerousness in Sentencing: Déjà Vu All Over Again, *Crime and Justice: A Review of Research* 48 (2019), 439.

 6 See *Ewing* v. *California*, 538 U.S. 11 (2003).
 7 For the history of the passage and the racial impact of the federal crack cocaine law passed in 1986, see Crack Cocaine Sentencing Policy: Unjustified and Unreasonable, *The Sentencing Project*, available at: www.prisonpolicy.org/scans/sp/1003.pdf.
 8 For an excellent account of the way Willie Horton figured in the 1988 presidential campaign between George H.W. Bush and Michael Dukakis, see Michael O'Hear, *The Failed Promise of Sentencing Reform* (Santa Barbara, CA: Praeger, 2017), 14–17.
 9 Ibid., 14.
10 See Jazmine Ulloa, California Expands Punishment for Rape after Brown Signs Bills Inspired by Brock Turner Case, *Los Angeles Times*, September 13, 2016, available at: www.latimes.com/politics/essential/la-pol-sac-essential-politics-updates-california-expands-punishment-for-rape-1475260488-htmlstory.html.
11 See *Furman* v. *Georgia*, 408 U.S. 238 (1972).
12 See Scooby Axson, Judge in Brock Turner Case Recalled, *Sports Illustrated*, June 6, 2018, available at: www.si.com/more-sports/2018/06/06/brock-turner-stanford-rape-case-judge-recalled.
13 See R. David Lacourse, Jr, Three-Strikes You're Out: A Review, *Washington Policy Review*, January 1, 1997, available at www.washingtonpolicy.org/publications/detail/three-strikes-youre-out-a-review.
14 See John H. Langbein, *The Origins of the Adversary Criminal Trial* (Oxford: Oxford University Press, 2003), 11.
15 See generally William T. Pizzi and Walter Perron, Crime Victims in German Courtrooms: A Comparative Perspective on American Problems 32 *Stanford Journal of International Law* 37 (1996).
16 See Declaration of Basic Principles of Justice for Victims of Crime and Abuse of Power, Resolution 40/34, November 29, 1985, available at: www.un.org/en/genocideprevention/documents/atrocity-crimes/Doc.29_declaration%20victims%20crime%20and%20abuse%20of%20power.pdf.
17 Article 68(3) of the Rome Statute setting up the International Criminal Court is titled Protection of the Victims and Witnesses and their Participation in the Proceedings, available at: www.icc-cpi.int/resourcelibrary/official-journal/rome-statute.aspx#article68. The reasons for the adoption of Article 68(3) are explained in Charles P. Trumbull, The Victims of Victim Participation in International Criminal Proceedings, *Michigan Journal of International Law* 29(4) (2008): 777–826.
18 Betty Jane Spencer, A Crime Victim's Views on a Constitutional Amendment, *Wayne Law Review* 34(1) (1987), 2.
19 See, for example, Florida Constitution Art I S. 16(b)7(a).
20 See generally Paul G. Cassell and Margaret Garvin, Policy Paper: The Need to Enhance Victims' Rights in the Florida Constitution to Fully Protect Crime Victims' Rights, *Utah Law Faculty Scholarship* (2017), 78, available at: https://dc.law.utah.edu/scholarship/78.
21 See *Mapp* v. *Ohio*, 367 U.S. 643 (1961).
22 See *Faretta* v. *California*, 422 U.S. 806 (1975).
23 See *Booth* v. *Maryland*, 482 U.S. 496 (1987).
24 See *South Carolina* v. *Gathers*, 490 U.S. 805 (1989).
25 See *Payne* v. *Tennessee* 501 U.S. 808 (1991).
26 The history of NOVA is available at: www.trynova.org/about/.
27 The National Center for Victims of Crime was only established in 1985. The history of this organization is set out at https://victimsofcrime.org/about-us/our-history.
28 The Office for Victims of Crime within the Justice Department was set up in 1984 as a result of the Victims of Crime Act, which was passed by Congress in 1984; see www.ojp.usdoj.gov/ovc/welcovc/voca.html.
29 See Evelyn Nieves, Our Towns: Lost Crusader Inspires "Jenna's Law," *New York Times*, May 3, 1998, available at: www.nytimes.com/1998/05/03/nyregion/our-towns-lost-crusader-inspires-jenna-s-law.html.
30 See Chris Hawke, Fla. Gets Tough New Child-Sex Law, *CBS News*, May 2, 2005, available at: www.cbsnews.com/stories/2005/05/02/national/main692465.html.
31 For a full account of the political machinations behind the passage of California's three-strikes law, see Franklin E. Zimring, Gordon Hawkins, and Sam Kamin, *Punishment and Democracy: Three Strikes and You're Out in California* (New York: Oxford University Press, 2001).

7

PLEA BARGAINING IN THE UNITED STATES

Coercing Guilty Pleas

As our criminal justice system moved away from an emphasis on rehabilitation in sentencing and as sentencing became harsher by degrees, prosecutors gained more control over plea bargaining. How they decided to charge could put tremendous pressure on defendants to plead guilty. What can happen today in courtrooms in the United States can be scandalous. The plea-bargaining pressures on defendants are often extreme. In order to understand the transformation of our criminal justice system away from trials, there is no better way to get an introduction to our plea-bargaining culture than to understand the way a famous metaphor of our criminal justice system has been turned on its head. The metaphor is that of the "gatehouse" and the "mansion."

The Gatehouse and the Mansion

The criminal procedure revolution focused tremendous attention on police questioning of suspects at the police station. One of the important influences on the direction of the Court in *Miranda* v. *Arizona* and its progeny was a 1965 essay by a law professor, Yale Kamisar, then at Michigan Law School. In his essay, titled "Equal Justice in the Gatehouses and Mansions of American Criminal Procedure: From *Powell* to *Gideon*, from *Escobedo* to …," Kamisar did a scholarly review of the Warren Court decisions up to that pre-*Miranda* v. *Arizona* point that were aimed at leveling the playing field for rich and poor citizens in our criminal justice system by providing stronger protections for all citizens accused of crimes against the power of the state.[1] The essay thus discusses the major right to counsel cases, the due process cases, and the Fourth Amendment cases that had been decided up to that point. In short, the cases that were the start of what came to be known as the "criminal procedure revolution."

The main thrust of the essay was to urge the Court to take the next logical step and do something about the questioning of suspects in police stations. The ellipsis at the end of the title makes the point that it was time for the Court, having become concerned about what was happening in interrogation rooms, in cases such as *Spano* v. *New York*[2] and *Escobedo* v. *Illinois*,[3] to take stronger measures to protect suspects against the pressures that are brought to bear on them by the police in order to obtain incriminating admissions that will lead to their convictions.

The essay's title alerts the reader to the metaphors that Professor Kamisar uses to condemn the treatment of suspects being questioned at police stations after they have been arrested. The mansion, of course, is the courthouse, but it is the gatehouse—the back room of the police station—that is the focus of the essay. In his words:

> The courtroom is a splendid place where defense attorneys bellow and strut and prosecuting attorneys are hemmed in at many turns. But what happens before an accused reaches the safety and enjoys the comfort of this veritable mansion? Ah, there's the rub. Typically he must pass through a much less pretentious edifice, a police station with bare back rooms and locked doors.[4]

Quoting from the infamous interrogation manual of Fred E. Inbau and John E. Reid[5]—later relied on heavily by the Supreme Court in *Miranda* v. *Arizona*—Kamisar tells us that in the gatehouse:

> the enemy of the state is a depersonalized "subject" to be "sized up" and subject to "interrogation tactics and techniques most appropriate for the occasion"; he is "game" to be stalked and cornered. Here ideals are checked at the door, "realities" faced, and the prestige of law enforcement vindicated.[6]

Kamisar warns us that what takes place at the police station is tawdry and sometimes shocking, as police work on the suspect, often for hours, in an effort to break down the suspect and get him to admit to committing the crime in question. This conduct is possible because the interrogation room is hidden from public view and there is no record of what goes on as officers cajole, trick, or directly coerce incriminating admissions from the suspect. In the gatehouse, there is no protection for suspects against the pressures the police can bring to bear on them.

But, continuing the metaphor, after arrestees have been cajoled, tricked, or coerced into making incriminating admissions, the case now moves to the courthouse where the situation is quite different: "Once [the suspect] leaves the 'gatehouse' and enters the 'mansion,' … the enemy of the state is repersonalized, even dignified, the public invited, and a stirring ceremony in honor of individual freedom from law enforcement celebrated."[7]

In the mansion, there will, of course, be a lawyer to represent the accused and a judge who will warn defendants of their rights and make sure that any courtroom waiver by the accused is knowing, intelligent, and voluntary.

Physically, of course, the courtroom is very different from the interrogation room—the courtroom is open to the public, and there are court reporters to record all that is said—a marked contrast to the "bare back rooms and locked doors" the suspect encounters in the police station.

The obvious point of the essay is that the protections of the Constitution mean so much in the courtroom, but "so little in the police station." But the protections in the mansion arrive too late for the accused because his confession is powerful evidence of guilt and the suspect will have difficulty convincing the judge or a jury that the confession was forced from him. Likely, it will be the suspect's word against that of the officers, who will deny pressuring the suspect to confess and insist that the suspect readily answered their questions. Thus, the essay urges the Court to complete its work by requiring, at a minimum, that officers warn suspects in the interrogation room of their right to remain silent and require that counsel be provided to all suspects, rich or poor, who indicate they want counsel before being questioned.

The Court in *Miranda* v. *Arizona* closely tracked Kamisar's essay, relying heavily on the same interrogation manual of Inbau and Reid as evidence of the pressures and trickery that police use to force confessions from arrestees.

Today, the metaphor has broken down completely. What happens in the police station is much less important in the vast majority of criminal cases. The real pressure on suspects will come in the mansion. Far from being "hemmed in," prosecutors often have powers with which to compel guilty pleas that make police trickery in the interrogation room look like child's play. That the defendant has a lawyer present or that the pressure takes place in front of a judge does not change the nature of the threats—if a defendant does not admit guilt and dares to go to trial, the defendant will face a sentence that will be many times higher than the offer that was made.[8]

The courtroom as a "splendid place" of "safety" and "comfort"? Not any longer. The next sections will consider two cases—one federal and one state—to show the extreme pressures that can be put on defendants in courtrooms.

Coercion in Federal Courts: *United States* v. *Kupa*

The federal system is not greatly different from state systems in having some powerful statutes that threaten very heavy mandatory sentences for defendants with prior criminal records. The threat of charging a defendant under one of these statutes is powerful leverage to force the defendant to plead guilty.

How often this occurs is not easy to determine because what is a matter of record in most cases is usually only the defendants' guilty pleas to the charges that spare them the threatened mandatory sanction with no record of what took place to get to the point of a guilty plea. But, every so often, a judicial opinion sweeps aside the plea-bargaining curtain and shows the power mandatory minimums give prosecutors and how they wield that power. One such opinion is *United States* v. *Kupa*,[9] describing the plea bargaining that took place in a drug case in federal court in New York. This shocking opinion became national news that was picked up in articles in the *New York Times* and the *Washington Post*.

The principle plea-bargaining weapon at the center of the *United States* v. *Kupa* decision is known as a "prior felony information," which is a document that may be filed by prosecutors for sentencing purposes in drug cases under Section 28 U.S.C. §851. At the time *United States* v. *Kupa* was decided, if a prosecutor filed a prior felony information and the defendant had a prior felony conviction, the drug sentence for the present crime was raised from ten years to life to twenty years to life. Thus, a defendant would receive at least twenty years in prison if convicted. And if the defendant had two prior drug convictions, the sentence was raised from twenty years to life to a mandatory life sentence without parole if convicted. (This statute has since been amended and a defendant with one prior serious drug felony conviction would receive fifteen years to life if a prior felony information is filed and a defendant with two prior convictions would face twenty-five years to life—both are still brutally long sentences.)

In *United States* v. *Kupa*, the defendant, Lulzim Kupa had two prior felony convictions for conspiring to distribute marijuana and he was charged, along with other defendants, with distributing more than 5 kilograms of cocaine. The offense with this amount of cocaine stipulated as an element carried a mandatory minimum sentence of ten years in prison and a maximum of life in prison, often referred to as a "10–life count" in the vernacular of federal drug laws.

The government offered Kupa the following plea agreement: if Kupa pled guilty to distributing cocaine, the government would withdraw the count charging the amount that would trigger the 10–life sentence and recommend a sentence of 110–137 months in prison, which would allow Kupa to be released after serving seven years and ten months in prison. But it told Kupa that if he did not accept the plea, as a result of his prior criminal history, it would file a prior felony information against him and he would then get a mandatory life sentence without the possibility of parole if convicted. Kupa was given a day to accept the plea offer.

When Kupa did not accept the offer, the government duly filed the §851 prior felony information, which mandated life in prison upon conviction. However, it gave Kupa another chance to plead guilty: if Kupa pled guilty, the government would withdraw the §851 information and recommend a sentence in the range of 130–162 months. Thus, for not accepting the plea agreement offered a day earlier, Kupa now was being offered a sentence that would allow his release in nine years and four months. So, Kupa's delay in accepting the original offer would add an additional year and a half to his sentence. He was again given a day to think it over.

When he did not accept the plea agreement quickly enough, the government forwarded another proposed agreement: this time ratcheting up the sentence Kupa would receive upon pleading guilty to ten years. So, Kupa would now serve ten years in prison if he pled as opposed to a mandatory life sentence if he were convicted at trial. Kupa finally agreed to the proposal and told the sentencing judge—who detailed all of these negotiations in his opinion—that he wanted to plead guilty, "… before things got worse."

Judge John Gleeson, the judge before whom all this took place, wrote a scathing sixty-page opinion describing how the threat of a Section 851 prior felony information had been used in this case and how it is used in "countless others" to coerce guilty pleas from defendants. In his opinion, Judge Gleeson describes the threatened use of a prior felony information as the sentencing equivalent of "a two-by-four to the forehead." For those defendants who insist on exercising their right to trial, "prosecutors insist on the imposition of unjust punishments when the threatened defendants refuse to plead guilty." Judge Gleeson went on to say that the government's threatened use of prior felony information "coerces guilty pleas and produces sentences so excessively severe they take your breath away."[10]

Adding to the force of his opinion is the fact that Judge Gleeson was at one time the head of Special Prosecutions in the U.S. Attorney's Office for the Eastern District of New York and he was the lead prosecutor in the prosecution of John Gotti, the head of a notorious crime family.

Plea bargaining has been around for a long time in the United States, but plea bargaining was usually conceived of as offering defendants discounts from the sentences *they otherwise deserve* after conviction. But we cannot say that for the threats put to Kupa to force his plea. Today, prosecutors often have the ability, which they use freely, to threaten and deliver punishments after a trial that are way out of proportion for what the defendant did. In *United States* v. *Kupa*, Judge Gleeson went through case after case in federal courts around the country where defendants received twenty-year or life sentences that no one in the courtroom—not even the prosecutors—wanted them to receive, but they received them only because they insisted on going to trial:

> No one can reasonably argue that Tyquan Midyett's or Melissa Ross's 20-year prison term was fair. No one can reasonably argue that Charles Doutre, Dennis Capps, or Kenneth

Harvey deserved life in prison. No one, not even the government, wanted those defendants to receive their *sentences*. The only reason prior felony informations were used against them was because the government unsuccessfully tried to coerce them to plead guilty. And because other defendants have to know that the government isn't kidding when it threatens to use prior felony informations against those who have the audacity to go to trial, they became examples. Their sentences may be a natural result of the way prosecutors routinely deploy prior felony informations, and as discussed above there are numerous others just like them warehoused in our prisons. But the fact that they are business as usual doesn't alter the fact that these sentences should instill shame in all of us.[11]

The percentage of prisoners in federal prisons actually serving sentences dictated by mandatory minimums was estimated to be roughly 20 percent in 2016. Not all of these sentences are necessarily undeserved, but some certainly are. The point for purposes of our incarceration rate and the vanishing trial in federal courts is the power such statutes give prosecutors to threaten high mandatory minimums to coerce guilty pleas.

United States v. *Kupa* shows how radically power in the federal system has shifted from judges to prosecutors. In the 1960s and 1970s, judges had complete control over sentencing. Judges would come into sentencing armed with a presentence report from a probation officer and would hear from the defense and the defendant as to the appropriate sentence. Prosecutors were generally silent; sentencing was a matter for the judge.

Today, that has changed radically. Federal prosecutors can control sentencing by the way they charge and they often have powerful weapons with which to force defendants to plead guilty. Judges, like Judge Gleeson, have to preside over a hearing in which they have very little control. If they protest the way prosecutors are using mandatory minimums or "enhanced mandatory minimums" like those in *United States* v. *Kupa*, they will be told in effect by prosecutors, "This is our call. Not yours."

Coercion in State Courts: *Bordenkircher* v. *Hayes*

State prosecutors also have many "weapons" they can use to pressure guilty pleas. If a robbery was committed "with a deadly weapon" that can add years to a sentence or if the victim is elderly or very young that can double minimum length of the sentence. However, the big club in prosecutors' hands in state systems are the so-called "habitual offender" statutes that most states have adopted which can mandate severe sentences if the offender has prior felony convictions.

These statutes vary from state to state—some restricting the third felony to a serious one or a violent crime, some requiring that the prior felonies also be serious, and so on—but basically they threaten defendants with long sentences, even life sentences if they are convicted of a second or third felony and, if in addition, the defendant is charged and convicted under the habitual offender statute. Usually convicting a defendant as a habitual offender is a formality as the prior felonies are easily proved by introducing the judgments of conviction of the prior offenses and showing the defendant is the person named in the conviction papers.

Some states have two or more habitual offender statutes, triggering a different mandatory sentence of perhaps ten or fifteen years if the defendant has one or two prior convictions and an even harsher sentence—often life in prison—if the defendant has three prior convictions. In courthouse slang, in states with two versions of these statutes, you will sometimes hear these statutes referred to as the "little bitch" or the "big bitch."

A case that shows dramatically how the threat of a habitual sentence is used to try to force a guilty plea is a Kentucky case that ended up in the Supreme Court, *Bordenkircher v. Hayes*.[12] In *Bordenkircher v. Hayes*, the prosecutor offered to recommend a five-year sentence if Hayes pled guilty to uttering a forged instrument in the amount of $88.30, a minor crime. But the prosecutor threatened to indict Hayes as a habitual criminal, which mandated a life sentence, if he refused to "save the court the inconvenience and necessity of a trial." Amazingly, Hayes refused to waive his right to trial. The prosecutor followed through on the threat and filed a habitual offender charge. Hayes was convicted of uttering the forged instrument and of being a habitual offender. Hayes received a life sentence.

What was interesting about *Bordenkircher v. Hayes* was the naked admission of the prosecutor that a five-year sentence would have been appropriate for the crime and the offender and the warning that, if he refused to "save the court the inconvenience and necessity of a trial," he would receive a sentence that would probably end up being three or four times greater.

The case came to the Supreme Court—what would the Court do with such shocking facts? A trial penalty of 300 percent simply to save the "inconvenience" of a trial? The Court upheld this sentence in an opinion that said essentially "this is simply plea bargaining." This was at least an honest opinion because trial penalties of 300 percent or 400 percent are not unusual in the United States.[13] Maybe the prosecutor threatens a six-year mandatory sentence instead of two years with a plea or a fifteen-year sentence instead of five years, but this is what happens every day in U.S. courtrooms. Prosecutors use sentencing leverage to force plea bargains and usually there are plenty of statutes that provide that leverage.

Because of the nature of plea bargaining and the ability of prosecutors to threaten orally but not formally charge defendants with the harsher statute, it is not always easy—as is also true in the federal system—to know how many of the 97 percent or more of guilty pleas entered each year in a given state are compelled by the threat of harsh trial penalties, but we know it happens and, as *Bordenkircher v. Hayes* shows, it is constitutionally permissible.

Convicting the Innocent

One of the concerns with coercing plea agreements is the worry that defendants who are innocent are being convicted. As Judge Gleeson put it in *United States v. Kupa*: "the greater the trial penalty in any plea-bargaining situation, the greater the risk that innocent people will plead guilty."[14] While this is a concern in the federal system, it is an even greater concern in state systems. First of all, state systems have so many more cases that it is easier to overlook flaws when you have powerful weapons that coerce pleas. Second, many state cases, especially violent crimes, are interpersonal crimes between a defendant and a victim or victims who know each other. There will be competing versions of what happened or different explanations of reasons for what happened. These are cases that deserve to be heard and should be heard. But when the trial penalty is significant, defendants who should be heard have no choice but to plead guilty.

Comparative Perspectives on Plea Bargaining

Plea bargaining or bargaining for a simpler trial occurs in other countries, but there are not the same intense pressures put on defendants by prosecutors to plead guilty because other countries tend not to have the wide variety of harsh sentencing statutes that litter federal and state criminal codes in the United States. One reason is that other countries have much stronger substantive sentencing protections than the United States.

In a book comparing the attitudes toward punishment in the United States with those in Europe, Professor James Whitman explains why statutes visiting harsh sanctions on offenders, such as three-strikes laws, would be "impossible" in European systems:

> The European systems all subscribe to some version of the principle of proportionality. This principle holds that sentences, though indeterminate, cannot be disproportionate to the gravity of the offense; the legal system takes it very seriously; and it means that sentences of American severity are effectively impossible.[15]

The ability of prosecutors to threaten disproportionate sentences for the crime in question, and deliver on those threats in the rare case a defendant insists on trial, helps push trials to the vanishing point and permits many more cases to flow through the system. In cases like *United States* v. *Kupa*, we see the threat of a brutal sentence—disproportionate to the crime charged—used to force defendants to plead guilty. And, in *Bordenkircher* v. *Hayes*, we saw a case where a rare defendant who insisted on trial paid the price with a life sentence after conviction.

As pointed out earlier, in Chapter 1, because European trial systems differ from our trial system in important ways, so there is a tendency of U.S. lawyers to dismiss comparisons with those countries with the response, "… they have different systems." However, sentencing is not fundamentally different in continental systems. Here the procedural differences are minor. In any system, priorities have to be set on sentencing and difficult decisions have to be made—whether the decision is made by a single judge, a panel of judges, or judges working with lay people to craft a sentence.

Professor Whitman describes the overriding concern in Europe for proportionality in sentencing. We need to ask the obvious question: where does proportionality fit in U.S. sentencing? Chapter 8 will discuss the lack of substantive sentencing protections in the United States and the Supreme Court's difficulties with requiring proportionality under the Eighth Amendment. But, for now, it is important to see how a proportionality requirement helps discourage harsh mandatory minimum statutes like those employed against the defendants in *United States* v. *Kupa* and *Bordenkircher* v. *Hayes*. Those brutal statutes do not exist in countries committed to proportional sentences.

Returning again to England and Canada, we have seen that by having two trial models, there is a sentencing discount built into their systems that encourages prosecutors and defendants to avoid jury trials in favour of simpler trials. They are not forced to plead guilty as in the United States but rather to opt for a nonjury trial. Thus, the threats one sees in *United States* v. *Kupa* and *Bordenkircher* v. *Hayes* to add additional charges to coerce a guilty plea are not needed. England has even made such tactics unethical. The Code of Conduct for Crown Prosecutors in England states:

> **6.3** Prosecutors should never go ahead with more charges than are necessary just to encourage a defendant to plead guilty to a few. In the same way, they should never go ahead with a more serious charge just to encourage a defendant to plead guilty to a less serious one.[16]

England also regulates plea bargaining through a set of guidelines. The guidelines are based on the premise that the sentence for a plea bargain should be lower than would otherwise be appropriate for the crime in question. And a defendant, in deciding whether to plead guilty, can ask for guidance from the court on what the likely sentence would be if convicted at trial. The guidelines then set up a sliding scale to encourage early guilty pleas through reductions from that sentence. The guidelines state that a defendant should receive a one-third reduction if the defendant pleads guilty at the first reasonable opportunity, a one-quarter reduction for a guilty plea if the case had been set for trial, and a one-tenth reduction if the guilty plea is entered only at the start or during the trial.[17]

Fair and Proportional Sentences in the United States?

Much of the rest of the book is concerned with the obvious question which cases like *United States* v. *Kupa* and *Bordenkircher* v. *Hayes* raise: where are the protections for defendants in the United States against brutally harsh sentences such as the life sentence Hayes received for exercising his right to trial for a minor, nonviolent crime? At what point might a sentence be cruel and unusual punishment? Chapter 8 deals with the Court's uncertainties about whether the Constitution requires punishments to be proportional to the crime.

Notes

1 This essay by Yale Kamisar, Equal Justice in the Gatehouses and Mansions of American Criminal Procedure: From *Powell* to *Gideon*, from *Escobedo* to …, was one of three in A.E. Dick Howard (Ed.), *Criminal Justice in Our Time* 1 (Charlottesville, VA: University Press of Virginia, 1965). The authors of the other two essays were Fred E. Inbau and Thurman Arnold.
2 See *Spano* v. *New York*, 360 U.S. 315 (1959).
3 See *Escobedo* v. *Illinois*, 378 U.S. 478 (1964).
4 Kamisar, Equal Justice in the Gatehouses and Mansions of American Criminal Procedure, 9.
5 Fred E. Inbau and John E. Reid, *Criminal Interrogation and Confessions* (Baltimore, MD: Williams and Wilkins Co., 1962).
6 Kamisar, Equal Justice in the Gatehouses and Mansions of American Criminal Procedure, 20.
7 Kamisar, Equal Justice in the Gatehouses and Mansions of American Criminal Procedure, 20.
8 See William T. Pizzi, Revisiting the Mansions and Gatehouses of Criminal Procedure: Reflections on Yale Kamisar's Famous Essay, *Ohio State of Journal of Criminal Law* 12(2) (2015): 633–643.
9 See *United States* v. *Kupa*, 976 F.Supp. 2d 417 (E.D.N.Y. 2013).
10 See *United States* v. *Kupa*, 976 F.Supp. 2d at 419.
11 See *United States* v. *Kupa*, 976 F.Supp. 2d at 448–449.
12 See *Bordenkircher* v. *Hayes*, 434 U.S. 357 (1978).
13 See Candace McCoy, Bargaining in the Shadow of the Hammer: The Trial Penalty in in USA, in Douglas D. Koski (Ed.), *The Jury Trial in Criminal Justice* (Durham, NC: Carolina Academic Press, 2003), 27.
14 See *United States* v. *Kupa*, 976 F.Supp. 2d at 450.
15 James Q. Whitman, *Harsh Justice: Criminal Punishment and the Widening Divide Between America and Europe* (New York: Oxford University Press, 2003), 57.
16 See The Code for Crown Prosecutors 6.3 (2018), available at: www.cps.gov.uk/publications/code_for_crown_prosecutors/charges.html.
17 See Sentencing Guidelines Council, Reduction in Sentence for a Guilty Plea—First Hearing on or after 1 June 2017, available at: www.sentencingcouncil.org.uk/overarching-guides/crown-court/item/reduction-in-sentence-for-a-guilty-plea-first-hearing-on-or-after-1-june-2017/.

8

THE SUPREME COURT

Uncertain on Proportionality ...
Endorsing Deterrence

One avenue for reforming sentencing and better protecting defendants from harsh sentences would be to commit strongly to proportionality in sentencing. Mention was made previously of the European commitment to proportional sentences that bars the sorts of the harsh statutes that are common in the United States.

The problem we have in the United States is that we believe that all goals of sentencing are equally valid—rehabilitation, deterrence, retribution, and incapacitation. In other countries, retribution or proportional punishment for the offense and the offender is the dominant purpose of sentencing. Deterrence or incapacitation are valid goals of sentencing, but they must be accomplished within a sentence that is proportional.

This is not a radical idea or a new idea. Deterrence is traced back to the Italian political philosopher, Cesare Beccaria, who in 1764 published the famous essay *On Crimes and Punishment*, which expressed a theory of punishment based on deterrence as a goal of punishment.[1] In Chapter XII on *The Purpose of Punishment*, Beccaria wrote:

> The purpose of punishment, therefore, is none other than to prevent the criminal from doing fresh harm to fellow citizens and to deter others from doing the same. Therefore, punishments and the method of inflicting them must be chosen such that, in keeping with proportionality, they will make the most efficacious and lasting impression on the minds of men with the least torment to the body of the condemned.[2]

As a result of passages such as this one, Beccaria is credited with the insight that punishment has, at least in part, a preventative function, namely, that of deterring others from committing crime. Notice, however, that Beccaria is not endorsing deterrence through the imposition of *harsh* penalties. (Beccaria actually believed in mild penalties and was a strong opponent of the death penalty.) Rather, Beccaria declares that punishments must be chosen such that *"in keeping with proportionality,"* they will deter others from committing the same crime.

The four traditional purposes of punishment cannot be equal options for legislatures to pick among. Proportionality has to be a limit on deterrence and incapacitation. Other countries understand that. The United States is an exception.

In this chapter, I want to use a common law country, Canada, to show how that country's commitment to proportional sentences has permitted the Canadian Supreme Court to read a proportionality requirement into the protection against "cruel and unusual treatment or punishment," which is contained in Canada's Charter of Rights and Freedoms. The chapter will then discuss how our Supreme Court started down the road of requiring a proportionality requirement for noncapital offenses, but eventually backed away from taking that route.

The second half of the chapter will discuss *Mapp* v. *Ohio*[3] and the exclusionary rule created by the Court to deter violations of the Fourth Amendment. The problem is not the exclusion of evidence but the theory of the Court—its endorsement of a deterrent sanction that is often not proportional to the violation. Having created its own deterrent penalty, the Court is in an odd position in judging the harsh deterrent statutes that Congress or state legislatures readily adopt to deal with whatever crime is of public concern.

The Canadian Advantages in Fending Off Harsh Sentencing Statutes

Canada is a country that not only shares a border with the United States but also shares our common law tradition. In addition, the Canadian crime rates track the rise and fall of rates in the United States. When our crime rate was climbing in the period from 1970 to 1990, so did Canada's. And when our crime rate declined sharply from 1990 to the present, so also did Canada's decline.

Yet, what is instructive about Canada is the way that its incarceration rate has remained rather stable over the last fifty years. Today, it is roughly one-fifth of the U.S. rate: about 114 citizens incarcerated per 100,000 in Canada compared to 655 in the United States.[4] How are they able to keep their incarceration rate stable?

It is certainly not the case that horrible crimes in that country do not lead citizens to call for harsher sentencing laws nor is it the case that politicians do not sometimes see political advantage in proposing harsh mandatory sentence laws to show that they are "tough on crime."

However, the legal system, and especially Canadian courts, fight harsh sentences by insisting that sentences be proportional. The battle over mandatory sentencing laws is not always successful— there are mandatory sentences among their laws—but they are usually appropriate to the vast majority of offenders who have committed that offense and thus are not similar to the many laws in the United States, where the punishment is far harsher than the crime would usually merit.

One major advantage that Canada has is that proportionality in sentencing has always been a part of its criminal law tradition and it is now specifically enshrined in Section 718.1 of the Canadian Criminal Code, which states it to be a "fundamental principle" of the Code that:

> A sentence must be proportionate to the gravity of the offence and the degree of responsibility of the offender.[5]

Canada has a Charter of Rights and Freedoms with many provisions similar to the protections in the Bill of Rights. Section 12 of the Charter states: "Everyone has the right not to be subjected to any cruel and unusual treatment or punishment."[6] Because the Canadian Criminal Code demands proportionality in sentencing, the Supreme Court of Canada has read a proportionality requirement into the Charter protection.

One case that shows the power of this Charter protection is *R. v. Smith*,[7] decided in 1987, which involved a statute that mandated a seven-year minimum sentence on anyone importing drugs into Canada. Compared to some of the mandatory sentencing statutes in the United States that impose life sentences and even life sentences without parole, the statute at stake in *R. v. Smith* was rather mild in the punishment mandated.

The Court began its analysis in *R. v. Smith* by noting that the statutory minimum of seven years would be "grossly disproportionate" to some who might run afoul of this law. As an example, the Court mentioned the situation of a young person coming back into Canada from the United States, only to be caught entering Canada with a joint of marijuana.

In defending the statute, the Canadian government did not dispute that the minimum sentence would be grossly disproportionate for some offenders, but it defended the statute based on the need for a strong deterrent sanction against drug traffickers. Here is the classic conflict between proportionality and deterrence.

More specifically, the government argued that the statute in question was constitutional under Section 1 of the Charter that gives the government the right to place such "reasonable limits" on the rights in the Charter "as can be demonstrably justified in a free and democratic society."[8] The government insisted that an exception was needed to the proportionality requirement in the Charter to combat the scourge of drugs.

The Court agreed with the government that the fight against importing drugs might be an interest sufficient to limit rights in the Charter, but only if the government could show that a more limited impairment of rights was not possible. Here the Court pointed out that other options would likely be just as effective in the fight against drug trafficking, such as limiting the mandatory minimum to those importing a certain amount of drugs, or to those who are repeat offenders, or to those who fall into both categories. The Court concluded that, given other options, the government had not made the case for sustaining the statute under Section 1 of the Charter.

Our Supreme Court's Difficulties with Proportionality for Noncapital Crimes

Canada is better able to fend off harsh deterrent punishments because its criminal code, which is national, states the punishment must be proportional to the offense and the offender. The United States is a federal system, so our Supreme Court has struggled with the issue of proportionality.

The Court has interpreted the Eighth Amendment's protection against cruel and unusual punishment to include a proportionality requirement when it comes to death sentences. In *Coker v. Georgia*,[9] the defendant, while serving sentences for murder, rape, kidnapping, and aggravated assault, escaped from prison and entered the home of a couple. He threatened both with a knife, tied up the husband, raped the wife, took the husband's car, and drove away with the wife in the car. After he was apprehended, he was charged with escape, armed robbery, motor vehicle theft, kidnapping, and rape. He received the death penalty from the jury for the rape.

The Supreme Court reversed the conviction, ruling that a sentence of death is grossly disproportionate and excessive punishment for the crime of rape, and is therefore forbidden by the Eighth Amendment as cruel and unusual punishment.

In *Edmund* v. *Florida*,[10] the Court extended its capital punishment proportionality principle to spare Edmund the death penalty as he was the driver of the getaway car and he had neither attempted to kill anyone nor intended to kill anyone and was only liable for the murder under the felony murder doctrine, which makes accomplices responsible for killings done by other participants.

But what about grossly disproportionate sentences for less serious crimes? Hayes, in the case described in Chapter 7, received a life sentence when his third crime was forging a check in the amount of $88.30.

It appeared for a time that the Court might extend the requirement of proportionality to noncapital cases. In *Solem* v. *Helm*,[11] the defendant, was convicted of uttering a "no account" check for $100. He would have received a maximum sentence of up to five years in prison for this offense but because he had a string of six prior felony convictions—three for third-degree burglary, one for obtaining money under false pretenses, one for grand larceny, and one for driving while intoxicated—Solem was sentenced to life without parole under South Dakota's recidivist statute.

In striking down the sentence as violative of the Eighth Amendment, the Court stated boldly that the protection against cruel and unusual punishments includes a principle of proportionality that applies to prison sentences.

It seemed at this point that the United States was off and running on the application of the Eighth Amendment to brutally long prison sentences. In *Solem* v. *Helm*, the Court gave lower courts three factors to use in proportionality analysis. Courts were to:

1   Compare the nature and gravity of the offense and the harshness of the penalty;
2   Compare the sentences imposed on other criminals in the same jurisdiction to see whether more serious crimes are subject to the same penalty or to less serious penalties; and
3   Compare the sentences imposed for commission of the same crime in other jurisdictions.

This analysis perhaps looks easy, but in a federal system it would be difficult to apply. States can have very different statutes for the same crime and have very different approaches to sentencing. State A, plagued by the opioid crisis, passes a law making the illegal sale of fentanyl in any amount punishable by a mandatory ten-year sentence. Other states in the region do not have such a harsh law. The punishment in other states for the sale of fentanyl is typically zero to five years for a first offense and most offenders receive two- or three-year sentences.

How would this analysis work? If State A insists that its emergency services are stretched to the limit by the crisis and that fentanyl is a more serious problem than heroin, what is a federal court to do if asked to strike down the law as disproportional to the crime?

As for comparing the punishment for sale of fentanyl with the punishments for other crimes in State A, the conflict among sentencing goals again comes to the fore. Why can't a state say that we generally favor rehabilitation, if possible, but there are some crimes for which rehabilitation should not be possible because of the harm the crime entails for others, such as the sale of fentanyl?

And what does the new "proportionality" analysis mean for deterrence and incapacitation? Is the Court now saying that proportionality must trump other sentencing goals? Or is proportionality supposed to exist alongside these other goals?

Not surprisingly, the Court reversed course on proportionality review. In 1993, in *Harmelin* v. *Michigan*,[12] the Court upheld the infamous Michigan 650 Lifer Law, which mandated a life sentence without parole to anyone possessing 650 grams or more of cocaine. Harmelin was a first-time offender who had received a mandatory life sentence without parole for 672 grams of cocaine. This is a brutal sentence—one usually reserved in most states for murderers—but the Court concluded that neither the severity of the penalty nor its mandatory nature violated the Eighth Amendment.

It was a divided Court that upheld Harmelin's life sentence without parole. Harmelin had argued, using death penalty cases for support, that a mandatory sentence which allowed no possibility of mitigating factors—such as his clean prior record—violated the Eighth Amendment. However, the Court ruled that, although death penalty jurisprudence requires an individualized determination that the death penalty is appropriate for the case under consideration, this was limited to death penalty cases. Outside of capital cases, there is no such requirement. The special status of the death penalty—"the qualitative difference between death and all other penalties"—allowed the Court to confine its prior rulings to capital cases.

As far as a principle of proportionality in the Eighth Amendment, there was support for such a principle among a majority on the Court but it was very narrow. It would apply to "extreme sentences" that are "grossly disproportionate" to the crime in question. However, this principle was too narrow to spare Harmelin his life sentence without parole. In Harmelin's case, the large amount of cocaine he possessed showed that the crime had the potential to do significant harm to society. Thus, it could not be said that his sentence was grossly disproportionate to the crime.

The Court was challenged again in 2003 to extend proportionality review to a noncapital case, this time involving California's infamous three-strikes law. The case testing the law's constitutionality was *Ewing* v. *California*.[13] Ewing had received a mandated sentence of twenty-five years to life for his third offense. The offense was the theft of three golf clubs, clumsily stuffed down his pant leg, as he exited a golf course pro shop. He argued that this sentence of twenty-five years in prison was grossly disproportionate to his crime of stealing $1,200 worth of golf clubs.

In *Ewing* v. *California*, the Court basically shut the door on proportionality review in noncapital cases. Justice O'Connor's opinion recognized that three-strikes laws are "a new trend" in criminal sentencing passed in response to public concerns about a class of offenders who pose a threat to public safety. She noted that such laws serve the penological purposes of incapacitation and deterrence. Although such laws may be controversial, O'Connor stated that the Court "does not sit as a super legislature" to "second-guess" the policy choices of individual states. As for review for gross proportionality in the Eighth Amendment as applied to noncapital sentences, Justice O'Connor stated that it would only apply to an extreme sentence such as a life sentence for overtime parking.[14]

The Supreme Court's Endorsement of Deterrent Sanctions: *Mapp* v. *Ohio*

Justice Scalia, in his concurrence in *Ewing* v. *California*, put his finger on the problem the Court is facing with proportionality in sentencing. He noted that proportionality is consistent with retribution as the justification of punishment, but he quoted from the plurality opinion of Justice

O'Connor that "the Constitution does not mandate adoption of any one penological theory" and that a "sentence can have a variety of justifications, such as incapacitation, deterrence, retribution, or rehabilitation."[15] He wondered how one can apply proportionality when other goals of sentencing demand punishments that are inconsistent with retribution.

As suggested in Chapter 7, the lack of a commitment to proportional sentences separates us from European countries. And, as seen at the start of this chapter, it also separates us from Canada.

Lacking proportionality as a control on sentencing, legislatures have carte blanche to impose whatever penalty they wish for a crime, except in the death penalty area. Time and time again, legislatures give in to the allure of deterrence. One can understand why it is attractive as a solution to crime. Who would carry a gun in crime if it would mean a ten-year minimum sentence? Who would dare to transport 650 grams of heroin if the offender would get life without parole if caught? But human motivation is complicated and the deterrent effect of threatened harsh punishments is difficult, maybe impossible, to evaluate.

Unfortunately, as between proportionality and deterrence, the Court is not neutral. In one of its most famous opinions, *Mapp* v. *Ohio*,[16] which was decided in 1961, the Warren Court gave in to deterrence. *Mapp* v. *Ohio*, which established an exclusionary rule for violations of the Fourth Amendment, is eclipsed in the history of the Warren Court perhaps only by *Gideon* v. *Wainwright*[17] and *Miranda* v. *Arizona*.[18]

In *Mapp* v. *Ohio*, of course, the Court ruled that "all evidence obtained by searches or seizures in violation of the Constitution is … inadmissible in … court."[19] The rule is powerful because "all evidence" made inadmissible by the rule includes not just evidence directly seized in the illegal search or seizure, but even incriminating secondary evidence—the so-called "fruits of the poisonous tree"—that is obtained as a direct result of the illegal action.

The Court in *Mapp* v. *Ohio* seemed to base its exclusionary rule on both a judicial integrity rationale as well as a deterrence rationale. With respect to judicial integrity, the Court quoted Justice Brandeis' famous warning in his dissent in *Olmstead* v. *United States* that "[o]ur Government is the potent, the omnipresent teacher.… If the Government becomes a lawbreaker, it breeds contempt for law; it invites every man to become a law unto himself; it invites anarchy."[20]

But the Court in *Mapp* v. *Ohio* also based its decision on the need for a deterrent remedy to protect citizens from police misconduct. The majority opinion noted that in the years since *Wolf* v. *Colorado*[21] rejected imposing an exclusionary remedy on the states, a majority of states had adopted, by judicial decision or through legislation, forms of exclusionary rules designed to protect citizens from police violations of their Fourth Amendment rights. They did so, noted the Court, because other remedies to deter police wrongdoing have proven "worthless and futile."

The Court, however, in the ensuing years, shunted aside the judicial integrity rationale as the basis of the exclusionary rule in favor of deterrence. In 1976, for example, the Court stated that judicial integrity has only "a limited role [to play] … in the determination whether to apply the rule in a particular context."[22]

Instead, for close to four decades, the Court has returned repeatedly to deterrence to determine whether the exclusionary rule should be extended to new settings or whether an exception should be made to the exclusionary rule for certain types of errors.[23] At the same time that it was endorsing deterrence as the goal of the exclusionary rule, it was also making clear that exclusion was not a personal constitutional right of the citizen improperly treated.

In the many situations where the rule is applicable—for example, on-the-street "stop" or "arrest" situations—the rule is intended to have dramatic effect. Thus, even if a citizen is arrested in good faith and treated politely, and even if strong confirming evidence is developed within a few hours, if the arrest was not supported by probable cause, any evidence seized as the direct result of the arrest—whether it is a murder weapon or a confession—must be suppressed. The Court's theory is that deterrence requires a strong sanction if it is to keep the police mindful of the Constitution in their treatment of citizens.

But just as crimes punished by harsh deterrent punishments run the gamut from terrible acts to acts that are not nearly so serious, violations of the Fourth Amendment range from intentional violations of the Fourth Amendment to violations that are understandable and even reasonable. A punishment that treats them all the same lacks proportionality.

The rule sends a very bad message to legislatures that deterrence is effective and it is easy.

Deterring Crime Versus Deterring Illegal Arrests or Unlawful Searches

The initial problem with our exclusionary rule is that there is a big difference between deterring crime and deterring Fourth Amendment violations. When we pass criminal laws intended to deter a certain crime, we hope that potential criminals will stay far away from such criminal conduct. Thus, for example, we do not want shady characters perusing the fraud statutes in order to find a scheme that might fall just short of criminal fraud as defined in the statutes. Nor do we want those with a sexual motive studying criminal statutes to see whether certain enticements to young people to engage in certain types of conduct would constitute sexual exploitation of minors and slip through a "loophole" in the law. Rather, we pass criminal laws in the hope that citizens will stay far away from conduct that might violate the law.

It is different with arrests and searches by police. The nature of policing asks that officers who are trying to solve crimes make arrests as soon as they can because study after study shows that the sooner that police are able to make an arrest after the crime, the greater the likelihood of conviction. Thus, police have a fine line to tread: they need to make proper arrests or conduct proper searches, but if they act too quickly and they violate the Fourth Amendment, the evidence seized— no matter how reliable—will be excluded from use at trial because the officer was judged to have violated the suspect's constitutional rights. This puts tremendous pressure on the issue of where an officer should draw the line in a particular situation and, unfortunately, the Court has had a difficult time explaining what the line is.

At the heart of Fourth Amendment jurisprudence are two concepts that have proven problematic for the Court: probable cause and reasonable suspicion. Attempts to clarify these concepts are of limited usefulness because decisions are usually "fact-bound" and tell officers little about the next situation they will face, except the obvious: it is a close case.

To illustrate the problem with probable cause, consider the leading Supreme Court case on probable cause for warrants, *Illinois* v. *Gates*,[24] which was decided in 1983. The case began with an anonymous letter to the Bloomingdale Police Department reporting that Sue and Lance Gates were selling drugs out of their condominium and it gave their address. The letter also said that they bought their drugs in Florida and, when they made their buys, Sue drove their car to Florida, left it to be loaded with drugs, and then Lance flew down and drove the car back to Illinois. The letter reported that Sue would be driving down in a few days and Lance would then fly down and drive the car back with over $100,000 in drugs.

After receiving the letter, the police were able to corroborate some details consistent with the letter, including the Gates' Bloomingdale address as well as the fact that "L. Gates" had a reservation to fly to West Palm Beach, Florida in a couple of days.

Arrangements were made with Florida drug agents and when Lance Gates arrived in Florida, the agents followed him and observed him going to a room at a Holiday Inn rented by a "Susan Gates." Early the following day, Lance Gates was seen heading north on a highway with a woman in a car with Illinois plates. The police then confirmed through the car's registration that it belonged to the Gates.

All of this information was put in an affidavit for a search warrant with the anonymous letter attached. Now the question for the judge was whether there was probable cause to search the car and the Gates' home. The judge decided that there was probable cause and issued the warrant. The upshot was that when the Gates arrived at their home, police were waiting and a search of the car turned up 350 pounds of marijuana. (The police found more marijuana, weapons, and other contraband in the home.)

The evidence was suppressed at the trial level and the case went up on appeal. There are, unfortunately, very few guidelines for judges on probable cause. Law professors love to debate even such a basic issue as how "probable" probable cause needs to be. The Supreme Court has said that probable does not mean "more likely than not," but what if the odds are only one out of five or even one out of ten? Or is probable cause maybe to be determined using a sliding scale in which the nature of the items sought—bomb-making materials versus a small amount of drugs—might allow the probability of their being found to vary along the scale?[25]

We do not know the answer to many of these questions. But there was one decision that the Court had handed down to help judges with warrants involving anonymous informants, like the warrant in *Illinois* v. *Gates*. That case was *Spinelli* v. *United States*,[26] which required such warrants to satisfy a "two-pronged test." The first prong required that the warrant must indicate to the issuing judge the basis of knowledge for the anonymous tip and the second prong required that the warrant provide facts that showed either the veracity of the informant or the reliability of the information given by the informant.

So was the Gates' warrant acceptable under the two-pronged test in *Spinelli* v. *United States*? Well, the Illinois Supreme Court split on the issue with the majority saying that it did not satisfy the two-pronged test but two justices said this warrant was fine under the test in *Spinelli* v. *United States*.

The case then went to the United States Supreme Court and again we have a badly split court on probable cause. Justice White reasoned that the warrant met the standard of *Spinelli* v. *United States* because the police work after the receipt of the letter corroborated "quite suspicious" behavior by the Gates and hence showed both that the informer was credible and that the informant had gathered the information in the letter in a reliable manner.[27]

The majority suggested disagreement with Justice White on whether the warrant really satisfied the two-pronged test of *Spinelli* v. *United States* because even though there was corroboration of some information in the letter, the majority worried that this did not permit "a sufficiently clear inference regarding the letter writer's 'basis of knowledge.'" But the majority then decided to abandon the two-pronged test and set lower courts free to review warrants simply by considering the "totality of circumstances" and whether, looking at the warrant, there is "a fair probability that contraband will be found in a particular place." Using this standard, the majority concluded that the warrant passes with flying colors.

But the saga does not end there, because there were two dissenters on the probable cause issue: Justices Stevens and Brennan. They dissected the warrant very differently from the majority and came to the opposite conclusion. Even under the totality of circumstances test, they concluded that the warrant did not show probable cause because there were important discrepancies between the letter and subsequent events. In particular, they noted that the letter said that Sue Gates drove the car down and *flew back*, but the affidavit showed that Sue Gates was actually traveling north with Lance Gates, an activity which the dissenters described as suggesting nothing "unusual" or "probative of criminal activity."

This litany of opinions from the Illinois Supreme Court and the United States Supreme Court is embarrassing. We have judges armed with a bevy of law clerks and weeks of time to study case law and scholarship, yet in analyzing the exact same warrant using two different standards for probable cause, the judges cannot agree whether this warrant was supported by probable cause *under either standard*.

It is not surprising that, after the shambles of *Illinois* v. *Gates*, the Court tried to withdraw somewhat from the world of probable cause determinations by announcing, a year later, a reasonable good faith exception for warrants so that, in close cases, a warrant would be upheld if the judge acted in reasonable good faith in approving the warrant.[28] This is rather ironic. Warrants present the best case for close appellate review of probable cause as the reviewing court has in front of it the exact same information presented to the authorizing magistrate. When it comes to probable cause or reasonable suspicion determinations on the street, a reviewing court will usually have much less information than the officer had when they decided to arrest or stop a suspect whom they suspected of committing a crime.

More importantly, the lack of a reasonable good faith exception for arrests on the street is simply unfair to police who are trying to do the right thing.

Consider, for example, a Colorado case I would sometimes use in class to introduce students to probable cause issues. The facts of the case are as follows:

> On September 29, 1981, at 12:45 p.m., a resident was sweeping the porch of her home in Denver. It was a hot day and the temperature was in the 80's. She saw a man, later identified as Fidel Quintero, walking on the opposite side of the street and watched him go up on the porch of the house opposite, stand at the front door for approximately twenty seconds, and then saw him stand at the front window so that he could peer into the front of the house for another twenty seconds. He then left the porch and appeared to be looking at the windows on the side of the house. He then walked down the street, stopped at another house, and then was out of sight of the resident. The resident again saw the same man an hour later and he was at a bus stop in front of her house. He had taken off his shirt and used it to cover a television set. He was pacing nervously and was trying to thumb a ride or hitchhike while waiting for the bus to arrive. The resident thought he looked quite "antsy" and called the police.
>
> The police radio dispatcher reported that a possible burglary suspect was at the bus stop at the corner where the resident lived. Officer Freeman, a twenty-one-year police veteran,

was the first to respond and arrived approximately five minutes after the call was made. He asked Quintero for identification and Quintero had none. Other officers who arrived at the scene assisted in the investigation.

Quintero claimed that he had bought the television set from someone in the neighborhood for $100 and was trying to go home with it. He was in an undershirt and had brown wool gloves in his back pocket which were found in a "pat down" search for weapons. While he was being questioned, the resident came out of the house and made herself known to the officers as the woman who had called the police and reported what she had seen. At this point, Quintero was arrested.

Under the shirt the police found the television set and a video game. (The police also found $140 in cash, five rings including two class rings bearing different initials and class years, and some ladies jewelry in Quintero's pants pockets when he was searched at the police station.) After the arrest was made, the officers checked the neighborhood and were unable to determine that a burglary had occurred.

Later that day the owners of a house one block south of the resident's house reported that they had been burglarized and that a television set and a video game had been stolen. The television set and video game that were in the possession of Quintero when he was arrested were identified as the items taken in the burglary.

Did Officer Freeman have probable cause to arrest Quintero? The Colorado Supreme Court split on the issue in *People* v. *Quintero*,[29] with the majority finding that there was insufficient evidence of a burglary while the dissent said that Officer Freeman would have been "derelict in his duty"[30] not to have arrested Quintero.

Probable cause—like many legal issues—is a classic judgment call in which reasonable judges will differ. There is no getting around it; there is no "probable cause meter" one can point at a situation, push a button, and get an answer.

Our exclusionary rule compounds the problem. Should Officer Freeman be disciplined by his Denver superiors for violating the Constitution, when a Colorado Supreme Court justice thinks he did exactly the right thing?

And what have we learned from *People* v. *Quintero* for the next case? What if Quintero had started to run when Officer Freeman approached? What if he had a long screwdriver in his back pocket when approached? What if the gloves and screwdriver had paint chips on them? And so on. Would there now be probable cause? All we can say is these are "close cases."

I could go on and do a similar analysis of the standard for forcible stops on the street, which requires "reasonable suspicion" that a crime is afoot. Suffice it to say that in 1996, a federal district court judge suppressed forty-six kilograms of cocaine and two kilograms of heroin with a street value of $4 million found in the trunk of a car driven by Carol Bayless that drug officers had stopped at 5 a.m., after what they perceived to be a large, orchestrated drug drop in Washington Heights, a part of New York City known for its prolific drug trafficking.[31] In *United States* v. *Bayless*,[32] the judge "explained" away every suspicious factor to conclude the officers lacked reasonable suspicion to stop the vehicle.

This was an arrogant opinion that the judge eventually reversed after a firestorm of publicity reached every political level up to the White House. But the case—suppression or not—shows the problems with the exclusionary rule, which requires subtle after-the-fact assessments under a test like reasonable suspicion that has no edges to it. Even if the officers did not have quite enough reasonable suspicion to stop Ms. Bayless, they were drug officers doing what they were supposed to be doing and where is any sense of proportion in suppressing $4 million in drugs to punish the officers for their transgression?

Concepts like probable cause and reasonable suspicion make sense as rough markers of when an arrest or a forcible stop should take place but they cannot bear the weight that our exclusionary rule puts on them.

"Proportional" Exclusionary Rules

It is important to emphasize that these criticisms of the U.S. exclusionary rule are not aimed at exclusionary rules per se, but at a bold exclusionary rule, which asks only if there is a violation of the Fourth Amendment without taking into account the circumstances surrounding the violation. England,[33] Canada,[34] and New Zealand[35] all have exclusionary rules, but none base their rules on deterrence. They are not trying to remedy police misconduct but are concerned with the effect on the administration of justice when unconstitutionally seized evidence is admitted at a trial. They balance a range of factors to see if exclusion is appropriate, such as the extent of the breach, the good faith or not of the officer involved, the seriousness of the crime, and the reliability and probative value of the evidence.

None of the criticisms offered in this chapter of the U.S. exclusionary rule are meant to suggest that the rule results in too many offenders avoiding convictions. There are plenty of exceptions built into the rule and, if the crime is serious, courts will often use them to find the police arrest or search constitutional. A New Zealand scholar comparing the proportional approach to exclusion that one finds in other common law countries with the theoretically unforgiving deterrent approach to police errors in the United States, suggests that "in reality, courts [in all systems] balance interests: the only question being whether they do it explicitly in their decisions, or implicitly behind the language of rules."[36]

Do Harsh Mandatory Punishments Deter?

Because of the proliferation of harsh laws aimed at deterrence and the Court's approval of the concept of deterrence, the obvious question becomes: do harsh deterrent sanctions work?

This is a difficult question with which our legal system has struggled for many, many years. The answer is that we are unsure of the answer to this question. Perhaps in 1961, when the Court decided *Mapp* v. *Ohio*, the efficacy of strong deterrent punishments may have seemed self-evident. Now, close to sixty years later, we can say after considerable experience attempting to measure the effects of powerful deterrent punishments that deterrence is more complicated than we thought.

The classic case is the death penalty. The death penalty would seem a perfect instrument against which to determine whether the penalty of death has a strong deterrent effect when compared with the lesser punishment of life imprisonment. There are states that have had the death penalty for many years and some that have never had the death penalty. There are careful statistics on murder rates over the years so we know where the rates are increasing and declining. We also have developed powerful mathematical tools, such as multivariate regression analysis, that can be applied to the data to help determine whether the death penalty deters. But what we have observed with the death penalty, an issue that is more straightforward than the exclusionary rule, is that we do not know if the death penalty deters. Instead, what we see is an ebb and flow as an economist or statistician publishes an article claiming to show a deterrent effect from the death penalty, which is then followed by a barrage of articles claiming that the variables used were not independent or that the data failed to include certain other influences or some other shortcoming that casts doubt on the validity of the findings in the original study.

When it comes to the Fourth Amendment, it is extremely doubtful that the exclusionary rule deters the sorts of aggressive police confrontations on the street that have been the subject of inner-city anger for many years. First, many such violations will not be reflected in a statistical database because they will not lead to a formal arrest or prosecution. If the goal of the officer is simply to harass and humiliate the citizen, then that goal is achieved by the constitutional violation alone. Second, many citizens who are the subject of unconstitutional actions will be reluctant to report such abuse to police authorities, perhaps feeling that it would only make them subject to greater abuse in the future (especially if the abuse took place in the jurisdiction in which they live) or perhaps feeling that they would not be believed by police authorities who are inclined to believe "one of their own."

Rethinking *Mapp* v. *Ohio*?

In fairness, *Mapp* v. *Ohio* is a very old case and we know much more about deterrence today but this is the problem with establishing rules and procedures using the Constitution: we have to live today with decisions which we may regret down the road.

Mapp v. *Ohio* was decided by a Court overconfident in what it was doing. The Fourth Amendment issue was never briefed, as the issue before the Court was whether the possession of obscene materials found in the search of Dollree Mapp's house was protected by the First Amendment. As suggested in discussing the victims' movement earlier in the book, the legal world has changed dramatically over the past decades. The Court would have much more input on the issue and much more information about deterrence if the issue had come up thirty or forty years later.

However, for purposes of our incarceration rate, the important point is not the exclusionary rule but the Court's endorsement of a deterrent sanction that trumps proportionality. As this chapter shows, this is not traditional deterrence theory and it is not the way other countries view the relationship between deterrence and proportionality. Instead, in one of its most famous criminal procedure opinions, the Court gave its imprimatur to tough deterrent sanctions where the punishment will often far exceed the sanction the violation deserves.

In turn, the legislative response to calls from the public to do something about a given crime is to up the punishment for the crime or even add a dramatic sanction in the pursuit of deterrence. These statutes give prosecutors power in plea bargaining that they do not have in other countries where proportional punishments rule.

Notes

1 See Cesare Beccaria, *On Crimes and Punishments, and Other Writings*, translated by Aaron Thomas and Jeremy Parzan, edited by Aaron Thomas (Toronto: University of Toronto Press, 2008) (Translation of *Dei delitti e delle pena*, published 1764).
2 Ibid., 28 (Chapter XII).

3 See *Mapp* v. *Ohio*, 367 U.S. 643 (1961).

4 See World Prison Population List, *World Prison Brief* (2018 data), available at: www.prisonstudies.org/sites/default/files/resources/downloads/wppl_12.pdf.

5 S. 718.1, *Martin's Annual Canadian Criminal Code* (Toronto: Thomson Reuters, 2018).

6 Section 12, The Canadian Charter of Rights and Freedoms, available at: https://laws-lois.justice.gc.ca/eng/Const/page-15.html.

7 See *R.* v. *Smith*, [1987] 1 S.C.R. 1045.

8 Section 1, The Canadian Charter of Rights and Freedoms, available at: https://laws-lois.justice.gc.ca/eng/Const/page-15.html.

9 See *Coker* v. *Georgia*, 433 U.S. 584 (1977).

10 See *Edmund* v. *Florida*, 459 U.S. 782 (1982).

11 See *Solem* v. *Helm*, 463 U.S. 277 (1983).

12 See *Harmelin* v. *Michigan*, 501 U.S. 957 (1991).

13 See *Ewing* v. *California*, 538 U.S. 11 (2013).

14 See *Ewing* v. *California*, 538 U.S. 11 at 28.

15 See *Ewing* v. *California*, 538 U.S. 11 at 31 (Scalia, J. concurring).

16 See *Mapp* v. *Ohio*, 367 U.S. 643 (1961).

17 See *Gideon* v. *Wainwright*, 372 U.S. 335 (1963).

18 See *Miranda* v. *Arizona*, 384 U.S. 436 (1966).

19 See *Mapp* v. *Ohio*, 367 U.S. at 655.

20 See *Mapp* v. *Ohio*, 367 U.S. 643, 659 (1961), quoting from *Olmstead* v. *New York*, 237 U.S. 438, 485 (1928).

21 See *Wolf* v. *Colorado*, 338 U.S. 25 (1949),

22 See *Stone* v. *Powell*, 428 U.S. 433, 446 (1976).

23 See, for example, *Illinois* v. *Krull*, 480 U.S. 340 (1987); *I.N.S.* v. *Lopez-Mendoza*, 468 U.S. 1032 (1984); and *Stone* v. *Powell*, 428 U.S. 465 (1976).

24 See *Illinois* v. *Gates*, 462 U.S. 213 (1983).

25 See Ronald M. Gould and Simon Stern, Catastrophic Threats and the Fourth Amendment, *Southern California Law Review* 77(4) (2004): 777–833.

26 See *Spinelli* v. *United States*, 393 U.S. 410 (1969), overruled *Illinois* v. *Gates*, 462 U.S. 213 (1983).

27 See *Illinois* v. *Gates*, 462 U.S. at 269, 271–272 (White, J., concurring).

28 See *Leon* v. *United States*, 468 U.S. 897 (1984).

29 See *People* v. *Quintero*, 657 P.2d 948 (Colo. 1983).

30 Ibid., at 951 (Rovira, J. dissenting).

31 See *United States* v. *Bayless*, 913 F.Supp. 232 (S.D.N.Y.), vacated on reconsideration, 921 F.Supp. 211 (S.D.N.Y 1996).

32 See *United States* v. *Bayless*, 913 F.Supp. 232.

33 The Charter of Rights and Freedoms in Canada contains a specific exclusionary provision that states that evidence found by a court to have been obtained in violation of a right in the Charter "shall be excluded if it is established that, having regard to all the circumstances, the admission of it in the proceedings would bring the administration of justice into disrepute." Section 24(2) The Canadian Charter of Rights and Freedoms, available at: https://laws-lois.justice.gc.ca/eng/Const/page-15.html.

34 See *Collins* v. *The Queen* (1987) 1 S.C.R. 265.

35 See *R.* v. *Shaheed* [2002] 2 *New Zealand Law Review* 377(CA).

36 Simon Mount, *R.* v. *Shaheed: The Prima Facie Exclusion Rule Re-Examined*, 2003 *New Zealand Law Review* 45, 65.

9

LIMITING JUDICIAL POWER AT SENTENCING

The Emergence of Sentencing Guidelines Systems

The previous chapters gave some indication of the way sentencing power has shifted from judges to prosecutors. In both the *United States* v. *Kupa* and *Bordenkircher* v. *Hayes* cases described in Chapter 7, prosecutors had weapons—the threat of brutal sentences in the offing if the defendants do not plead guilty—with which to try to induce guilty pleas. But these are extreme cases—not many defendants qualify to be charged using prior felony information in federal court or a habitual offender statute in state courts.

Apart from these harsh statutes, sentencing authority in the federal system and in most state systems has shifted considerably toward prosecutors. Prosecutors often use that power to force guilty pleas by threatening sentences that are clearly inappropriate for the crime and the offender.

It is a familiar mantra these days for critics of mandatory minimum statutes to declare, "Judges should sentence, not prosecutors." But those critics often forget that broad judicial sentencing discretion had many problems which led some legislatures to try different alternatives such as tight sentencing ranges or sentencing guidelines to try to curb the nearly unbridled discretion judges typically wielded at sentencing.

This chapter will explain the emergence of guidelines systems in some state systems and the federal system; to understand these efforts to impose some controls on sentencing, it is important to understand the problems that emerged when judges had complete control of sentencing.

The U.S. Tradition: No Appellate Review of Sentencing Decisions

Judges in the United States had tremendous power when it came to sentencing defendants in the 1960s and 1970s. It was common in the federal system and state systems to see judges with discretion to sentence a defendant to anywhere from zero to twenty, zero to forty, or zero to sixty years.

Going in front of a judge who could sentence the defendant to two, ten, or twenty years is frightening, even if it is a first offense and the chance of twenty years is unlikely.

Obviously, many defendants know that the evidence against them is strong and they have little chance of an acquittal at trial, so the question that dominates their thinking is: what sentence will I receive and how much time might I spend in jail or prison? But given the broad sentencing power vested in judges at that time, it was not always easy to predict the sentence likely to be imposed.

One reason is that judges often had their own value systems and this added to the uncertainty. Some judges viewed any crime committed with a firearm to be very serious and deserving of a stiff sentence, even though some crimes with a firearm are rather pathetic. Some judges were loath to send a woman with children to prison but others were moved by the adage, "If you do the crime, you pay the time."

What is strange about sentencing in the United States is not only the breadth in terms of possible years that trial judges could choose in their sentencing decisions, but also the absolute nature of the decision. As long as the sentence was within the statutory limits, there was no appellate review of the sentence. A treatise on sentencing in the United States puts the situation rather bluntly:

> Despite significant sentencing reform in the late 20th Century, the dominant principle of appellate sentence review remains unchanged: Unless trial court discretion was abused, sentences within constitutional and statutory boundaries are not reviewable.[1]

The unwillingness of appellate courts to review criminal sentences was frequently criticized by sentencing scholars, bar associations, and others concerned about fairness in our criminal justice system. In 1968, while pressing for reform of sentencing, the American Bar Association put it bluntly:

> It is shocking, to say the least, that the United States is the only country in the free world where not only can a single man sentence without explaining why, but where there is no channel for review of his work.[2]

As this quote makes clear, vesting unreviewable and sweeping sentencing power in a single person made the United States an outlier among other countries where sentencing decisions, given their importance, are subject to appellate review. While a judge in the United States might sentence a defendant to four, fourteen, or even forty years with no review, it is not unusual for an appellate court in other countries to decide that twelve months is too long for a defendant and a lesser sentence would be appropriate.[3]

Vesting unreviewable sentencing discretion in a trial judge was typically defended with three rationales. The first is that trial judges actually get to see the defendant and are therefore in a better position to know the appropriate sentence for the crime and the offender.

The second is that appellate courts should confine their review from lower courts to "issues of law." A sentencing decision, it is said, is distinguishable from an issue of law because it is a question of judgment that needs to be left to the trial judge.

The third rationale is that allowing sentencing review would bury appellate courts in frivolous appeals.

If these rationales had force at one time, that time has long since passed.

Deference to a trial judge's sentencing decision because of a trial judge's ability to "size up" the defendant in court is more myth than reality in a world where the plea-bargaining rate is 96 or

97 percent. A few mumbled words as the defendant pleads guilty—"I am so sorry, judge. I embarrassed my family …"—hardly provides much insight into how the defendant should be sentenced.

The defendant's participation at sentencing is rarely illuminating. Defendants rarely say much at sentencing and are often counseled by their lawyers to keep comments short. There will, of course, be a strong case made for a lenient sentence from the defendant's lawyer, but any information put forward to support that sentence would be fully available to an appellate court in the transcript.

The most important information for sentencing will be contained in the presentence report, where the judge can read:

(1) details of the crime (sometimes with more information and more background than was brought out at trial);
(2) interviews with the victim, family members, friends, employers, counselors, and others;
(3) information about the defendant's prior criminal behavior;
(4) information about any psychological or addiction problems; and
(5) information about the defendant's prospects for improvement or reform.

In short, the report will have any information that might help the judge determine the moral gravity of the crime, understand the offender's role in the crime, and decide on a sentence appropriate for this offender. But all of this information would be available to the appellate court as well.

As for sentencing as "a matter of judgment," rather than "an issue of law," this flies in the face of the reality that appellate courts review rulings that are matters of judgment all the time. Mention was made in Chapter 4 of the problems with appellate review of a trial judge's decision not to remove a prospective juror for cause—this is a typical appellate issue after trial. Compared to sentencing, a denial of a challenge for cause is an issue on which a trial judge would have much *more* information than an appellate court because the judge could observe the juror's body language while the juror answered questions.

In contrast, appellate courts that review sentences regularly would have not only the same basic information a trial judge had—the presentence report—but also more information than a trial judge. The appellate court would have a broad palette of prior sentencings with which to compare the sentence under review. The appellate court could thus compare the sentence being challenged with the sentences judges in other parts of the jurisdiction have handed down for similar crimes and similar offenders.

In addition, there is another important reason for appellate review of sentences. Crimes can arouse strong feelings in a community. Maybe the children and friends of the family will be in court during sentencing, hoping for a sentence appropriate to their terrible loss. This can put a lot of pressure on judges in sentencing to impose a harsh sentence on a convicted defendant. Obviously, this pressure is magnified in state systems where almost all judges are elected or are subject to recall.

Today, victim impact statements add to the pressure at sentencing. The victim impact statement may help the judge see the terrible consequences of the particular crime. But as emotional as such evidence can be, the legal system, including the Supreme Court as explained in Chapter 8, struggles with the relevance of the victim's background to the sentence the crime deserves.

Given the emotion that horrible crimes engender, it is important to have an appellate venue separate, and perhaps distant, from the court of conviction to make sure the sentence is fair and appropriate to the crime and offender.

The last objection to appellate review of sentencing—that appellate courts might be inundated with frivolous appeals—seems moot today because appeals are effectively mandated by *Anders* v. *California*, which was discussed in Chapter 4. If a trial court's many rulings in the course of a criminal case are to be reviewed for possible error, the most important decision in a criminal case for many defendants should not be immunized from appellate review.

The Federal Courts, the Supreme Court, and Sentencing Review

The federal position on appellate review of sentencing decisions was no different from the general state position: there was no appellate review of a sentence that was within the statutory limits.

Consider the case of Miguel Rodriquez,[4] a case that is typical of many hundreds such cases in the 1960s and 1970s, where a defendant tried to appeal his sentence. Rodriquez's problems began in 1968, when he and two co-defendants were convicted of transporting and concealing 101 pounds of marijuana. At sentencing, the judge sentenced Rodriquez to twelve years in prison, although his co-defendants had only received five-year sentences. Rodriquez appealed his sentence to the Court of Appeals for the Fifth Circuit, claiming that the sentence he received was disproportionate to the crime and also arbitrary given the much lighter sentences his co-defendants had received.

It may be the case that the heavier sentence was completely explainable— maybe Rodriquez played the central role in the drug crime or maybe Rodriquez had a prior criminal record. However, the appellate court refused to review Rodriquez's sentence other than to note the sentence range for the crime was five to twenty years. Since Rodriquez's sentence of twelve years was within the sentence range for the offense, the court stopped its analysis at that point, referring to the "universality of court decisions" that appellate courts have no control over a sentence within the lawful sentencing range.

One might have expected that the Supreme Court, as part of the criminal procedure revolution, would have insisted on appellate review of sentencing given the central importance of the issue and the line of cases showing considerable distrust of the decisions of trial judges. If juries, according to *Duncan* v. *Louisiana*, are needed as protection against a "biased, compliant or eccentric judge" on the issue of guilt,[5] wouldn't that mandate review of sentences imposed by such a possible judge? But the Supreme Court endorsed the hands-off approach of appellate courts to trial court sentencing decisions. In 1974, the Court stated:

> If there is one rule in the federal criminal practice which is firmly established, it is that the appellate court has no control over a sentence which is within the limits allowed by a statute.[6]

To return to the sentence of Miguel Rodriquez, twelve years in prison versus five years may not seem much when, unfortunately, we have become accustomed to hearing of sentences of gargantuan lengths: eighty-seven years, 126 years, 268 years, etc. But to Rodriquez, the seven additional years he had to serve while his co-defendants would have been released to their communities deserved review.

The Erosion of Judicial Sentencing Authority

Like an unstable compound, this conflicted view of trial judges—needing close appellate oversight after every trial, but nearly infallible on sentencing issues—could not last. It was bound to explode. In the 1970s, sentencing by trial judges, especially by federal trial judges, came under sustained attacks.

One of the most influential critics of sentencing at that time was a federal judge in New York City, Marvin E. Frankel, who called for reform in a book, *Criminal Sentences: Law Without Order*, published in 1973 that attacked the broad sentencing discretion that had been vested in judges:

> [T]he almost wholly unchecked and sweeping powers we give to judges in the fashioning of sentences are terrifying and intolerable for a society that professes devotion to the rule of law.[7]

As he was an outstanding judge and a scholar, who was writing from "inside" the federal system, Judge Frankel's exposé of the sentencing system was very influential. He called for a sentencing commission that would put limits on the sentences that could be imposed for individual crimes.

During the same period, there were also studies published which showed that judges given the exact same sentencing files arrived at very different, sometimes wildly different, sentencing decisions. In one study, fifty federal trial judges in the United States Court of Appeal for the Second Circuit were given twenty identical files and asked what sentence they would impose on each defendant.[8] The results showed a "glaring disparity" where, for example, one judge gave a union official convicted of extortionate credit transactions twenty years' imprisonment and a $65,000 fine, where another judge would have sentenced the same defendant to three years' imprisonment and no fine.[9] In short, judges had very different views of how much punishment was deserved.

These studies should not be surprising. While there is strong evidence that across demographic lines, sexes, and even cultures, there is broad shared intuition on the comparative seriousness of particular crimes,[10] when it comes to what the punishment should be for a particular crime, our opinions often diverge sharply. If a defendant has burgled an apartment and stolen jewelry, some would consider a sentence of a year in prison a significant punishment while others might consider it a slap on the wrist.

In addition to differing opinions as to the blameworthiness of a certain criminal act, sentencing can vary among judges because, as Chapter 8 makes clear, jurisdictions in the United States do not have a single controlling sentencing objective. If a state statute speaks about sentencing, it usually lists the four traditional purposes for sentencing with no priority among them.

Judges, in sentencing offenders, may be more or less influenced by one of these factors. A judge may say,

> You deserve three years for that crime, but I also see you have a good chance at rehabilitation and you have already started down that road.... Therefore, I am only going to give you an eight-month sentence which can be served in our jail so you can continue your program....

Another judge may see the priorities differently and put deterrence ahead of rehabilitation when sentencing the same offender,

I see you have a good chance at rehabilitation and you have started a program … but at the same time, I have seen too many young people your age come through this court in recent years who have done what you did. I need to assure others who are tempted to do the same crime that stiff punishments await them if they persist in their ways. For that reason, I am imposing a five-year sentence. It is a tough sentence, but it sends the right message. We need to put a stop to this crime that has plagued our community too often.

Still another judge may agree on the progress the defendant has started on in rehabilitation, but conclude, "… that nonetheless retribution is needed and for a serious crime such as this a three-year sentence is appropriate."

Finally, in addition to differences among judges on the priorities to pursue in sentencing, there were often regional differences in sentencing that were troubling. For example, federal judges in the South tended to punish defendants far more harshly for the same crime compared to federal judges in northern states. It was common in the 1970s for defendants who were arrested in a northern city for a crime that took place in a southern state to plead guilty in the northern city so they could be sentenced by a northern judge rather than being returned to the south for trial and sentencing. A federal rule of criminal procedure permits a defendant to be sentenced in the district of arrest if the defendant pleads guilty.[11] Pleading guilty to a likely two-year or four-year sentence was very attractive compared to returning to the south to face a likely ten- or twenty-year sentence if convicted.

Sentencing "Reform"—Sentencing Guidelines

In other countries, the sorts of disparities that occurred in the United States from judge to judge did not occur with the frequency one found in the United States because, as shown in Chapter 8, there is often a strong commitment to proportionality. This makes appellate review possible as there is a single goal for sentencing and appellate opinions are able to provide guidance on the sentences that should be imposed on similar offenders who have committed a particular offense.[12]

The problem in the United States is that there is no single goal of sentencing and the jurisprudence of sentencing is scant. On top of that, sentencing ranges are typically very broad in the United States.

The federal government as well as many states were aware of the well-documented problems with sentencing brought out by Judge Frankel and others in the 1970s. A few pioneering states put sentencing guidelines systems in place in the early 1980s.

Sentencing reform in the federal system was slower to develop. Senator Ted Kennedy began sponsoring legislation calling for guidelines in 1975, but it was not until 1984 that legislation setting up a federal guidelines commission was enacted and the guidelines themselves did not come into effect until 1987.

The objectives and broad outlines behind the state guidelines systems and the federal guidelines system were the same but, as will be explained, the state models and the federal model were very different in practical operation.

The theory was that there would be a permanent agency—a sentencing guidelines commission, which would draft guidelines for individual crimes, often starting from historical data on sentences for different crimes.

The commission would be a nonpartisan body with experts on sentencing, corrections, statistics, treatment options, imprisonment options, and so on. The commission would draft guidelines, which would consider a variety of sentencing factors to determine a specific sentencing range within which a judge would be required to sentence. The guidelines would have the force of law and, hopefully, they would give judges sufficient range to handle the great bulk of the particular crime. However, judges would be permitted to depart from the guideline range, either up or down, in unusual situations where the judge felt the range was inappropriate for the particular offender and the particular offense. Hence, the guidelines were often referred to as "presumptive guidelines."

Such departures would need to be explained and justified and they would be subject to appellate review.

The sentencing ranges under the guidelines were not meant to be set in stone. If the sentencing commission found that departures were frequent for a particular reason, they could adjust the guidelines to account for that in the sentencing range. And, because they would be expected to draft guidelines that would make the best use of the jurisdiction's resources, the commission might adjust guideline ranges up or down to avoid overcrowding prisons and to make sure those sent to prison were those most deserving of incarceration.

Guidelines with the force of law meant that legislators had to cede control over sentences to the commission but there would be gains for legislators. First, a guidelines commission could take some of the heat off of legislators "to do something about crime X." Second, sentences would be more consistent over a range of crimes as the commission could see a sentence for an individual crime against the way other crimes were to be punished. Legislators usually do not have that perspective.

In 1980, Minnesota was the first state to adopt a guidelines system, which is often considered the model of the way a guidelines system should work, as it has proven successful in bringing consistency to sentencing and in allowing for a more efficient use of prison and other resources. It also lowered sentences overall.

The state of Washington also was an early adapter of a guidelines sentencing model that had worked well. It set up a guidelines system in 1981.

There will be more on state guidelines systems in Chapter 10 as state systems, such as those in Minnesota, Washington, Pennsylvania, and Virginia, were the basis on which a reform model put forward by the American Law Institute was built. The next section deals with the federal system's sentencing guidelines, which had a very different outcome from state guidelines systems. In sum, they were a disaster.

The reason for discussing the federal guidelines prior to describing the state guidelines models is that most citizens are familiar with the criticisms of the federal guidelines because they are national in scope and because of the prestige of the federal system. That they proved such a disaster is unfortunate as the theory behind the guidelines was sound and something needed to be done to reform sentencing in the United States. Well-constructed guidelines systems offer the best alternative for reform.

The Disaster of the Federal Sentencing Guidelines

The Sentencing Reform Act of 1984 set up a Sentencing Guidelines Commission within the judicial branch charged with enacting guidelines for each offense. It all looked promising at the start with: an executive director, Kay Knapp, who was a true expert on guidelines systems and had been director of the Minnesota commission; a large staff of seventy; and a sizable budget.

Unfortuantely, things fell apart quickly. Ms. Knapp was forced out before a year had passed. The guidelines that were developed were overly severe, way too detailed, and failed to take advantage of what had proven successful in the existing state guidelines commissions. The commission also failed to work with federal judges to get their input.

Going from a system that treated each defendant as a separate individual at sentencing, the Federal Sentencing Guidelines (FSG) put forward a heavily computational view of sentencing. Sentencing ranges were determined by a grid with 258 boxes. The horizontal axis of the grid titled, "Criminal History Category" adjusts severity based on the offender's prior conviction record. The vertical axis dealt with what was titled the "Offense Level," which adjusts severity based on the factors of the defendant's criminal behavior that the Sentencing Commission has deemed relevant to sentencing. The box where the criminal history and offense level intersected determined the range within which the judge must sentence, which was a very narrow range.

This was a highly computational approach to sentencing. Lawyers and judges started with the base level assigned for the crime—a specific point count—and then added factors about the crime that might raise or lower that point total such as "the crime involved more than minimal planning," or "the actor used a dangerous weapon in the crime," or "the amount taken exceeded X dollars."

In addition, information about the actor, in particular the actor's criminal history, might factor into the final number used to calculate the defendant's sentence, depending on the seriousness of the prior conviction and the time since its occurrence. Thus, if, for example, the defendant committed the crime while on probation or parole for another crime, this would increase the points total and thereby increase the defendant's sentencing exposure.

The large sentencing grid to be employed in calculating the sentence range in an individual case does not give the full picture of the extreme complexity of the FSG. Accompanying the FSG was a manual that attempted to draw very fine distinctions among sentencing factors, such as that between a defendant whose participation in the crime was "minor" compared to one whose participation was "minimal."

When all was said and done, a judge would have a very specific and quite narrow range in a box in the grid within which the judge had to sentence.

The FSG were a blow to federal judges and were detested by them. Imagine changing from having complete control over sentencing which you take seriously, and then suddenly, having to adjust to a system in which you add up points to calculate a sentence where your ability to deviate is limited. To understand how things were turned upside down, under the FSG some factors of a defendant's personal history were specifically *not* to be taken into account at sentencing, such as an offender's education and vocational skills, an offender's drug or alcohol dependence, · an offender's family ties and responsibilities, an offender's community ties, or an offender's difficult upbringing.

Sentencing had previously been a matter of judgment. The defect during the "broad discretion years" was not in the exercise of judgment but in the failure of the system to give judges the principles and criteria needed to guide that judgment and to provide for appellate review of these crucial decisions.

Kate Stith, a law professor, and José Cabranes, a federal district judge, in a book titled *Fear of Judging: Sentencing Guidelines in the Federal Courts*, summed up what happened under the FSG as follows:

> The federal Sentencing Guidelines retained the traditional venue of sentencing while effectively abandoning the substance of the traditional sentencing rite. The Guidelines have replaced the traditional judicial role of deliberation and moral judgment (inherently imperfect) with complex quantitative calculations that convey the impression of scientific precision and objectivity. The federal Sentencing Guidelines as they are now constructed seek not to *augment* but to *replace* the knowledge and experience of judges.[13]

In reining in the sentencing power of judges, the FSG shifted power to the prosecutors and defense lawyers. Under the guidelines, defendants were supposed to be sentenced for the "real crime," not the crime to which the defendant pled guilty or the crime of conviction. Thus, the way a crime was described could move a sentence up or down—was there "more than minimal planning" or "was a weapon displayed"? If so, that would add points to the score. By the same token, if "the defendant only participated minimally" in the crime or if "the defendant accepted responsibility" for the crime, that would decrease the sentencing number by a fixed amount.

Sentencing under the FSG became corrupted as a federal prosecutor and a defense lawyer would sometimes team up to work out a "description" of the crime that enabled them to reach a plea-bargain sentencing range that worked for both sides. The probation officers who had previously presented judges with the views of both sides were put in an impossible position—should they now give their account of the crime based on case files or after talking to law enforcement? Or should they accept the account of the crime expressed by the prosecutor, or sometimes, the prosecutor and the defense attorney? Were probation officers now fact-finders for judges?

Further complicating the position of probation officers was the fact that sometimes defense attorneys told their clients and their families not to talk to probation officers out of a fear that it might raise the offense level.

The bottom line of the FSG was that control over sentencing shifted heavily to federal prosecutors. Previously, federal prosecutors had little control over sentencing but now prosecutors had a major hand in the sentence that would be imposed because of the way the description of the crime affected the sentence, as well as tools that prosecutors had to affect the sentence.

One of the tools in the hands of prosecutors was the aforementioned "acceptance of responsibility," which prosecutors would not agree to unless the defendant pled guilty. Another such tool was the prosecutor's affirmation that the defendant had provided "substantial assistance" to the prosecution in the prosecution of the case. If a defendant has provided substantial assistance, the FSG permitted a reduction of the sentence by one-third to one-half. Obviously, prosecutors would not agree that a defendant provided substantial assistance if the defendant insisted on trial.

The Impacts of the FSG

The direct impact of the FSG was an increase in the severity of sentences. In principle, the Federal Sentencing Commission was supposed to start sentencing calculations using historical sentencing data so that sentences would not increase, but the Commission decided that some offenses needed to be punished more severely, such as white-collar offenses and drug offenses. Instead of being more lenient on offenders or at least neutral on sentence lengths when compared to prior sentences, sentence lengths grew under the FSG: the length of sentences for federal prisoners more than doubled between 1988 and 2012.[14] (Not all of this was due to the FSG as Congress also passed statutory minimums during this era, especially for drugs, however, much of the increased severity was due to the FSG.)

As probation was more difficult to obtain under the FSG and parole had been abolished, a greater proportion of federal offenders were sentenced to prison where they stayed for a longer period. Under the FSG, prisoners had to spend 85 percent of their sentence in prison before they could be released for good behavior.[15]

The federal system only incarcerates 13 percent of our citizens. It is thus limited in terms of its impact on our incarceration rate, however, as the federal system is national in scope and because of its prestige, the failures of the FSG overshadowed the successes of state systems. Whenever the topic of sentencing guidelines came up in the legal community or even in the press, guidelines were immediately linked with a system that was harsh, overly technical, and that robbed judges of discretion to sentence defendants fairly.

This is unfortunate, as the theory behind the sentencing guidelines model is sound and other alternatives for reforming sentencing—voluntary guidelines or narrow determinate sentencing ranges, for example—have not proven effective in reducing the disparities in the way similar offenders are sentenced for the same crime.

Mandating appellate review of sentencing is also not going to be effective without standards or priorities against which courts can review and compare sentences.

It was against this background that, in 1999, the American Law Institute began to build a reform model for state sentencing systems based on the state guideline model. Unfortunately, as Chapter 10 will explain, the Court undercut that effort just as it was beginning to come to fruition.

Notes

1 See Arthur W. Campbell, *Law of Sentencing*, 3rd edn (St. Paul, MN: Thomson, West, 2004), Section 14:4.
2 American Bar Association, Standards Relating to Appellate Review of Sentences 26 (1968).
3 See, for example, *R. v. Priest*, 30 OR (3d) 538 (Canada 1996) (defendant's sentence of one year for breaking and entering reduced to time served and probation).
4 See *Rodriquez v. United States*, 395 F.2d 825 (Fifth Cir. 1968).
5 See *Duncan v. Louisiana*, 391 U.S. at 156.
6 See *Dorsynzki v. United States* 418 U.S. 424, 440–441 (1974) (quoting from *Gurera v. United States*, 40 F.2d 338, 340–341 (Eighth Cir. 1930).
7 See Marvin E. Frankel, *Criminal Sentences: Law Without Order* (New York: Hill and Wang, 1973).
8 This study and others showing similar inconsistencies were reported by Alan M. Dershowitz, Background Paper, in *Fair and Certain Punishment: Report of the Twentieth Century Fund Task Force on Criminal Sentencing* (New York: McGraw-Hill, 1976), 67 and 102–105.
9 Ibid.
10 See Paul H. Robinson, Robert Kurzban, and Owen D. Jones, The Origins of Shared Intuitions of Justice, *Vanderbilt Law Review* 60 (2007): 1633–1680; and Paul H. Robinson and John M. Darley, Intuitions of Justice: Implications for Criminal Law and Justice Policy, *Southern California Law Review* 81(1) (2007): 1–68.
11 See Federal Rule of Criminal Procedure, Rule 20 Transfer for Plea and Sentence, available at: www.law.cornell.edu/rules/frcrmp/rule_20.

12 For an excellent summary of the history of sentencing decisions in England, including guideline judgments, see Andrew Ashworth, *Sentencing and Criminal Justice*, 5th edn (Cambridge: Cambridge University
Press, 2010), 34–39.

13 Kate Stith and José A. Cabranes, *Fear of Judging: Sentencing Guidelines in the Federal Courts* (Chicago, IL:
University of Chicago Press, 1998), 22 (emphasis in the original).

14 See Prison Time Surges for Federal Inmates, *The Pew Charitable Trusts*, November 18, 2015, available
at: www.pewtrusts.org/en/research-and-analysis/issue-briefs/2015/11/prison-time-surges-for-federal-
inmates

15 Ibid.

10

THE SUPREME COURT

An Obstacle to Reform

One of the themes of this book is that building a strong criminal justice system through a series of Supreme Court decisions was a risky undertaking. The Court can only tackle issues in isolation, it has a more limited range of options than legislative bodies, it lacks sufficient expertise on issues, and cannot easily gather the needed expertise.

While it is tempting to rely on the Court in our federal system to impose sweeping reforms on the states, the sorts of comprehensive reforms that are often needed on problems of criminal justice have to come from other sources.

There are states that are laggards on criminal justice issues, but there are also states that are aware of their problems and that are trying novel approaches to solve some of these problems. If one looks carefully, one finds that some states are making progress in improving their systems.

There are also organizations, like the American Bar Association, that can study and then develop sets of standards or rules that can be models for reform for our federal and state systems.

This chapter turns to a major reform effort that had strengths behind it that the Court lacks: broad expertise, the ability to tackle a group of related issues together, the ability to gather input as reform efforts develop, and the luxury of time to propose and revise. The reform to be discussed is the American Law Institute's attempt to build a model code of sentencing that the states could look to for reform options.

U.S. Sentencing Problems

As we know from the previous chapters, the United States has serious sentencing problems. We have no priority among the traditional sentencing goals. While the death penalty requires proportionality, that requirement is not applicable to other criminal statutes. States can pass statutes that aim at retribution for a crime, but they can also pass statutes that try to deter such crimes by threatening harsh sentences that are not proportional to the crime.

We have no strong tradition of appellate review of sentences, so there is very little guidance coming from appellate courts and very little protection for defendants who receive sentences that are much harsher than similarly situated offenders have received. Judges have their own beliefs about the seriousness of different crimes and they have their own priorities on what they are trying to achieve in individual sentences. This is not the fault of the individual judges, but of the sentencing system.

There are other problems with sentencing even where prison sentences are not imposed. It is a common criticism of putting defendants on probation that it does not work well because the structure sets up offenders up to fail. This failure is part of the enormous churn of citizens through our jails.

Pressures on judges and legislators are also much greater than they are in other countries. One reason is that criminal laws are national in other countries, but criminal law is a state matter in the United States. This means that horrible crimes—parolees who commit a violent crime, for example—will put pressure on state legislators to respond. In other countries, the pressure will be less because the crime took place at distance from many legislators.

An additional pressure in the United States is that state judges are elected. This increases the pressure on judges to be stern in sentencing. Mentioned in Chapter 6 was the recall of a trial judge in California, who gave a Stanford swimmer a six-month sentence for sexual assault, which had been recommended by the probation office. Recalls are rare, but judges know it can happen and there is little a judge can do if a firestorm builds around a particular sentence.

The victims' movement in the United States, also discussed earlier, is now a powerful and well-organized force that can put tremendous pressure on legislators and can also initiate its own legislation through ballot initiatives.

Other countries can better deflect some of the pressure on legislators because there is often a justice ministry that studies legislation and weighs in on its merits or its flaws. It may be titled a justice ministry or a department of justice but it is a body with nonpartisan experts on a broad range of legal issues including criminal justice matters. If a legislator proposes a mandatory sentence for a certain crime, the justice ministry can be expected to analyze the proposal and estimate its strength and weakness, and assess what the costs of passage would be for the trial system, for the probation system, for the prison system, and so on.

This does not mean no unwise legislation is passed, but a justice ministry provides a buffer between the public and legislators and, if the justice ministry does not support the legislation, most legislative proposals will go no farther. It will usually be very difficult for a piece of legislation to be passed without the backing of the justice ministry. There is a department of justice that serves that function in Canada, but we lack such a buffer in the United States and the pressure on legislators can be intense.

It is against the above background of sentencing problems in the United States that the American Law Institute undertook to offer a major sentencing reform.

The American Law Institute and Its Law Reform History

The American Law Institute (ALI) is an independent organization that produces scholarly work that aims to clarify, modernize, and standardize important areas of law in the United States. It plays an important role in our federal system because states (and Congress as well) need guidance in developing coherent bodies of law on legal topics that affect citizens on a daily basis. States looking to improve their contract law, election law, family law, and so on, will often look to and rely on the ALI for guidance on the best alternatives.

In setting the path for reform, the ALI brings together a body of experts in the particular legal area to discuss, evaluate, and eventually put forward a treatise—often referred to as a "restatement" of the law in the particular area. Because the drafters of the restatements will include academics, practitioners, state and federal judges, and others who work in the area of law, the ALI restatements incorporate the "best thinking" on subjects in that legal field.

The criminal area is different from most other areas of the law. It makes good sense for states to have similar laws in commercial areas because interstate commerce works more efficiently if lawyers in different states handle legal issues in the same or similar ways. There is thus a push for a certain uniformity and predictability in many areas of the law.

The criminal area differs from commercial areas of the law. States are free to take their own approaches on criminal law issues. There is not the same impetus and need for uniformity as there is in many other areas of the law. But recognizing that states still needed a source for guidance on criminal law issues, the ALI developed over a ten-year period starting in 1952 a Model Penal Code (MPC), which attempted to build a model for drafting criminal statutes or even complete criminal codes. The MPC was finally adopted in 1962, after many drafts over the preceding years.

The MPC offered states, for the first time, a coherent and philosophically justified body of statutes that set out the contours and limits of criminal sanctions. Over the years, the MPC has had a dominant role in standardizing criminal statutes in terms of the way crimes and defenses are defined and the majority of states have adopted many of the provisions of the Code. Thus, if a state wants to know the best approach to take in allowing duress as a defense to a crime or wants to see the best way to handle criminal liability for a person who assists someone to commit a crime, the starting point is the MPC.

But even where a provision of the MPC is not adopted, courts often looked to the MPC for guidance in interpreting statutes because the MPC incorporates the best thinking on most criminal law issues. The MPC became the most successful criminal justice law reform endeavor in United States history.

Because of its influence on criminal statutes, criminal law casebooks for law students almost uniformly contain an appendix with selected provisions from the MPC to use as a point of comparison to the various state laws in the cases contained in the book. Any U.S. lawyer who has taken a criminal law course over the last fifty years will be familiar the MPC and its general approach to criminal law issues.

But one weakness in the MPC that developed over time was its treatment of sentencing, which was not emphasized and had very little influence in the ensuing years. The reason for this stems from the philosophy of sentencing that was dominant in the 1950s and early 1960s when the MPC was taking shape. As explained earlier, rehabilitation dominated thinking on sentencing at that time and a central tenet of that commitment to rehabilitation was the need to allow judges and, especially, parole boards very broad discretion to permit the individualized treatment of offenders. Due to the consensus on rehabilitation, which had its roots in the Progressive Movement of the late nineteenth century, "indeterminate sentencing" predominated and the MPC provisions on sentencing were built on that foundation.

But those original MPC provisions on sentencing became largely irrelevant as the country's commitment to rehabilitation waned and states began pursuing other objectives. Some states abolished parole, some established sentencing commissions with guidelines, some focused on intermediate sanctions, some stayed with broad sentencing discretion vested in the trial judge, and so on.

In 1999, the ALI realized that the time was right to return to the MPC and embark on a comprehensive treatment of sentencing. The Federal Sentencing Guidelines (FSG), which took effect in 1987, had proven a disaster and they have had no influence on state sentencing procedures. But there were states that had been working to reform their sentencing systems even prior to the FSG and these states had been far more successful in providing consistency in punishment, while still allowing judges room to tailor sentences to individual circumstances.

The hope was that a revised MPC on sentencing—what became the Model Penal Code: Sentencing (MPCS)—would help states reform their sentencing laws. It would function as the MPC by offering a model for sentencing that would cover a broad range of issues from probation to prison sentences to parole. Ideally, the MPCS would help ensure that defendants were treated fairly and consistently when it came to sentencing and it would help states use their prison resources more wisely and more effectively.

The advisors to the MPCS project included a large group of federal judges, state judges, practitioners, state court administrators, criminologists, and academics from around the country and even from abroad. It hardly needs to be said that the advisors and consultants that drafted the MPCS included many scholars who had been working on sentencing for most of their careers and, in the case of the many judges and practitioners, had personal experience with the difficulties that sentencing presents.

The Structure and Sentencing Goal of the MPCS

The structure adopted by the drafters of the MPCS was modeled heavily on the sentencing commission/guidelines systems begun in Minnesota and Washington. When the drafters of the MPCS began work on sentencing, there were sixteen states that had considerable experience with such systems. These systems had proven to function well.

In opting to build on a sentencing commission/guidelines model, the drafters of the ALI project faced a serious initial problem: "guidelines" were associated in the legal community and even in the public mind with the Federal Sentencing Guidelines (FSG). There were thus heavily negative connotations associated with the concept of "guidelines" because the FSG had proven to be such a failure. The FSG had increased the severity of sentences and they were strongly disliked by judges because they were so restrictive in what could be considered about an offender, so narrow in their ranges, and so mechanistic in their application. It was a frequent complaint of judges that they were no longer sentencing, but rather computing.

But state guidelines systems, by comparison, generally reduced the severity of sentences and these systems gave judges considerable discretion to depart from the guidelines and, in addition, the ranges under the guidelines were broader than under the federal guidelines. They had brought greater consistency to the states that used such systems, while still allowing judges considerable room to tailor sentences to the offender.

In the end, and after considering other alternatives, the drafters concluded that the state commission/guidelines model was the only alternative that would be effective in controlling the arbitrariness and lawlessness that otherwise often characterized sentencing in the United States.

In putting forward a sentencing commission-guidelines model, the ALI consultants and advisors also had support from the American Bar Association, which in 1994, in its *Criminal Justice Standards for Sentencing*, had put forward a sentencing commission/guidelines model.

But the drafters of the MPCS were not naïve about the negative connotation of "guidelines" and drafts of the MPCS, as the project developed, usually included an explanation by the Reporter on the MPCS project, Professor Kevin Reitz, of the important differences between the guidelines system the MPCS was putting forward and the FSG. Thus, for example, the 2003 progress report to the main body of the ALI included a ten-page section titled, "Major Points of Distinction between the Proposed Model Penal Code Sentencing System and the Federal Sentencing System."[1]

The Advantages of the State Sentencing Commission/Guidelines Model

There are several advantages of the sentencing commission/guidelines model that make it attractive. First of all, a permanent sentencing commission with experts able to gather and analyze sentencing data will have a much broader perspective on a proposed sentencing change than legislators. It should be able to determine if a proposed sentence change for a particular crime is in line with punishments for less serious and more serious crimes. The commission could also use its expertise for other important purposes, such as making sure prison facilities are being used wisely or making sure there is not an unfair disparate impact of certain sentences on racial or ethnic groups.

The permanent sentencing commission that the MPCS envisaged would have the authority to set "presumptive" sentencing guidelines, meaning guidelines that would have legal force but which would be subject to judicial departures based on "substantial reasons." There would also be appellate review of sentences under the MPCS model with authority granted to the appellate court to reverse any sentence, even if it is a sentence that is legislatively mandated, if the sentence is determined to be disproportionately severe. Appellate courts would also help bring consistency to sentencing departures by resolving conflicts among trial judges in the interpretation and application of the grounds for departures in the guidelines. It was the hope of drafters of the MPCS that appellate review would help a "common law" of sentencing to develop in each state.

Presumptive guidelines would help take some pressure off sentencing judges because the guidelines would help them explain and defend their sentencing decisions.

On the goals of sentencing, the MPCS is not neutral among the four traditional goals of sentencing. It gives priority in sentencing to proportionality. The MPCS requires that judges should render sentences "in all cases within a range of severity proportionate to the gravity of offenses, the harms done to crime victims, and the blameworthiness of offenders."[2] Other goals of sentencing, such as "rehabilitation, general deterrence, incapacitation of dangerous offenders, restitution to crime victims, preservation of families, and reintegration of offenders into the law-abiding community" are to be achieved "when reasonably feasible" only "within the boundaries set by proportionality."[3] In short, utilitarian goals of sentencing should not be permitted to result in a penalty that violates proportionality because it is too lenient or too harsh.

The emphasis on proportionality runs throughout the entire MPCS structure, for example, it does not want judges adding years to a sentence for deterrence purposes.[4] And while it acknowledges the reality that states are unlikely to rush to repeal statutes that have mandatory punishments attached to a conviction, the MPCS gives appellate courts the ability to review and modify even mandated sentences and adjust punishments to ensure they are proportional to the offense and the offender. In short, the drafters of the MPCS understood well that proportionality cannot be simply a sentencing option; it requires a commitment.

The structure and the sentencing goal are two important features of the MPCS. However, given its attempt to offer a global model for sentencing, the MPCS has provisions on many other important topics, such as: probation and parole, economic penalties, collateral consequences of conviction, victims' rights at sentencing, mechanisms to help manage correctional resources wisely, mechanisms to assess and address racial and other disparate impacts in punishment, sentencing of juveniles as adults, and mechanisms to address prosecutorial control of sentencing outcomes.

This is a very quick sketch of the MPCS. It is a comprehensive document on the law of sentencing writ large. The Proposed Final Draft runs to more than 500 pages as the drafters carefully explain what the theory is behind each provision, why that provision was chosen among other alternatives, and how they expect the provision to work.

Thus, if a jurisdiction wants to know the best ideas for modifying a sentence due to physical infirmity[5] or whether a judge should be permitted to consider in sentencing criminal conduct for which the defendant has not been charged or convicted,[6] the MPCS must be the starting point.

The drafters did not expect states to jump to embrace all the features of the MPCS. They were fully aware that some were controversial and might not be adopted as an initial matter. However, it was hoped that states would adopt the basic structure of the ALI model and in the years ahead see the wisdom of other provisions on, for example, economic penalties or probation, as the need arises.

The Supreme Court's Blow to the MPCS

But, in 2004, as the MPCS was approaching the latter stages of the project and after the MPCS had determined that the overall structure would be that of a sentencing commission/presumptive guidelines system, the reform effort was delivered a major setback by the Supreme Court.

In a case from the state of Washington, *Blakely* v. *Washington*,[7] the Supreme Court struck down a provision that allowed a judge to give an aggravated sentence above the standard sentencing range if the trial judge found "substantial and compelling reasons" that the standard sentencing range would not best serve the purposes of sentencing. When judges departed from the standard sentencing range—and the vast majority of departures are departures below the sentencing range—a judge had to make written findings of fact and such departures were subject to appeal. But that was insufficient for the Court—the findings of fact that supported an upward departure had to be found by a jury.

In the specific case of Blakely, he had pled guilty to kidnapping which carried a maximum sentence of ten years. Given Blakely's prior record and the fact that he had admitted to using a firearm in the crime, the standard range would have been 49–53 months. But because Blakely, in the trial judge's eyes, had committed acts of "domestic violence plus deliberate cruelty," the judge imposed a sentence of ninety months, which was thirty-seven months above the upper limit of the standard guideline range. The facts were that Blakely had kidnapped his estranged wife, threatened her life as well as that of their thirteen-year-old son, attempted to force her to withdraw their divorce proceedings, duct-taped her and sealed her in a coffin-like wooden box for several hours, and drove her from Washington to Montana. He also forced their son to accompany them with threats to kill the victim with a shotgun if the son failed to comply.

Blakely challenged the upward departure to his sentence, so the judge held a three-day hearing in which the judge heard testimony from Blakely, his wife and son, a police officer, and medical experts. At the conclusion of the hearing, the judge made thirty-two findings of fact in support of his ruling that the crime had been committed with deliberate cruelty.

Although the ninety-month sentence was well within the ten-year maximum for the crime, the Supreme Court in a 5–4 opinion ruled that Blakely had been denied his Sixth Amendment right to a jury trial because the sentence imposed was more than the upper limit of the presumptive guideline range of fifty-three months.

Understanding the *Blakely* v. *Washington* Problem

The issue *Blakely* v. *Washington* raised is an important one, at least theoretically, because jury trials are increasingly rare. The issue is: where is the line to be drawn between elements of the crime that a jury must decide at trial on guilt and factual issues that a judge can determine to increase a sentence.

The background to *Blakely* v. *Washington* was *Jones* v. *United States*,[8] decided in 1999. *Jones* v. *United States* involved the federal carjacking statute, which provided for a sentence of zero to fifteen years, but the statute stated that it would be zero to twenty-five years if the victim suffered serious bodily injury and zero to life if the victim died.

Jones v. *United States* was really a case of statutory interpretation in which the Court had to decide whether a victim's injury was an element of the aggravated offenses or whether it was intended as a sentencing factor. In deciding that bodily injury was really an element of the offense, the Court concluded that to read the statute otherwise would raise serious constitutional problems under the Sixth Amendment.

The implication of *Jones* v. *United States* was clear—a legislature needs to be careful it does not deprive a defendant of the right to a jury trial on an important element by shifting it from an element of the crime to simply a sentencing factor that would not require a jury to decide the issue. Thus, under the carjacking statute, it would likely be unconstitutional for a judge to sentence a defendant to twenty years in prison due to the fact that the victim had suffered serious bodily injury but that factor had never been presented to a jury.

This seems to make sense because we are accustomed to criminal statutes that define an escalating series of crimes based on whether a defendant injured someone, caused serious bodily injury to someone, or caused the death of someone. Thus, for example, one sees assault crimes escalating in that way.

But *Blakely* v. *Washington* presented a very different issue: was the crime, in this case, kidnapping of a mother and son, committed with "deliberate cruelty" so as to permit a judge to depart from the normal sentencing range and impose a longer sentence? Death penalty statutes—which the Court has reviewed on occasion[9]—often list among the aggravating factors the manner in which the crime was committed such as being committed in a particularly "vile," "heinous" or "cruel" manner. Against this background, kidnapping committed with "deliberate cruelty" seems properly an issue for sentencing.

To get to its holding that the upward departure exceeds the "maximum" for second-degree kidnapping statute, the Court has to term the normal guideline upper limit for Blakely's specific actions to be the "maximum" for second-degree kidnapping. This is a novel use of the word "maximum." If Blakely had asked a criminal defense attorney before his plea, what sentence he was likely to receive for second-degree kidnapping, any defense lawyer would have told Blakely:

> This is the normal sentencing range, but the statute permits an upward departure above the range if the judge sees fit and you may well get such a departure under the facts of the case as the way you treated your wife was extreme.

What Justice Scalia is doing in the majority opinion in *Blakely* v. *Washington* is telling us—as Humpty Dumpty in Lewis Carroll's *Through the Looking-Glass*—"when I use a word it means what I choose it to mean" and "maximum" means the upper limit for the particular guideline range adjusted for the way the particular crime was committed and the background of the offender. Thus, if Washington were a non-guidelines state, the obvious answer to the question "what is the maximum for second-degree kidnapping?" would be ten years as it is a class B felony. But in *Blakely*-speak, once there are guidelines in place, the new "maximum" is a moving target depending on the contours of the particular crime.

In non-guidelines states, where judges have broad ranges within which to sentence, limitations on matters judges may consider are traditionally few. The leading case for seven decades has been *Williams* v. *New York*,[10] where the defendant, after being convicted of murder during a burglary, was brought into court for sentencing. In imposing a death sentence on the defendant, the judge took into account factors about the defendant's background which could not have been brought out at trial and also the fact that defendant had committed some thirty other burglaries, though the defendant had not been convicted of some of these crimes. The judge also made mention of some other activities of the defendant contained in the presentence report that showed the defendant possessed "a morbid sexuality" and was "a menace to society." The judge imposed the death penalty.

In the case before the Court, Williams had argued that relying on materials such as these denied him due process of law as he had not been given a chance to confront witnesses who had provided this information.

The Court denied Williams' claim, emphasizing that individualized punishment requires that a sentencing judge obtain a broad range of information about the defendant that would be denied "by a requirement of rigid adherence to restrictive rules of evidence properly applicable at the trial."[11]

Williams v. *New York* has continued to be cited by the Court to the present day when indicating that judges have broad latitude to take into account almost any information they consider relevant to sentencing. Not only can a judge therefore base a sentence on other crimes for which the defendant has not been charged, but the Court in 1997 even ruled that a crime for which the defendant has been *acquitted* can be considered in deciding punishment.[12]

The Court in *Blakely* v. *Washington* distinguished the sentencing from that in *Williams* v. *New York* in this way:

> *Williams* involved an indeterminate-sentencing regime that allowed a judge (but did not compel him) to rely on facts outside the trial record in determining whether to sentence a defendant to death. The judge could have "sentenced [the defendant] to death giving no reason at all."[13]

The upshot of this quote is that it is fine for a state to give judges wide-open discretion to sentence within range of zero to sixty years and allow them to do what they want within that range, but once there are restrictions on sentencing within such a range, a jury is needed.

Against this background, *Blakely* v. *Washington* is a shocking decision. First of all, when one considers the traditional broad discretion given judges in sentencing, one might assume that the greater includes the lesser. If Washington could give judges discretion to sentence a defendant for second-degree kidnapping anywhere from zero to ten years, one might assume that Washington could legislate some structures to ensure consistent sentences within that broad sentencing range. To insist that broad discretion is preferred under the Constitution rather than structured discretion ignores the serious problems we have experienced with broad sentencing discretion in a system where there is no priority among the goals of sentencing and where appellate review is not available or underdeveloped.

This is not to deny the possibility that legislatures might shift traditional elements of crimes from the trial phase to sentencing. Factors justifying an upward departure such as that the defendant "used a firearm" in the course of a crime, or "caused injury," or "caused serious bodily injury" should be constitutionally suspect. But shouldn't the Court examine the particular factor in an individual case rather than jeopardize the whole sentencing edifice? What the Court did in *Blakely* v. *Washington* was to hold unconstitutional the entire presumptive guideline approach to sentencing unless juries make findings of fact beyond a reasonable doubt on upward departure factors.

To make matters even more bizarre, the Court has upheld a finding of fact by less than proof beyond a reasonable doubt by a judge that requires the imposition of a mandatory minimum sentence. In *Harris* v. *New York*,[14] the defendant was convicted of various drug and firearms crimes. One of the drug statutes Harris violated required a seven-year minimum if a defendant "brandished" a firearm during a drug sale. The judge made no such finding at the trial, which was a bench trial, but found by a preponderance of evidence that Harris had brandished a gun and imposed the seven-year minimum. Here the sentence of seven years was required upon finding this fact. In *Blakely* v. *Washington*, by contrast, no upward departure was necessarily required if the judge found deliberate cruelty.

The Sad Implications of *Blakely* v. *Washington*

There is a serious lack of depth to *Blakely* v. *Washington*. The Court does not seem to understand the hard issues which the decision raises. Consider two of them: who should sentence; and how adversarial should sentencing be? In *Blakely* v. *Washington*, it was the judge who thought an upward departure might be appropriate, not the prosecutor.

As mentioned earlier in discussing the way prosecutors are free to use mandatory minimums to determine a defendant's sentence, it is a familiar refrain to insist that "judges should sentence, not prosecutors." Here the judge was doing exactly that—the judge felt an upward departure was warranted even though the prosecutor was satisfied by a sentence within the normal guideline range.

But *Blakely* v. *Washington* puts control over upward departures in sentencing in the hands of prosecutors. If there is to be a trial on upward departure factors, prosecutors will control whether those factors are raised or not. It will become another plea-bargaining weapon to be added to the risk of trial:

> If you don't accept a plea to second-degree kidnapping, I will add upward-departure factors to the issues to be decided by the jury. When the jury finds deliberate cruelty, I am going to ask for the statutory maximum. With the victim in the courtroom, what do you think the judge will do?

And, of course, if a defendant does plead to the charge, a prosecutor will make sure the waiver of a jury trial extends to the sentencing phase if the prosecutor wants to keep an upward departure in play.

Or perhaps it will play out as follows: the prosecutor will agree as part of a plea bargain not to seek an upward departure.

Now it gets interesting: what if the judge thinks an upward departure is mandated by the extreme facts of the crime. Who is going to try the upward departure issue? Is the prosecutor going to be happy to go to a jury trial for an upward departure that might raise the sentence only a year or two, or maybe not at all? The fact-finding in *Blakely* v. *Washington* took three days, even without a jury. What if the prosecutor says, "I don't think a sentence above the normal range is needed and I told the defendant I would not seek an upward departure."

Maybe judges in presumptive-guidelines jurisdictions will refuse to take guilty pleas that tie their sentencing hands by foreclosing upward departures. Some judges to this day refuse to take "sentence bargains" feeling that sentencing is their call. (Judges will accept "charge bargains" in which the defendant pleads to less than the full range of charges, but usually that leaves broad sentencing discretion in the hands of the judge.) But accepting guilty pleas to the crime only—which would keep the possibility of upward departures open would be far more awkward—as judges are not in a position to force a jury trial if they think an upward departure should be considered.

The Court really does not understand the different role of judges at sentencing compared to trial or even the different roles the advocates play at sentencing compared to trial.

The irony is that the Court thinks it is protecting defendants by expanding the Sixth Amendment to sentencing. But it will be a much tougher world for defendants in the rare case there is a trial on upward departure factors. Consider the role of victims—perhaps they will push prosecutors to seek upward departures. Today, almost every state gives prosecutors a responsibility to consult victims on plea bargains. Now that prosecutors control upward departures, won't victims in a case like *Blakely* v. *Washington* be more likely to say, "Second-degree kidnapping is okay with me, but I want you to seek an upward departure as I want to testify to what he put me through." And, if there is to be an adversary trial on aggravating issues like "deliberate cruelty" and victims testify on the issue, it is not hard to predict the outcome of the trial. And when juries return verdicts supporting an upward departure, shouldn't we expect that prosecutors will recommend upward departures close to the maximum?

The Court does not understand that there are differences between a trial and a sentencing hearing. Certainly, we have very adversarial hearings at sentencing in death penalty cases, but that is the exception. Traditionally, sentencing has been in the hands of judges who can sometimes sentence more leniently than the defense proposes or more harshly than the prosecutor wishes. Gradually, judges have lost much of this power through mandatory minimums and tight sentencing ranges. Washington was a jurisdiction that tried to preserve some of the ability of judges to act independently of the advocates on sentencing. *Blakely* v. *Washington* takes away that independence. It will be the rare case in which a judge seeks an upward departure that the prosecutor does not wish to pursue.

Like many Supreme Court opinions, the Court in *Blakely* v. *Washington* overlooks and ignores victims in its analysis. The implication of the opinion is that a judge or maybe a prosecutor might want an upward departure. But what if the victim wants an upward departure? This is not a trial on guilt but on sentencing. It is not hard to envision a world in which a victim might say, "I will prove deliberate cruelty even if the prosecutor won't."

As indicated earlier, the Court has struggled to figure out what to do with victim impact statements, finally deciding they are admissible. The notion of a sentencing trial on upward departure factors invites a slew of additional issues relating to victims. European countries often give victims of sexual assault or domestic violence the right to participate at trial through counsel. Our two-sided adversary trial system would seem to exclude such a role for victims at trial but sentencing is a different world.

These are issues that the Court did not consider and, in a Supreme Court opinion, that is understandable—they are not experts. However, that is exactly the problem with building a criminal justice system ruling on isolated issues only. The implications of *Blakely* v. *Washington* are more complicated than the Court made them appear.

The Revised MPCS

Blakely v. *Washington* stunned the drafters of the MPCS and took the wind out of the sails of the project. It took many years for the drafters to recover and rework the MPCS. The revised MPCS was finally approved by the ALI membership in 2017.

The MPCS adjusted to *Blakely* v. *Washington* as well as it could. It continued to prefer the sentencing commission/presumptive guidelines model for states but it had to add changes. One of them requires the prosecution to give twenty days' notice prior to guilty plea or trial "of its intention to establish one or more penalty-ceiling enhancement factors."[15] But the result of a jury determination beyond reasonable doubt that one of the penalty-ceiling enhancement factors exists does not mandate the judge to impose a sentence above the guideline range.

In the end, we have a sentencing "trial" that is neither fish nor fowl—it is a bit like the death penalty with enhancement seeming to be in the hands of the prosecution, yet the provision wants to keep sentencing as the prerogative of the judge in the final analysis.

In addition, a judge under the revised MPCS "may on its own motion" raise any penalty-ceiling enhancement factor and "invite the parties to present evidence and arguments on the issue at trial or at a bifurcated proceeding."[16] Obviously, this is an invitation to the prosecution. And if the prosecution declines …?

The MPCS also put forward an alternative for saving the MPCS from the *Blakely* v. *Washington* problem, though clearly this is a much less preferred option. The second alternative is for a state to simply make the guidelines "advisory," meaning that judges could follow them or not when they sentence. The Supreme Court, in a decision after *Blakely* v. *Washington*, made the FSG "advisory." (This case, *United States* v. *Booker*,[17] will be discussed in Chapter 11).

Making the guidelines advisory undercuts most of the advantages of the original MPCS proposal—a sentencing commission with the power to control sentences and take pressure off legislators, guidelines ranges applicable to the vast majority of cases so that commissions could predict the impact of sentencing changes, the development of a common law of sentencing, and so on.

Once judges are free to follow or not follow the guidelines, the basic structure becomes largely ineffective. Early in their work, the drafters of the MPCS had considered voluntary guidelines among the alternatives for solving the problems plaguing sentencing in the United States, but had concluded that voluntary guidelines did not solve the serious problems we face.

Mass Incarceration and *Blakely* v. *Washington*

The problem of mass incarceration was very much at the heart of the reforms put forward in the MPCS. The choice of a system based on the Washington and Minnesota models was due in part to the success of several of those states in achieving slow growth in prison populations in the period from 1980–2001. In addition, many elements in MPCS were directed at countering the harsh deterrent statutes that litter most state criminal codes today as well as the many statutes, such as three-strikes laws, based on a theory of incapacitation that has been largely discredited. One of the MPCS central features was to establish proportional punishment as a restraint on other utilitarian purposes of punishment.

Obviously, the MPCS, as a model that states or the federal system can adapt to their particular criminal justice system, still exists. States can use its provisions for guidance on important issues such as probation, parole, the purposes of sentencing, limitations on prosecutorial control of sentencing, and so on. But the heart of the structure—the sentencing commission/guidelines model—was undercut by *Blakely* v. *Washington*.

There is an arrogance to *Blakely* v. *Washington* that is shocking. The decision has been called many things in print—a legal earthquake, a bombshell, and a forty-car pile-up[18]—and many less polite things in private. Every federal circuit that had considered the claim that the Sixth Amendment required a jury determination of upward departure factors had rejected the claim. And the forty or so judges, scholars, and lawyers in the field who had put in years of work on the MPCS obviously did not think they were putting forward a proposal that had a major constitutional deficiency.

The Court had to know that it was undercutting the ALI project in *Blakely* v. *Washington*. The dissent of Justice O'Connor warned the decision would wreak "havoc ... on trial courts across the country"[19] and she ended her dissent with the lament that "[o]ver 20 years of sentencing reform are all but lost...."[20]

Notes

1 American Law Institute, Model Penal Code: Sentencing, Report (April 11, 2003): 115–125.
2 Section 1.02(2)(2)(a)(i), American Law Institute, Model Penal Code: Sentencing (Proposed Final Draft 2017).
3 Section 1.02(2)(a)(ii), American Law Institute, Model Penal Code: Sentencing (Proposed Final Draft 2017).
4 See Comment f. to Section 6.06 (2) at 155, American Law Institute, Model Penal Code: Sentencing (Proposed Final Draft 2017). This limiting provision was much debated as some members felt that adding years to a sentence in a white-collar cases was needed to "send a message" to potential offenders; see Kevin R. Reitz and Cecelia M. Klingele, Model Penal Code: Sentencing—Workable Limits on Mass Punishment, *Crime and Justice* 48 (2019), 281 n. 24, available at: www.journals.uchicago.edu/doi/full/10.1086/701796.
5 Section 305.7, American Law Institute, Model Penal Code: Sentencing (Proposed Final Draft 2017).

6 See Section 7.03(2)(b), American Law Institute, Model Penal Code: Sentencing (Proposed Final Draft 2017).
7 See *Blakely* v. *Washington*, 542 U.S. 296 (2004).
8 See *Jones* v. *United States*, 526 U.S. 227 (1999).
9 See, for example, *Arave* v. *Creech*, 507 U.S. 463 (1993) (aggravating factor was "utter disregard for human life"); *Richmond* v. *Lewis*, 506 U.S. 40 (1992) (aggravating factor was "especially heinous, cruel or depraved").
10 See *Williams* v. *New York*, 337 U.S. 241 (1949)
11 See *Williams* v. *New York*, 337 U.S. at 246.
12 See *United States* v. *Watts*, 519 U.S. 148 (1997).
13 See *Blakely* v. *Washington*, 542 U.S. at 305 (quoting *Williams* v. *New York*, 337 U.S. at 252).
14 See *Harris* v. *New York*, 536 U.S. 545 (2002).
15 Section 7.07B(3)(a), American Law Institute, Model Penal Code: Sentencing (Proposed Final Draft 2017).
16 Section 7.07B(7), American Law Institute, Model Penal Code: Sentencing (Proposed Final Draft 2017).
17 See *United States* v. *Booker*, 543 U.S. 220 (2005).
18 See Kevin R. Reitz, The New Sentencing Conundrum: Policy and Constitutional Law at Cross-Purposes, *Columbia Law Review* 105(4) (2005): 1086 n. 18.
19 See *Blakely* v. *Washington*, 542 U.S. at 324.
20 See *Blakely* v. *Washington*, 542 U.S. at 326.

11

EXTREME ADVERSARIALISM, MUTED ADVERSARIALISM, AND THE SLOW DEATH OF TRIALS

The Vanishing Trial

A main thesis of this book is that a strong criminal justice system needs trials to keep incarceration rates in check. The prospect of a trial forces investigators to do more thorough investigations of crimes and to make sure they have all the relevant evidence in the case and, just as important, to make sure that evidence such as witnesses' statements are reliable and consistent with other evidence. When there is no prospect of a trial, sloppy and incomplete investigations are more likely to occur.

A strong trial system also forces prosecutors to be careful in charging. For example, there are cases by the hundreds in every state court involving *mens rea* where it is going to be difficult to prove beyond a reasonable doubt, for example, that the defendant knew the item was government property, knew the item was stolen, knew the item was counterfeit, and so on. The prospect of a trial makes prosecutors necessarily cautious in charging cases where there is a weakness.

But trials are no longer routine, they are exceptional events. This allows the system to handle many more cases. There is a price for such efficiency. Professor Darryl Brown explains the result for our incarceration rate:

> Put bluntly, efficient criminal process is an important cause of the contemporary carceral state. Having eliminated too much beneficial friction, hyper-efficient procedures led the state to reduce its financial investment in adjudication, especially in courts, prosecution, and public defense. Proportionately less spending on that stage of the criminal justice system allows (even implicitly encourages) proportionately more on policing—which supplies more cases for prosecutors and courts—and on prisons, which administer the consequences of those judgments that criminal courts churn out ever more efficiently.[1]

This chapter returns to the vanishing trial to try to explain why it is occurring. Some of the explanation has already been covered previously, for example, the existence of harsh sentencing statutes that compel plea bargains discussed in Chapter 7, and the use of complex procedures in misdemeanor courts to wear down defendants discussed in Chapter 5.

But many defendants face trials where there are no harsh sentencing statutes threatening them, yet defendants plead guilty. This chapter will show that our systematic avoidance of trials is in part a rejection of a trial system that permits and encourages an extreme type of advocacy that is not permitted in other trial systems.

The chapter begins with the experience in federal courts after judges were freed from the restrictions of the Federal Sentencing Guidelines and—to the confoundment of experts—trials continued to decline in numbers and percentages.

The Vanishing Trial in Federal Court Under the "Advisory" Guidelines

The federal system has resources, talented judges and lawyers, but almost no trials. The standard story put forward to explain the decline was, for many years, the claim that the decline could be traced to the Federal Sentencing Guidelines (FSG).[2] We have previously seen how the guidelines transferred more control over sentencing to prosecutor or to prosecutors working with defense attorneys. Judges hated the guidelines and often ceded control over sentences to prosecutors and defense attorneys.

However, this explanation for the decline of trials in our most prestigious trial system becomes inadequate and incomplete when we consider what happened after the Supreme Court restored considerable control over sentencing to judges.

In *United States* v. *Booker*,[3] a follow-up case to *Blakely* v. *Washington*, discussed in Chapter 10, the Supreme Court restored a great deal of their traditional sentencing authority to federal judges. In *United States* v. *Booker*, the Court declared that the FSG were no longer mandatory but only "advisory."[4] While the FSG were to remain a factor in sentencing, the Court said that judges were free to consider other factors such as (a) the circumstances of the offense and the history and characteristics of the defendant; (b) the need for the sentence to reflect the four primary purposes of sentencing, that is, retribution, deterrence, incapacitation, and rehabilitation; and (c) the need to avoid unwarranted sentencing disparities among similarly situated defendants.

Notice what *United States* v. *Booker* did. Judges could consider the history and characteristics of the offender. Other than the defendant's criminal history, the FSG cared not a whit about the defendant's deprived upbringing or family circumstances.

Second, instead of a tight retributive sentencing range that tied judges' hands at sentencing, now judges would return to a consideration of the other traditional goals of sentencing—deterrence, incapacitation, and rehabilitation.

United States v. *Booker* opened sentencing up once again to traditional sentencing advocacy as lawyers could try to convince a judge to depart from the FSG range and impose a sentence appropriate to the offender's background and personal circumstances. We seemed to be back close to the pre-FSG era with talented judges with lifetime appointments once again in control of sentencing. And, in fact, judges have been willing to depart more and more frequently from the FSG ranges, usually departing down from what the FSG would have required. In 2017, less than half of all sentences were within the FSG range for the offense.[5]

The expectation in the wake of *United States* v. *Booker* was that the number of trials would rise because a defendant could refuse a prosecutor's offer, challenge the government's evidence at trial, and still have a chance to receive a light sentence if the defense lawyer was persuasive at sentencing. And, if the defendant had a colorable defense, there was the chance of an acquittal.[6]

A leading scholar on sentencing, Douglas Berman, predicted that *United States* v. *Booker* "will make it difficult to convince defendants to plea bargain, because they may think they'll get a better deal from a judge."[7] But what happened was the opposite: in the period 2006–2016, the absolute number of criminal trials in federal courts declined 47 percent.[8]

The general decline in the percentage of convictions from trials also continued its steady decline. In 1997, in the middle of the mandatory-FSG era, 5 percent of convictions came from trials.[9] But in 2015, ten years after the FSG had become advisory only, the percentage of convictions from trials had dropped to 2 percent.[10]

Why have federal trials continued to decline in recent years when scholars predicted there would be more trials in this period? Freed of the FSG, why not take a chance of an acquittal at trial as defendants still could catch a break at sentencing?

To understand why, one has to understand the difference between the type of advocacy that our trial system values and the type of advocacy that is required at sentencing. Trials in the U.S. esteem what might be called "extreme adversarialism." But sentencing requires "muted adversarialism." (I have borrowed the latter term from cultural ethnographers who have studied national trial systems and have used the term to describe the English criminal trial system.[11]) The next section will explain extreme adversarialism using the example of the *O.J. Simpson* trial.

The *O.J. Simpson* Trial and Extreme Adversarialism

Most readers will no doubt be familiar with the *O.J. Simpson* trial in outline—a double murder that was going to show citizens our trial system at its best. There were experienced prosecutors from a well-funded district attorney's office; a "dream team" of well-known defense lawyers; and a well-respected judge in a state system usually considered a strong system among the states.

So confident were U.S. lawyers about what would take place that Professor Charles Nesson of Harvard Law School announced that he would use the trial as it unfolded to teach a course on trial advocacy. Students would presumably see excellent lawyering and learn as the lawyers displayed their considerable skills.

But what happened was a trial that quickly spun out of control. The trial drifted for weeks as the judge overseeing the trial was clearly loath to put any limits on the lawyers. He sat up on the bench sipping coffee while chaos reigned. On many days, the jury heard no witnesses at all, as trial time was taken up with squabbles that often had nothing to do with the merits of the case. The case itself was a serious one—a double homicide—but it was not that complicated that it should need eight months of trial time.

The art of advocacy? Defense lawyers wearing ties of kente cloth—a traditional Ghanaian fabric—intended to reach out to black jurors who share an African racial heritage. The lead prosecutor wore angel earrings to show sympathy with one of the victims. Is this the art of advocacy students should learn? This is acting not advocacy—but this is U.S. advocacy.

The defense asked the trial judge to not allow the family of victims to sit in the first row of the public gallery, which the judge took "under advisement" so he could consider the merits of a ridiculous request.

The defense challenged every single strike of a black juror by the prosecution as being made solely on the basis of race. (The way the "race card" was used over and over by the defense caused dissension even among defense lawyers.) Again, we are dealing with extreme adversarialism, which has few limits.

Then, at the end of the trial, a jury that had been instructed, as all juries are, not to discuss the evidence before the end of the trial but to keep an open mind until deliberations, was able to digest and discuss eight months of evidence in four hours before it reached a verdict.

It was typical of lawyers in the aftermath to try to excuse the trial. For example, that the prosecutors picked the "wrong" jurors—they thought that women, white or black, would be sympathetic to Nicole Simpson because of the abuse she had suffered from O.J. So, apparently, the prosecution would have won if they had struck black women on the basis of race? But what about the evidence in the case? What are we saying about U.S. trials?

In some common law countries, the lawyers ask no questions of prospective jurors or if questions are even permitted, they will be few and will be asked by the judge to make sure the person can be fair. By contrast, in the *O.J. Simpson* case, jury selection took two months. To assist in the process, the prosecution and defense both had the benefit of a seventy-nine-page, 297-question questionnaire that all potential jurors had filled out before jury selection in an effort to assure *O.J. Simpson* "a jury of his peers." In addition, both the prosecution team and the defense team, though experienced trial attorneys, used jury selection consultants to help them pick the "right" jurors.

The mistake, according to others, was filing the case in Los Angeles instead of in Santa Monica as the jury pool would have included a larger percentage of white potential jurors in the latter venue. Again—why should who you get on the jury determine the outcome?

Another frequent refrain from lawyers around the country about the trial was that the trial would have stayed on track "if only it had taken place in front of Judge Perfect who knows how to handle major cases." No doubt there are some excellent judges who might have done better in controlling the trial. But does it take an extraordinary judge to handle a case where the evidence is not that complicated?

But what does this have to do with the Supreme Court? It is true the Court does not control legal ethics or determine most of the procedures on jury selection but the Court has tremendous influence by the way it treats these topics. Mention was made in Chapter 4 of the Court's dismissive attitude to a lawyer who tried to follow the rule of ethics which state that a lawyer should not "assert ... an issue ... unless there is a basis in law and fact for doing so that is not frivolous...."[12] The Court described the lawyer as acting as "amicus curiae." The Court seemed to imply that wealthy defendants will find sleazy lawyers who would not worry about ethical details, so appointed lawyers should not worry about them either.

The Court has added another layer to the complexity of jury selection through the decision in *Batson* v. *Kentucky*, discussed in Chapter 2. As pointed out, the Court was warned by a few trial judges not to do what it hinted it was going to do—that it would be time-consuming and ineffective—but the Court went ahead nonetheless.

Admittedly, these were maybe indirect and minor influences on the *O.J. Simpson* trial but there were plenty of issues in the *O.J. Simpson* debacle for which the Court bears direct responsibility, such as the tension between guaranteeing a fair trial and freedom of the press. A number of witnesses in the case—some of whom were called and some of whom were not called—had sold their stories to the press, damaging their credibility (one of them had sold Simpson a stiletto knife). Were they embellishing their accounts to make them more attractive to the news sources?

Reputable news sources condemn this behavior—sometimes called "cash for trash" or "witness whoring"—but, in high-publicity cases, there is an insatiable market for these kinds of "stories" and tabloid publications will eagerly buy stories from witnesses.

There is a way to try to stop this practice and that is to bar publication of witness accounts—other than the testimony at trial—at the pre-trial stage or during the trial. Many countries would do that automatically in a high-publicity case. As mentioned previously in this book, they would also close hearings where witnesses will discuss evidence that might jeopardize a fair trial if released to the public.

The Supreme Court has made it nearly impossible to do these things. As this book has tried to show, whether it is the Fifth Amendment, the Fourth Amendment, the Sixth Amendment, or the First Amendment, the Supreme Court takes quite an extreme and expansive view of these rights. Expanding rights is easy; building a reliable, efficient, and respected trial system is not easy.

The U.S. "solution" to the "fair trial versus free press" tension is to sequester a jury in a hotel for the duration of the trial. The *O.J. Simpson* jury was sequestered for eight months. It is expensive, raises its own problems (think Stockholm syndrome), and, today, in the world of cell phones, one suspects it would be nearly impossible to keep juries in the dark about matters they should not hear or should not research.

Other countries balance the values differently. Canada, for example, is very reluctant to sequester juries, believing that jury service is burden enough to put on citizens without having to lock them away from their families and friends. Canada will close hearings and bar publication of accounts that might jeopardize a fair trial. Might the U.S. balance of values between free press and fair trial be wrong? Are we confident today that the Court got it right?

Arguing for restrictions on press freedom is a losing proposition in the United States. Constitutional scholar Erwin Chermerinsky opined in an op-ed that there is "little evidence" that the practice of witnesses selling their stories to the press poses "a threat to the fair administration of justice."[13] But what evidence could one produce? Is it not enough that the prosecution kept some witnesses from testifying who had sold their stories to the press?

What is missing in the Chermerinsky analysis that insists on "a threat to the administration of justice" in order to restrain the press is the lack of the respect for the dignity of the court in what the tabloid press was doing. The Supreme Court has taken away the tools trial courts need to defend that dignity.

Three jurors writing a tell-all book about the trial from their perspective? Might that have influenced them during deliberations? How could we limit their freedom of expression in order to make a buck on the trial? This would be contempt of court or a crime in other common law countries but is acceptable in the United States.

Lawyers trying their case in the press every day of the trial? How can the public know whether they are speaking as advocates or from their own expertise when they condemn an adverse ruling that day at trial? Who knows and who cares? We cannot have "gag orders." (Many trial lawyers who prefer to keep their advocacy in the courtroom like to be bound during a trial by "unconstitutional" restrictions on any statements to the press.)

Lawyers and judges insist to this day that the *O.J. Simpson* trial was an exception made extreme by the level of publicity and it was not typical at all of trials that take place around the country each day. This claim is no doubt true—juries generally do a good job, trials take place in an orderly fashion, and verdicts are entirely defensible no matter what the decision. However, while high-publicity cases stress trial structures, those are cases that should show how resilient that structure is. Instead, the *O.J. Simpson* trial held a mirror up to the faces of our legal profession and said, "This is what you look like." It was painful.

Extreme Adversarialism, Muted Adversarialism, and the Decline of Trials

One of the few people to probe the counter-intuitive decline in trials in federal courts in the post-FSG era is a federal judge from North Carolina, Robert Conrad, who wrote an article with a law clerk titled "The Vanishing Criminal Jury Trial: From Trial Judges to Sentencing Judges."[14] The goal of the article is to try to understand why lawyers, even after the Federal Sentencing Guidelines were reduced to simply one factor among several in sentencing, prefer to avoid trials and concentrate their efforts on sentencing. As the title suggests, Judge Conrad worries that federal trial judges are becoming more and more only federal sentencing judges.

Judge Conrad's worries are well founded. In 2016, the *New York Times* had an article on the dearth of trials in the Southern District of New York, once the most prestigious trial court bench in the federal system. The article was titled, "Trial by Jury, a Hallowed American Right, Is Vanishing."[15] The article stated that in 2015 a bench with forty district court judges heard only fifty criminal trials that year. The article mentioned one judge who had presided over only four criminal trials in six years on the bench and another judge who has not had a criminal trial for eighteen months. Trials have indeed vanished.

Judge Conrad puts forward suggestions for the continued decline in trials including the expense of trials, the fact that evidence is stronger today due to technology, the worry of trial judges about reversals, and the negative career effects on federal prosecutors of trial "losses" as factors in trial avoidance.

None of these are very convincing. As for the fact that cases are stronger today due to technology, this would seem to be true in other Western countries where there is no talk about trials becoming "extinct" as there is in the United States. And many trials are not about whether the defendant did the act but about whether the defendant had the *mens rea* for the crime—an issue on which technology is not usually helpful.

As for the worry of trial judges about reversals or the worry among federal prosecutors about the effect of a trial "loss," those reasons—if they have any validity—have existed for decades and certainly have not changed significantly between 1997 and 2015 to account for a 50 percent decline in the percentage of convictions from trials in that period.

Finally, the concern over the costs of trials is probably a big factor in state systems—how many counties in the United States could afford to put on a trial like the *O.J. Simpson* trial? But federal courts have tremendous resources and, again, was there an increase in the costs of trials between 1997 and 2015 that made trials suddenly costlier?

There is a more direct reason for the systematic avoidance of trials in federal courts: the tension between the extreme adversarialism prized at trials and the muted adversarialism that is called for at sentencing. These different types of advocacy do not mix.

Extreme adversarialism insists that lawyers go to extreme lengths to defend their clients at trial. You concede nothing at trial and if there are gray areas of ethics you go there—in fact, some would argue defense lawyers have to go there. As Alan Dershowitz, former Harvard law professor and sometimes defense lawyer, put it while attempting to justify the defense tactics in the *O.J. Simpson* case, "What a defense attorney 'may' do, he *must* do, if it is necessary to defend his client."[16]

If it is to your advantage to draw out the trial, you do it. If it is to your advantage to distract the jury and break up the continuity of your opponent's powerful cross-examination of your witness, you figure out a way to do it. If you can get under the skin of the judge and it is to your benefit, you do it. If it requires time and expense for a laboratory technician to come to court in order to testify to the results of a blood test the results of which you do not challenge, you make the opponent produce the technician. If it is to your advantage to challenge opposing counsel as unethical, you do it. If you have a question that has an impermissible factual assumption, you ask it and make the other side object.

Extreme adversarialism extends to the pre-trial stage (recall Justice Warren's dubious assertion in *Miranda* v. *Arizona* that the adversary process begins as far back as the point of arrest). If it is a sexual assault trial, you want to do as much as possible to try to keep the case from ever coming to trial. Even if you doubt it will be admissible, you make inquiries or let it be known you will make inquiries into the victim's intimate relations with others, or a defense lawyer may let the court or the prosecutor know that it will be difficult to protect the victim's identity if the case continues to trial.

However, when it comes to sentencing, it is a different type of advocacy that will be effective. To be effective at sentencing, the defense needs to get the judge to understand the defendant, maybe to sympathize with the defendant's background, or the circumstances that led to the crime. This can be very powerful advocacy, but it has to be done within a muted range. To explain the crime but stop short of excusing the crime is an art and it can be very moving. Though the defendant did something quite terrible, a good defense lawyer can make the judge understand that this act is not the defendant. The judge will no doubt have a sentence in mind at the start but a lawyer can move the judge off that number.

The advocacy at sentencing has to be muted in relation to the victim as well. Perhaps there is a victim impact statement or maybe the victim even gives evidence of the impact of the crime. The defense lawyer has to walk a fine line—respecting the victim and acknowledging the impact of the crime, but explaining to the judge why that impact should not increase the defendant's sentence.

Sentencing is also muted for other reasons, some of which were brought out in Chapter 10. The role of the judge at sentencing is not that of the neutral referee one sees at trial. The judge at sentencing is making a judgment about the sentence that is warranted for this crime and this offender. In *Blakely* v. *Washington*, we saw a judge doing what judges are theoretically supposed to be doing: stepping forward and acting independently of the prosecutor in deciding that an upward departure might be warranted. The judge is not bound by the wishes of the parties.

Similarly, a prosecutor's role is more muted compared to the role at trial. Sentencing has traditionally been the judge's function and a prosecutor is often ill-equipped to decide a sentence. The presentence report is prepared for the judge by a probation officer who works for the judiciary. It can contain very private information about the defendant and the defendant's family or friends. Some of the information may need to be kept confidential. The presentence report is not prepared for the prosecutor and, in some jurisdictions, it is not made available to the prosecutor because sentencing is not their job.

The above differences in the advocacy at trial versus that at sentencing is one of the reasons Chapter 10 was critical of the Court's decision to insert a jury into sentencing decisions. Sentencing has always been very different from a trial.

Obviously, this is an oversimplification as there are heated adversary battles in death penalty cases but that is an exception brought about because of the penalty at stake.

The different type of advocacy needed at sentencing compared to trial helps explain why freeing judges from the control of the FSG has led to fewer trials. The FSG gave defense lawyers almost no room for advocacy at sentencing. It was a computation and the most important factors raising or lowering the guidelines' sentence were controlled by prosecutors. Defense lawyers hated the guidelines, as traditional sentencing advocacy had no role in the sentencing decision. Judges hated them because there was no "judging" involved in the sentencing decision.

Once the guidelines were made advisory, it opened the door to traditional sentencing advocacy. Not surprisingly, lawyers preferred to use their skills to try to shave years off a defendant's sentence either in plea negotiation (which is also muted advocacy) or at sentencing. Excellent advocacy takes place in federal courts every day but it happens in plea bargaining and at sentencing, not at trials. Statistics showing a high percentage of downward departures from the "advisory" sentencing range suggest lawyers are making the right choice.

Understanding Muted Adversarialism at Trials in Other Common Law Countries

One might wonder why trials have declined to near the vanishing point in the United States while trials seem robust by comparison in other common law countries. Part of the answer, as shown in Chapter 5, is that they use simpler trial procedures for the vast majority of their cases and save jury trials for serious crimes. Trials for the vast majority of criminal cases are informal; punishments are lenient.

However, even when jury trials take place in those countries, there is not the same extremely adversarial trial culture that one saw on display in the *O.J. Simpson* case in other countries. The relationship of lawyers to the court is different; the relationship of a defense lawyer to the client is different; the structure of the courtroom is different; and the respect lawyers must show each other is different.

I will use England as an example of the way adversarialism at trial is muted because it is so evident in every aspect of their jury trial system—in the training of barristers, in the way barristers are paid, in the structure of the courtroom, in the code of ethics for barristers, and even in the rules of evidence. All of these features contrast sharply with the United States.

A more obvious reason for using England is that we trace our jury trial system to England and to our shared common law history. For this reason, the Court often draws support in its ruling from eighteenth- and nineteenth-century English legal authorities, for example, the Court quotes Blackstone's *Commentaries on the Law of England* in both *Duncan* v. *Louisiana*[17] and *Blakely* v. *Washington*.[18] The Commentaries are a four-volume treatise originally published in the years between 1765 to 1770 that summarize the development of the common law in different legal fields, including criminal law, at that point in time.

But though descended from the same common law roots, trials have evolved very differently in England compared to the United States. The starting point is that England has a divided bar. There are solicitors, who are the general criminal practitioners—they will go to the police station if a client is to be interviewed, they will handle applications for bail, they will investigate, they will work with the client to see if a plea bargain is appropriate, and they will interview witnesses. But at the point of trial, they will engage a barrister to present the case in Crown Court where there will be a jury trial. Barristers are trial specialists.[19]

The same is true on the prosecution side—the Crown Prosecution Service will review the crime information, make the charging decisions, and interview witnesses, but a barrister will present the case in Crown Court.

Barristers are independent lawyers who practice together in a chambers with a group of other barristers, but they are not partners. They share a clerk with the other barristers but they get paid only for their work at trials (minus a share to the clerk whose job it is to keep the barristers busy).[20]

A key to understanding muted adversarialism starts with the way barristers get paid: barristers only get paid for being on their feet at a trial.[21] What this means is that barristers, especially young barristers, want to be on trial as much as they can.

To do jury trial after jury trial the way young barristers do would be impossible for a prosecutor or defense lawyer in the United States. It would be too physically and emotionally draining. U.S. trial lawyers are like heavyweight fighters—they may do battle once or twice a year. What makes it possible to do trials every week in England is that there are structures in place that keep adversarial battles within limits.

Pre-trial preparation is much more extensive in the United States for prosecutors and defense lawyers. Barristers work from a summary of what the solicitor expects from the witnesses or the defendant. If there is deviation from that summary, barristers deal with it.

Another check on adversary excess is that barristers come from a tradition of switching sides. Young barristers, hungry for work, will prosecute a case one week and defend in another the following week. Barristers are supposed to be skilled advocates, who can take either side of a case and do it justice.

Because neither side wears a white hat, this makes it easier for barristers to agree on what the issues are, what points can be stipulated, and which witnesses will be necessary. It is, for example, easier for a prosecuting barrister to be sympathetic and give some leeway for a problem the defense barrister is having because the prosecuting barrister knows they may have the same problem next week and need some leeway when they may be defending.

If there is going to be something unusual about the trial, a barrister will inform the opposing barrister so that the opposing barrister can be prepared and the trial will not be unduly delayed. There is an etiquette among barristers that demands that they treat each other with respect—the typical way barristers refer to each other in court is "my learned friend."

There are financial reasons for being upfront about issues as barristers have reasons to try to keep the trial within the limits set for it. If a trial has been set for three days, but it extends from three to four or five days, it will mean the next cases the barristers were set to try in different courts will be handed to other barristers and they will likely have no income for those lost trial days.

The legal structure in England with a solicitor preparing a case for trial in Crown Court and then another lawyer presenting the case is antiquated and is starting to break down a bit as now solicitors can sometimes do trials that were once exclusively done by barristers. But to make it survive, barristers need to be skilled at what they do and to make the case that they increase the efficiency of trials. Many who train to be barristers do not make it. If they are not good advocates and are not efficient in what they do, they will not get repeat work from solicitors and will turn to other legal employment.

The muted adversariness of the English trial system is also evident in the structure of the courtroom—the opposing barristers sit at a bench near each other at the front of the courtroom. They will move to a podium that is between them to question witnesses, but they do not move around the well of the courtroom.

There is no dressing for adversary advantage in Crown Court as the barristers wear robes, dicky collars, and wigs. Solicitors will be in the courtroom a few benches behind the barristers.

The defendant does not sit next to the defense barrister, but instead is in a separate box at the back or the side of the courtroom referred to as "the dock." This is symbolic of the fact the relationship of a defense barrister is not as close to the defendant as is true in the United States. The barrister comes into the case late in the process and is hired by the solicitor, not the defendant. Indeed, the barrister may only meet the defendant shortly before the trial or even on the day of trial.

This is all very different from the United States where prosecutors and defense lawyers sit at separate tables, where the client sits next to the defense lawyer, and where lawyers usually have freedom to move around the well of the courtroom.

The rules of pre-trial procedure and the rules of evidence mute the adversariness of English jury trials. First of all, as detailed in Chapter 3 in discussing *Miranda* v. *Arizona*, there is greater access to the suspect as a source of evidence compared to the United States. The suspect had best disclose their defense when interviewed or suffer an adverse inference if the defense is first mentioned at trial. In addition, as trial approaches, the prosecution has to fully disclose the evidence it will use at trial and the defense has to fill out a rather detailed disclosure form explaining its defense in detail, the witnesses it will call and their contact information, and indicating those facts on which it agrees with the prosecution and those which it challenges.[22]

The defendant's defense is evident even in the prosecution's presentation of witnesses as the defense has to "put their case" to the Crown's witnesses. One frequently hears a defense barrister put a question in the following form: "I submit to you, constable, that the defendant running from the scene is consistent with possible self-defense in the stabbing, is it not?" The defense needs to lay a foundation for self-defense in its questioning.

An important evidentiary restriction on adversariness in the English system is a rule that forbids the prosecution from attacking the character of a defense witnesses unless the defense has attacked the character of a prosecution witness.[23] This means that a defendant who has prior convictions will not be impeached with those convictions unless the defense has attacked a prosecution witness. Defense barristers will be careful in calling into question the character of, for example, a police officer. They will suggest that the officer "misheard" what the defendant said when making the arrest or that the officer may be "misremembering" some other incriminating detail. But to attack the officer for lying may have consequences for defense witnesses, including the defendant if the defendant has prior convictions.

A final distinction—and maybe the most important distinction between U.S. lawyering and that in England—is the contrasting level of respect for the court and the justice system built into the rules of ethics for barristers. The Code of Conduct for barristers states that barristers have "an overriding duty to the Court to act with independence in the interests of justice: he must assist the Court in the administration of justice and must not deceive or knowingly or recklessly mislead the Court."[24] The Code also states that barristers must not do anything that is "likely to diminish public confidence in the legal profession or the administration of justice or otherwise bring the legal profession into disrepute."[25] A barrister must also "in all his professional activities be courteous … and take all reasonable and practicable steps to avoid … wasting the Court's time…."[26]

A responsibility to the court or to the administration of justice separate from the obligation to represent the interests of the client is not part of the duty of criminal defense attorneys under the ABA Standards. Instead, the American Bar Association Standards for the Defense Function state that "the basic duty defense counsel owes to the administration of justice and as an officer of the court is to serve as the accused counsel and advocate with courage and devotion and to render effective, quality representation."[27]

As far as wasting the Court's time, the Model Rules of Professional Conduct require a lawyer to "make reasonable efforts to expedite litigation" but hedge it by adding "consistent with the interests of the client."[28] Again, a lawyer's obligation to the court is secondary to the interest of the client.

This is a very brief and necessarily incomplete account of advocacy in England. There are other ways advocacy is muted in England compared to the United States, such as the background of judges and the more active roles that judges are expected to play at trials. However, this excursion into English advocacy is not meant to suggest that the United States needs to divide its bar into solicitors and barristers. Nor it is to suggest that the English system does not have weaknesses in its trial system. They have had miscarriages of justice, too. Rather, the point is to show that there are different types of advocacy and the advocacy we have come to accept in the United States and that we saw on display in the *O.J. Simpson* case is not the advocacy that exists in other common law countries. Nor is it the advocacy that will be effective at sentencing.

Notes

1 Darryl K. Brown, *Free Market Criminal Justice: How Democracy and Laissez Faire Undermine the Rule of Law* (New York: Oxford University Press, 2016), 149.
2 See, for example, Frank O. Bowman, III, American Buffalo: Vanishing Acquittals and the Gradual Extinction of the Federal Criminal Trial Lawyers, *University of Pennsylvania Law Review PENNumbra* 156 (2007): 227–229; and Ronald F. Wright, Trial Distortion and the End of Innocence in Federal Criminal Justice, *University of Pennsylvania Law Review* 154 (2005): 129–132.
3 See *United States* v. *Booker*, 543 U.S. 220 (2005).
4 This was a bizarre ruling in itself. How could the Court turn a system of presumptive guidelines into a system of advisory-only guidelines by constitutional fiat? See Morris B. Hoffman, Booker, Pragmatism and the Moral Jury, *George Mason Law Review* 13(3) (2005): 455–510.
5 See U.S. Sentencing Comm'n Sourcebook of Federal Sentencing Statistics Table N (2017), available at: www. ussc.gov/sites/default/files/pdf/research-and-publications/annual-reports-and-sourcebooks/2017/ TableN.pdf.
6 See, for example, Wright, Trial Distortion and the End of Innocence in Federal Criminal Justice, 133.
7 See Robert J. Conrad, Jr. and Katy L. Clements, The Vanishing Criminal Jury Trial: From Trial Judges to Sentencing Judges, *George Washington Law Review* 86(1) (2018), 132 (quoting from Professor Berman's January 30, 2005 blog post on *Sentencing Law and Policy*, at: https://sentencing.typepad.com/sentencing_ law_and_policy/).
8 Ibid., 103–104.
9 Benjamin Weiser, Trial by Jury, a Hallowed American Right, Is Vanishing, *New York Times*, August 7, 2016, available at: www.nytimes.com/2016/08/08/nyregion/jury-trials-vanish-and-justice-is-served-behind-closed-doors.html.
10 The *New York Times* reported that, in 2015, there were 81,000 criminal convictions in federal courts but only 1,650 convictions after trials, see ibid.

11 See Thomas Scheffer, Kati Hannken-Illjes, and Alexander Kozin, *Criminal Defence and Procedure: Comparative Ethnographies in the United Kingdom, Germany and the United States* (Basingstoke: Palgrave Macmillan, 2010), 138–147.

12 American Bar Association, Model Rules of Professional Conduct, Rule 3.1 (dealing with the role of the lawyer as Advocate), available at: www.americanbar.org/groups/professional_responsibility/publications/model_rules_of_professional_conduct/rule_3_1_meritorious_claims_contentions/.

13 Erwin Chermerinsky, Should Witnesses Be Allowed to Sell Their Stories Before the Trial: Yes, There is Insufficient Cause to Override the First Amendment and Ban the Selling of Stories for Profit, *Los Angeles Times*, August 22, 1994, available at: www.latimes.com/archives/la-xpm-1994-08-22-me-29878-story.html.

14 Conrad and Clements, The Vanishing Criminal Jury Trial, 99.

15 Weiser, Trial by Jury, a Hallowed American Right, Is Vanishing.

16 Alan M. Dershowitz, *Reasonable Doubts: The O.J. Simpson Case and the Criminal Justice System* (New York: Simon & Schuster, 1996), 145.

17 *Duncan* v. *Louisiana*, 391 U.S. at 151.

18 *Blakely* v. *Washington*, 542 U.S. at 301.

19 A lovely book comparing in detail barristers and defense lawyers is Peter W. Tague, *Effective Advocacy for the Criminal Defendant: The Barrister vs. The Lawyer* (Buffalo, NY: William S. Hein, 1996).

20 Ibid., 19–26 and 264–266.

21 See Ibid., 81–85.

22 The form which the defense must complete in advance of trial is titled, Defence Statement, and it is available at: www.justice.gov.uk/courts/procedure-rules/criminal/forms-2015#Anchor4.

23 Section 101(1) of the Criminal Justice Act of 2003 provides: "In criminal proceedings evidence of the defendant's bad character is admissible if, but only if … the defendant has made an attack on another person's character."; available at: www.legislation.gov.uk/ukpga/2003/44/section/101.

24 Provision 302, Code of Conduct for the Bar of England and Wales, 8th edn (London: Bar Standards Board, 2004), ARCHBOLD Third Supplement to the 2010 edition at 689 (2011).

25 Ibid., Provision 301 (iii).

26 Ibid., Provision 701, 694.

27 See Standards 4–1.2 (b), American Bar Association, Standards Relating to the Administration of Criminal Justice, The Defense Function, available at: www.americanbar.org/groups/criminal_justice/standards/DefenseFunctionFourthEdition/.

28 Rule 3.2, American Bar Association, Model Rules of Professional Conduct, available at: www.americanbar.org/groups/professional_responsibility/publications/model_rules_of_professional_conduct/rule_3_2_expediting_litigation/.

12

WHERE DO WE GO FROM HERE?

The Reform Movement

We are in a period when citizens are open to criminal justice reform. There is a broad consensus that we have too many people in prison and we can do better. Crime, including violent crime, is down dramatically and this makes it politically possible to do things that would have been difficult twenty or thirty years ago.

State budgets are also stretched tight and legislators have come to realize that warehousing so many citizens is very expensive when the money could be spent more wisely on other priorities. Even states not normally considered to be at the forefront of criminal justice reform, such as Oklahoma, Texas, and Arkansas, have tried to lower their incarceration rates.

This section will discuss a series of reforms of laws and policies that have taken place or are taking place around the country.

Probably, the reform that is most widespread is that of drug laws. In 2010, the federal government did away with the 100–1 disparity between crack cocaine and powder cocaine as well as the mandatory minimum for crack crimes.[1] These provisions have been made retroactive, resulting in the release of some 6,000 federal prisoners.

The reform of federal drug laws continued in 2018 with The First Step Act.[2] The Act expanded a safety valve provision that permitted judges to sentence certain low-level, nonviolent drug offenders to less than the mandatory minimum set out for the offense.

Among its other provisions was a modification of the mandatory minimum prison term for some drug traffickers who have prior convictions. (This was the statute that was threatened against Lulzim Kupa to force his guilty plea which was discussed in Chapter 7.) The statute increased the threshold for the prior convictions that trigger the higher punishments and it reduced the twenty-year mandatory minimum to fifteen years for offenders with one prior qualifying conviction. For those with two prior qualifying convictions, the mandatory minimum is reduced from a life sentence to a sentence of twenty-five years.

The bipartisan reforms of drug laws in the federal system are important as they signal an end or, perhaps, at least a ceasefire in the "war on drugs." Unfortunately, the effect on our incarceration rate is not great because the number of prisoners in federal prisons and jails is a small percentage of those incarcerated in the states. The federal authorities have 221,000 citizens incarcerated, while the states incarcerate 1,918,000.

However, there have been important reform efforts in the states. States as diverse as Connecticut, Mississippi, Rhode Island, Michigan, and South Carolina have reformed their laws and achieved reductions in their prison populations ranging from 14 to 25 percent, resulting in a cumulative total of 23,646 fewer people in prison.[3] California, New York, and New Jersey also reduced their prison populations by 26 percent between 1999 and 2014 by lowering drug penalties, decriminalizing some drugs, and reducing many felony sanctions to misdemeanors.

Some evidence of a public now open to criminal justice reform was the passage in California in 2014 of Proposition 47, which downgraded many minor nonviolent felonies such as shoplifting, theft, and forgery to the misdemeanor level. There was opposition to the measure from some district attorneys and some in the law enforcement community, but it passed easily. That a state that had enacted one of the first and harshest three-strikes laws in the country would pass a major sentencing reform with 59 percent voting in favor of the proposal is a testament to a shift in the public mood about crime.

In addition to laws lowering criminal sanctions, the change in the public mood about crime is evident in major cities which have elected so-called "progressive prosecutors," who ran on tickets promising to combat mass incarceration and the mistreatment of citizens by the police. Among those elected are: Kim Ogg in Houston, Charles Todd Henderson in Birmingham, Mark Gonzalez in Corpus Christi, Rachael Rollins in Boston, and Kim Foxx in Chicago. Instead of running on traditional tickets promising to be "tough on crime," these prosecutors ran on tickets promising to hold police accountable in their confrontations with citizens and to fight mass incarceration by being much more careful in whom they prosecute and how they prosecute.

One such prosecutor, who has received a great deal of press coverage because he ran for office after a career as a committed defense attorney, is Larry Krasner, who was elected district attorney in Philadelphia. The *New Yorker* ran an article on Krasner under the title, "Larry Krasner's Campaign to End Mass Incarceration." In the article, Krasner condemned his predecessor for embracing "bigger, meaner mandatory sentencing" and for casting a "very wide net" to bring "black and brown citizens from less prosperous neighborhoods into the [criminal justice] system when that was in fact unnecessary and destructive."[4]

A related aspect of prosecutorial reform in our cities is the changes in policing for minor crimes in recent years. Police are beginning to understand that aggressive arrest policies are creating more problems for society than they solve. Misdemeanor arrests are down significantly from their peak in 2010 in California and New York (and in other regions as well) with arrests of young black men down dramatically. The *Wall Street Journal* reported that the arrest rate in St. Louis for black men fell by 80 percent between 2005 and 2017. In Durham, North Carolina, as well as New York City, the arrest rate for black men fell by 50 percent.[5] Fewer arrests will help keep more people out of jails and jails too often start citizens down a path that ends up in prison.[6]

Some of the decline in arrests is attributable to the decriminalization of possession of marijuana and small amounts of other drugs, but some of it is the result of a new mindset about the proper relationship between the police and public. On the change in policing, the article quotes the chief strategy officer of the Seattle Police Department (another city with a steep decline in arrests): "There started to be a realization that you were often exacerbating the problem."[7]

In addition to arresting fewer citizens, cities are trying to reform bail to keep those they do arrest out of jail. One reform is the attempt to eliminate or nearly eliminate cash bail, which keeps arrestees in jails until their families can pull together the resources to post the required bail—if they ever can. New York passed a sweeping bail reform that sharply curtailed the use of cash bail in an effort to get more arrestees released quickly. New Jersey took similar steps and bail reform is being attempted in California as well.

Sober Reflections on Reform Efforts

The reforms described above are important steps symbolically in reforming our criminal justice system, but we have to be frank that they have had only a very limited impact on our incarceration rate. The incarceration rate declined only 7 percent in the period from its high point in 2009–2017. If you take California out of the picture, which was forced to comply with a court order to reduce prison overcrowding, the decline has been even less.

The *New York Times* reported in 2019:

> For all the talk of curbing mass incarceration and bipartisan support for reducing prison sentences, the number of people incarcerated in the United States declined only slightly in 2017, according to data released … by the Bureau of Justice Statistics.[8]

Rachel Barkow, a sentencing expert at New York University, saw the significance of the report not in the decline but in how minor the decline was. She states in the article: "The kinds of reforms we're seeing now are really modest. I am glad we are getting them. But this is not transformative yet." She went on to give the timeline others have given, such as The Sentencing Project, that "[I]t is going to take us 75 years to reduce the population by half."[9]

Admittedly, we do not know the impact of some of the reforms described above. Will the change in policing in major cities and more careful use of cash bail lower our incarceration rate significantly five or ten years down the road? Will progressive prosecutors be able to achieve their goals of reducing incarceration rates by the way they charge offenders or in the way they prosecute or decline to prosecute certain crimes?

One hopes that these reforms will have an impact on prison admissions and on our incarceration rate, but there are reasons for caution. Reforms such as these are frail. They can be reversed if the public mood shifts. The broad bail reform enacted in New York State is already under stiff attack. It has been reported that there has been a spike in major crime of 22.5 percent compared to the previous year and both the police and New York City Mayor Bill de Blasio attribute the spike to the bail reform.[10] More specifically, the police commissioner reported:

> In the first 58 days of 2020, 482 individuals who had already been arrested for committing a serious (felony) crime such as robbery or burglary were rearrested for committing an additional 846 crimes. Thirty-five percent, or 299, were for arrests in the seven major crime categories—murder, rape, robbery, felony assault, burglary, grand larceny and grand larceny auto—that is nearly triple the amount of those crimes committed in the same 58 days in 2019.[11]

Polls show that public opinion, that at one time supported the legislation, has turned against the legislation.[12] One suspects there will be reforms to the "elimination of cash bail" legislation.

In California, bail reform is on hold, in part, because of strong opposition to the legislation from the strange bedfellows of the law enforcement community and the American Civil Liberties Union. The reform is now a ballot issue to be decided by the voters in November 2020.

Similarly, progressive prosecutors promise reform, but will they be able to lower sentences generally and cut admissions to prisons? Will police and judges buy into their changes? It is too early to know. But, again, there are reasons to be cautious about their impact. Not every candidate who ran on a progressive ticket was successful. Incumbents in Sacramento and San Diego both beat back progressive challengers by large margins. There is also opposition forming to those who have been elected.[13] Voters can be fickle and, as we know from the Willie Horton episode in the 1988 presidential election,[14] the public mood can turn on a dime after a horrible crime.

In this regard, it is important to remember that the victims' movement is not over by a long shot. If things go wrong after the release of an offender as a result of sentencing reform or the decision of a progressive prosecutor, one can expect a strong reaction from victims' organizations. These are very powerful groups and when a terrible crime upsets them, the results can be dramatic and swift.

Finally, many of the legislative reforms enacted so far are considered by sentencing experts to be the proverbial "low-hanging fruit" of sentencing reform—nonviolent minor crimes. Going beyond these crimes to reform sentences broadly for violent crimes and serious property crimes, which are needed to reduce our incarceration rate, will be very difficult politically. Cutting sentences, as the First Step Act does, for drug traffickers with prior convictions from twenty years to fifteen years or from life to twenty-five years is a pretty timid reform.

The Supreme Court and Reform

We should continue to push legislative reforms—The Sentencing Project is trying to raise awareness of the extraordinary number of prisoners serving life sentences in the United States. The Sentencing Project reports that the U.S. warehouses 40 percent of those serving life sentences anywhere in the world and 83 percent of those serving life without parole.[15]

However, trying to reform our criminal justice system through legislation is a long and difficult path in the United States. As this book has explained, legislators in the United States do not have the buffer between them and the public that a justice ministry gives legislators in other countries. In addition, we have a federal system, so reforms have to go state by state.

When you consider our political system, you can see why seventy-plus years is the timeline for cutting our incarceration rate in half at the present rate of progress.

Avoiding the Elephant in the Room

This book has relied heavily on organizations such as The Sentencing Project and the Prison Policy Initiative that work full-time to reform sentencing laws with the aim of lowering our incarceration rate. This book also cites the work of many scholars in the field—John Pfaff, Issa Kohler-Hausmann, and Michael O'Hear, among others—who have studied our incarceration rate from many angles including charging by prosecutors, misdemeanor courts, sentencing laws, and so on. I am indebted to them for the understanding they bring to topics such as these.

What is missing, however, in the analysis of our incarceration problem by organizations and scholars such as these, is any discussion of the Supreme Court's role in our incarceration mess. It is a topic that no one touches, for example, consider Issa Kohler-Hausmann's book, *Misdemeanorland*, which was described in Chapter 5. The book takes us into the workings of misdemeanor courts in New York City and shows us what happens to those swept into a court system in which the adjudicative model has long been abandoned. It is a powerful book.

However, there is no discussion of or even a cite in the book to *Baldwin* v. *New York*, which extended jury trials to misdemeanors in those courts. Jury trials have strengths and they are part of our tradition, but they also have weaknesses. The present book has shown that the United States is very much an outlier in its jury trial commitment. Nonjury trials, not just for misdemeanors, but even felonies are common in England and Canada and they have built systems to encourage that option.

It is unlikely that we will make progress in lowering our incarceration rate until we roll up our sleeves and rethink many of the major planks of the criminal procedure revolution. Other solutions are not going to be effective. Consider two solutions put forward by John Pfaff in his wonderful book, *Locked In: The True Causes of Mass Incarceration and How to Achieve Real Reform*. This book, mentioned in Chapter 1, dismantles the "myths" about the causes of mass incarceration but when it comes to "real reform," Pfaff's suggestions are weak, and even likely to make matters worse.[16]

He suggests, for example, that we should provide more money for defense of indigent defendants. There is nothing wrong with this suggestion—criminal justice systems are always struggling with the burden of limited resources. So, let's double the resources for public defenders. But will it really solve our incarceration problem? The federal system has plenty of resources but no trials. The incentives are all wrong and the role of judges is confused and inconsistent.

Recall also "No Day in Court," the report from the Bronx Defenders discussed in Chapter 5, where the defense attorneys had fifty-four cases they wanted to take to trial, yet none came close to trial; none even had a full suppression hearing completed a year later, and the defendants paid steep prices in terms of their time for trying what they did to fight those cases. Those defendants had willing and able lawyers. It was not a lack of money that avoided trials, but a system of court appearances that cost the defendants dearly.

The "more money for defense" solution is symptomatic of much that has been written about incarceration in the United States. It is put forward without a word of criticism of the procedural system that the Supreme Court has created that requires enormous resources. Do we really need sufficient monies appropriated so that a defense lawyer can conduct an independent investigation, rehearse witnesses, draft pre-trial memos, conduct pre-trial hearings, spend a day or more picking a jury, conduct a full jury trial with opening and closing arguments, scrutinize the complete trial transcript for error, and file an appellate brief raising any not "wholly frivolous" issues for a store break-in, a car theft, or an assault in a bar? Is there not some responsibility on the criminal justice system to use resources more economically and wisely?

The thrust of this book is to show that other common law countries believe in simple trials for simple cases. They also achieve efficiencies in other ways that still allow citizen participation. Scotland use justices of the peace for less serious crimes and England uses lay magistrates even for less serious felonies. These are volunteers and work without pay. Very few criminal cases in England and Canada go to the jury trial court. It is to everyone's advantage to keep trials simple.

Might the differences in their trial systems have something to do with their ability to keep incarceration rates in check? Shouldn't we at least be exploring that issue?

Another of Pfaff's suggestions is that we do more to control what he sees as the real power in criminal justice systems today—prosecutors whom he considers to be "unregulated." He explains his proposal for mandated statewide prosecutorial guidelines as follows:

> Instead of leaving the decisions about whether to file a charge or dismiss the case, or whether to file a misdemeanor or felony charge, or whether to file a charge that carries a mandatory minimum or not, to the discretion of the prosecutor, the guideline could, say, instruct the prosecutor to dismiss all charges against a certain type of defendant in the presence of certain mitigating factors, or state that a mandatory minimum cannot be filed against a defendant with no prior criminal record, unless certain aggravating factors exist.[17]

There are many problems with this proposal, in addition to the political one that prosecutors are elected public officials and they run for office on their own policies, which may differ from other prosecutors in the same state. First, any sizable prosecutor's office will have guidelines in place for the way to charge and the way to treat high-volume routine criminal cases. Defense lawyers know these policies and so do judges. No one wants to see a prosecutor in one court giving a deferred prosecution to an offender charged with possession of heroin, while a prosecutor in another court throws the book at the offender. These guidelines are not typically announced to the public because prosecutors do not want to have them used against them when they run for reelection—"She gives lenient treatment to drug offenders …" (Nor would it be wise to let young people tempted by drugs know that arrest for a first offense will result in treatment, not prosecution.)

The real problem, however, with Pfaff's advancement of guidelines is that he buys into "Supreme Court thinking," which is: let's solve the problem with an additional layer of procedure. Guidelines are always going to have exceptions—that the assault was *vicious*, that the defendant took money from a *vulnerable* person, and so on. Who is going to decide these issues? And, one supposes, that Pfaff is thinking that defendants will challenge prosecutors for not following the guidelines, but might victims be able to challenge a decision not to prosecute as inconsistent with the guidelines? Or might victims go to the legislature, or whoever draws up these guidelines, to get the guidelines rewritten to make them harsher?

If we want the major reforms that our system desperately needs, this book has shown many options. Why not put in place rules to make jury trials simpler, less adversarial? Why not allow a state to adopt some of the ethics rules or evidence rules that have been discussed in this book? Why not allow a state to put more responsibility on judges to simplify issues for trial, to control trials better, and to clarify issues for jurors? Why not give judges more authority to handle pre-trial publicity in a world where social media can be as big or bigger a problem than the press? Can't we do better for victims, especially rape victims?

The problem with reforms such as these is that they would clash with Supreme Court decisions and would be attacked as watering down the right to counsel, the right to a public trial, the right to freedom of the press, the right to a jury trial, the privilege against self-incrimination, due process, and so on. But other countries that share our values and insist that they also protect these same fundamental rights do things differently. We are part of a rich and important historical tradition but there are different ways of doing things even within our common law tradition.

The Court has locked states into a single system of procedures and a particular concept of trial that is failing. There is nothing embarrassing about admitting our problems. Systems need to adjust and they do. English authorities are insisting that judges—hardly timid now in criminal trials—take a much more "robust" role in controlling complicated cases.[18] As mentioned in Chapter 4, New Zealand has given judges the authority to deny a defendant a jury trial (except in the most serious criminal cases) if the judge cannot facilitate the shortening of the trial sufficiently that it can be completed in twenty days.[19]

We can look down our noses at these suggestions and insist that the proper role of a trial judge is that of the passive referee, that we should never permit a defendant to be convicted of a felony by a judge alone, or that zealous advocacy, as opposed to muted advocacy, must be demanded of defense lawyers.

However, sooner or later, we have to account for the quintupling of our incarceration rate over the period when the rights of defendants were getting stronger and stronger. This is not to say that the criminal procedure revolution was "the cause" of the problem, but it is not an accident either. Things did not work out as we had thought they would. The Court created a system with major flaws that we need to acknowledge and try to correct. Most troubling to the author is the fact, as demonstrated in undercutting the *Model Penal Code: Sentencing*, that the Court has no appreciation of the fact that it is the major obstacle to meaningful reform.

The legal historian, Lawrence Friedman, observes that anthropologists have turned thinking about "progress" in criminal justice upside down. Anthropologists describe tribal criminal justice systems in positive terms—their courts are cheap, open to all, and informal. They are seen to restore social harmony and repair a tear in the social fabric. Western courts, by contrast, are seen as stiff, formal, and antidemocratic. They ignore and oppress the poor, and they are expensive to boot.[20]

This is a crude and simplistic comparison but it holds a warning the United States should heed. Criminal justice systems evolve over time and they do not necessarily always improve. Sometimes a human element is lost; sometimes costs drown benefits; sometimes values shift; and so on. We need not be frightened of change or intimidated by those who insist there is only one way of doing things. We can do much, much better.

Notes

1 See Section 2, Fair Sentencing Act of 2011, available at: www.congress.gov/111/plaws/publ220/PLAW-111publ220.pdf.

2 See Congressional Research Service, The First Step Act of 2018: An Overview, March 4, 2019, available at: https://crsreports.congress.gov/product/pdf/R/R45558.

3 Dennis Schrantz, Stephen T. DeBor, Marc Mauer, Decarceration Strategies: How 5 States Achieved Substantial Prison Population Reductions, *The Sentencing Project* (2018), available at: www.sentencingproject. org/publications/decarceration-strategies-5-states-achieved-substantial-prison-population-reductions/.

4 Jennifer Gonnerman, Larry Krasner's Campaign to End Mass Incarceration, *The New Yorker*, October 22, 2018, available at: www.newyorker.com/magazine/2018/10/29/larry-krasners-campaign-to-end-mass-incarceration.

5 Jacob Gershman, Arrests Drop Sharply for Minor Crimes, *Wall Street Journal*, October 7, 2019, available at: www.wsj.com/articles/arrests-for-low-level-crimes-are-plummeting-and-the-experts-are-flummoxed-11570354201?mod=searchresults&page=1&pos=2.

6 Ram Subramanian, Ruth Delaney, Stephen Roberts, Nancy Fishman, and Peggy McGarry, Incarceration's Front Door: The Misuse of Jails in America, *Vera Institute of Justice*, February 2015, available at: www.vera. org/downloads/publications/incarcerations-front-door-report_02.pdf.

7 Ibid.

8 Campbell Robertson, Crime Is Down, Yet U.S. Incarceration Rates are Still Among the Highest in the World, *New York Times*, April 25, 2019, available at: www.nytimes.com/2019/04/25/us/us-mass-incarceration-rate.html.

9 Ibid.

10 See Editorial, The "No Bail" Fiasco in New York, *Wall Street Journal*, March 7–8, 2020, available at: www.wsj.com/articles/the-no-bail-fiasco-in-new-yorkthe-no-bail-fiasco-in-new-york-11583534248?mod=searchresults&page=1&pos=1.

11 Ibid.

12 Carl Campanile, New York Voters have Turned Against Bail Reform, New Poll Says, *New York Post*, January 21, 2020, available at: https://nypost.com/2020/01/21/new-york-voters-have-turned-against-bail-reform-new-poll-says/.

13 See, for example, James D. Schultz, The Disastrous Consequences of DA Larry Krasner's "Reforms," *Philadelphia Magazine*, June 27, 2019, available at: www.phillymag.com/news/2019/06/27/larry-krasner-reforms-philadelphia; and Akela Lacy and Ryan Grim, Pennsylvania Lawmakers Move to Strip Reformist Prosecutor Larry Krasner of Authority, *The Intercept*, July 8, 2019 (describing legislation giving the state attorney general authority to prosecute firearms offenses in Philadelphia), available at: https://theintercept.com/2019/07/08/da-larry-krasner-pennsylvania-attorney-general.

14 This episode in the presidential election between George H.W. Bush and Michael Dukakis is discussed in Chapter 6.

15 See People Serving Life Exceeds Entire Prison Population of 1970, *The Sentencing Project*, February 20, 2020, available at: www.sentencingproject.org/publications/people-serving-life-exceeds-entire-prison-population-1970/.

16 John F. Pfaff, *Locked In: The True Causes of Mass Incarceration and How to Achieve Real Reform* (New York: Basic Books, 2017).

17 Ibid., 210–211.

18 See Ying Hui Tan, Law Report: Unnecessarily Long Indictment Led to Unmanageable Trial: *Regina* v. *Cohen and Others*—Court of Appeal (Criminal Division) (Lord Justice Mann, Mr Justice Ognall, and Mr Justice Buckley), July 28, 1992, *Independent*, July 29, 1992, available at: www.independent.co.uk/news/uk/law-report-unnecessarily-long-indictment-led-to-unmanageable-trial-regina-v-cohen-and-others-court-1536275.html; and *Regina* v. *Cohen*, Court of Appeal (Criminal Division) (England) July 28, 1992.

19 See Section 102, New Zealand Criminal Procedure Act of 2011, available at: www.legislation.govt.nz/act/public/2011/0081/latest/whole.html#DLM3360166.

20 See Lawrence M. Friedman, Courts Over Time: A Survey of Theories and Research, in Keith O. Boyum and Lynn Mather (Eds.), *Empirical Theories About Courts* (New Orleans, LA: Quid Pro Books, 2015), 14.

INDEX

For Product Safety Concerns and Information please contact our EU
representative GPSR@taylorandfrancis.com
Taylor & Francis Verlag GmbH, Kaufingerstraße 24, 80331 München, Germany